PROTEST AND PEDAGOGY

POLITICS AND CULTURE IN THE
TWENTIETH-CENTURY SOUTH

SERIES EDITORS

Bryant Simon, Temple University
Jane Dailey, University of Chicago

ADVISORY BOARD

Rebecca Brückmann, Carleton College
Erik Gellman, The University of North Carolina, Chapel Hill
Charles McKinney, Rhodes College
Sarah J. McNamara, Texas A&M University
Elizabeth McRae, Western Carolina University
La Shonda Mims, Middle Tennessee State University
Robert Norrell, University of Tennessee, Knoxville
Anke Ortlepp, Universität zu Köln
Vanessa Ribas, University of California, San Diego
J. Mills Thornton, University of Michigan
Allen Tullos, Emory University
Brian Ward, Northumbria University

PROTEST AND PEDAGOGY

Charlottesville's Black Freedom
Struggle and the Making of the
American High School

Alexander D. Hyres

THE UNIVERSITY OF GEORGIA PRESS | ATHENS

© 2026 by the University of Georgia Press
Athens, Georgia 30602
www.ugapress.org
All rights reserved

Set in Arno by Westchester Publishing Services

Use of any part of this book in training for any artificial intelligence (AI), large language model (LLM), machine learning technologies, or similar generative language system without license is expressly prohibited.

Printed digitally

EU Authorized Representative
Easy Access System Europe—Mustamäe tee 50, 10621 Tallinn, Estonia, gpsr.requests@easproject.com

Library of Congress Control Number: 2025022977
ISBN: 9780820375298 (hardback)
ISBN: 9780820375304 (paperback)
ISBN: 9780820375311 (epub)
ISBN: 9780820375328 (PDF)

To all the Black educators and students in the fight for freedom, justice, and liberation—past, present, and future.

I am reminded over and over again of the pain of my ancestors and all of the fighting that they had to go through for us to be where we are now. Quite frankly I am disgusted with the selective display of history in this city. There is more to Charlottesville than just the memories of Confederate fighters. There is more to this city that makes it great.

—Zyahna Bryant, "Change the Name of Lee Park and Remove the Statue," Change.Org Petition, 2016

CONTENTS

ix   List of Figures, Map, and Tables

xi   List of Abbreviations

xiii   Foreword, by Derrick P. Alridge

xv   Acknowledgments

xxi   Timeline

1   INTRODUCTION

PART ONE
The Rise and Fall of the Black High School

ONE

17   "A Long, Hard Struggle and a Lot of Agitation": The Fight for a Black High School, 1890–1926

TWO

38   "Pillars of This Town": Jefferson High School, 1926–1951

THREE

55   "To Take Their Places as Future Leaders": Jackson P. Burley High School, 1951–1967

PART TWO
The Origins and Limits of the Desegregated High School

FOUR

79   "A Little More Defiant, a Little More Militant": Lane High School, 1959–1974

FIVE

109   "Because Racism Was So Deeply Ingrained": Charlottesville High School, 1974–2001

CONCLUSION
127 "The Statues Coming Down Is the Tip of the Iceberg"

135 Notes

157 Bibliography

183 Index

LIST OF FIGURES, MAP, AND TABLES

Figures

11 "Triumph of the Charlottesville Twelve" historical marker at Venable Elementary School and Lane High School (2018)

57 Jackson P. Burley High School (2018)

83 Lane High School in *The Chain* yearbook (1962–1963)

96 "Black Studies... at Last" in *The Chain* yearbook (1971–1972)

112 Charlottesville High School (2018)

131 Charlottesville High School student walkout (2019)

Map

xix Map of Charlottesville

Tables

7 1. Population of Charlottesville, 2020

24 2. Population of Charlottesville, 1890–1920

39 3. Population of Charlottesville, 1930–1950

80 4. Black students at Lane High School, 1959–1963

130 5. Demographics of Charlottesville High School, 2020

ABBREVIATIONS

Albemarle County Schools Division (ACS)
American Civil Liberties Union (ACLU)
Association for the Study of Negro Life and History (ASNLH)
Charlottesville City Schools Division (CCS)
Charlottesville High School (CHS)
Jackson P. Burley High School (BHS)
Jefferson High School (JHS)
Lane High School (LHS)
National Association for the Advancement of Colored People (NAACP)
Student Nonviolent Coordinating Committee (SNCC)
Teachers in the Movement (TIM)
University of Virginia (UVA)
Virginia Council on Human Relations (VCHR)

FOREWORD

It is with great pleasure that I write the foreword to Alexander Hyres's *Protest and Pedagogy: Charlottesville's Black Freedom Struggle and the Making of the American High School*. This book is timely for several reasons. First, the United States is currently experiencing another culture war around the issues of race and education, among other issues. Second, the teaching of Black history in U.S. schools has become contested as states nationwide debate the appropriate content curriculum for students. This book responds to the current times by illuminating the issues of race, education, pedagogy, and curricula in debates in public high schools during the 1960s and 1970s.

Alex and I began working together nearly a decade ago on my research project, Teachers in the Movement (TIM) Project. The project explores the roles of teachers and teachers' pedagogy during the Civil Rights Movement. Our argument has been that teachers practiced a form of pedagogical activism that reveals an alternative form of engagement in civil rights beyond the more common picketing, boycotting, and marching typically associated with activism.

One of the first interviews for the project was with Florence C. Bryant, a well-known teacher and activist in Charlottesville, Virginia, who was instrumental in the desegregation of the Charlottesville City Schools Division. During the interview, Bryant gave our team a history lesson not only on Charlottesville and its schools, but also on the role of teachers within communities. In Charlottesville, she talked about what it was like to teach in segregated schools, the communal bonds between teachers and the Black community, and her teaching at desegregated schools in Charlottesville.

Alex and I also interviewed Wilbur T. Lewis, Charlottesville High School's first Black principal. During the interview, we not only learned about Lewis's challenges as a Black principal, but we also learned about his work as a math teacher and his upbringing in Lynchburg, Virginia. Alex's development of the questions and his oral history interviews and research skills paved the way for what I knew would be a promising career from him as an historian of education. He conducted interviews, accessed interviews from various collections, and dug deep into the archives. Alex played a crucial role in subsequent research for the TIM Project and interviews with teachers and administrators in Charlottesville and Richmond, Virginia.

In 2025, Alex published *Protest and Pedagogy*, a book based on several years of archival research in Charlottesville and across Virginia and the southeastern United States. His work has culminated in a treatise that broadly explores the role of teacher and student activism in high schools. It also reveals the relationship between protest and pedagogy in African American high schools. The book centers on Black high schools as sites of protest during the 1960s and 1970s. In this way, his book illuminates the need to provide a more comprehensive understanding of Black protest and Black Studies beyond the more familiar stories of protest and activism in universities.

Protest and Pedagogy taught me much about Charlottesville. The book shows how the Black students at Lane High School in Charlottesville sought a Black history course and advocated for hiring more Black teachers. It introduced me to the work of Virginia State University's Dr. Edgar Toppin, who developed a course for Virginia students titled "Americans from Africa: A History." The book takes us into the classrooms of Black school teachers and informs us much about the relationships between protest, activism, and curriculum. We learn about Black teachers and students, including Charles Alexander, Rebecca Fuller McGinnis, Benjamin Tonsler, Florence Bryant, and many legends in Charlottesville's Black community.

Alexander Hyres's *Protest and Pedagogy: Charlottesville's Black Freedom Struggle and the Making of the American High School* is necessary and welcomed in our time. Hyres offers a fresh examination of Black protests in schools during the 1970s and represents the impressive young scholars researching the activism of teachers and students in high schools. Well-written, thoroughly documented, and tightly executed, Hyres's book will teach us all about Black protest pedagogy and high schools in the decades to come.

Derrick P. Alridge
Philip J. Gibson, Professor of Education
University of Virginia

ACKNOWLEDGMENTS

Many people have supported and sustained me during the past decade as this project developed from an idea into a book. Derrick Alridge, my advisor and dissertation chair at the University of Virginia (UVA), supported me and this project from the beginning. His trust, encouragement, and critical feedback helped me become a better scholar, writer, and person. I was fortunate to work with Derrick during the early days of what became the TIM Project. Working closely with him and interviewing local teachers for the project helped develop my thinking about the participation of African American educators and students in the Black freedom struggle during the twentieth century. Thank you to all the people in Charlottesville, Virginia, who shared their experiences as educators and students with me and the other members of the TIM Project team.

Beyond the oral interviews from the TIM Project, this book benefitted from the work of local oral history projects at The Jefferson School—African American Heritage Center and the Albemarle County Historical Society. Thank you to the interviewers and interviewees who created a record for current and future generations to learn from the past. Several people at local archives and repositories also helped me locate additional source material to support the book's narrative and arguments. Thank you to the librarians and archivists at the Charlottesville City Schools Division, Charlottesville High School Media Center, the University of Virginia, and The Jefferson School—African American Heritage Center.

I am indebted to many other people at the University of Virginia who supported me and this project. Many professors and people at UVA helped me develop as a historian, writer, and thinker. Nancy Deutsch, Walt Heinecke, Diane Hoffman, and Rachel Wahl sharpened my understanding and analysis of education and schooling in the United States. Elizabeth Varon and Grace Hale reoriented how I see the social and political history of the South and the United States in profound ways. Allan Megill taught me how to read and write as a historian. Sidney Milkis sharpened my analysis of politics and history in the United States. Kwame Otu and Claudrena

Harold deepened my understanding of Black Studies as a field. They also challenged me to think about the entanglements between the past and present in Charlottesville, Virginia, the United States, and the Black Diaspora.

Fellow graduate students at UVA helped me endure the many peaks and valleys of earning a doctoral degree. Thank you to Monica Blair, Benji Cohen, Erik Erlandson, Carmen Foster, Andrew Frankel, Lindsey Jones, Allison Kelly, Chenyu Wang, and Danielle Wingfield. I am also appreciative to the many undergraduate students at UVA with whom I crossed paths in "Multicultural Education," "Introduction to Black Studies, I and II," and "Civil Rights Movement and Education." These students taught me much about teaching and learning and how to translate my research to broader audiences. I'm grateful for the students in the "Civil Rights Movement and Education" course during the spring of 2018. Your engagement in the class and encouragement with this project meant a lot to me as I was finishing my dissertation and seeking a job.

I was fortunate to land a job in the Education, Culture, and Society (ECS) department at the University of Utah. The development and completion of this book would not have been possible without the support, feedback, and love of my colleagues in ECS: Josephine Amoakoh, Cynthia Benally, Leticia Alvarez Gutiérrez, José Gutiérrez, Jeremy Horne, Karen Johnson, Harvey Kantor, Frankie Santos Laanan, Frank Margonis, Jason Newnum, Omi Salas-SantaCruz, William Smith, Wenyang Sun, Audrey Thompson, Veronica Valdez, Kēhualani Vaughn, Sarah Vorsheck, and Tuba Yilmaz. Thanks to all my students at the University of Utah, in both graduate and undergraduate classes, who have thought alongside me as I revised this manuscript. Your support and encouragement have helped sustain me these past couple of years.

My academic communities beyond the University of Utah have also been crucial to developing this book. I have benefitted from many formal and informal conversations at the History of Education Society, the Association for the Study of African American Life and History, and the American Educational Research Association. Thanks to Scott Baker, Nancy Beadie, Zoë Burkholder, Mahasan Chaney, Candace Cunningham, Dionne Danns, Jack Dougherty, Ansley Erickson, Jarvis Givens, Isaac Gottesman, Michael Hines, Hunter Holt, Ben Justice, Lauren Lefty, Tondra Loder-Jackson, Kristen McCullum, Phil Nichols, Amato Nocera, Michelle Purdy, Robert Robinson, Crystal Sanders, Christopher Span, Kyle Steele,

Derek Taira, Elizabeth Todd-Breland, Joy Williamson-Lott, and Vincent Willis for your research and your feedback on this project at various stages of its development.

While revising the dissertation into a book, I have worked on various related pieces across genres. Thanks to Brian Rosenwald and Nicole Hemmer at *The Washington Post*'s "Made by History" column for their feedback on a piece examining Black student organizing at Charlottesville High School. Working on that piece helped me think about the arc of this book and its contemporary relevance. Thanks to Pero Dagbovie and the anonymous reviewers at the *Journal of African American History* for their feedback on an article, which formed the basis for revisions across a couple of chapters. Thanks to the editors, Derrick Alridge, Jon N. Hale, Tondra Loder-Jackson, and the reviewers of my chapter on Florence Coleman Bryant in the edited volume, *Schooling the Movement*. Their feedback on the chapter helped me understand Bryant's life and work and make sense of how she fits within broader trends of African American educators during the Black freedom struggle. Finally, thanks to Linda Mahood and the anonymous reviewers at the *Journal of the History of Youth and Childhood* for their feedback on an article about Black male youth activists during the school desegregation era in Virginia. I appreciate these journals and presses permitting me to use material from those articles and chapters for this book.

Thanks to Nate Holly, Laura Price Yoder, and the University of Georgia Press for believing in the book and all you did to improve it. As a first-time author, I had a lot of questions about the process and struggled at various points, from submitting the proposal to getting the book into the publication pipeline. Nate answered all my questions with patience and understanding, steadfastly supporting me through some difficult moments. Most importantly, he found great external reviewers for the manuscript. The anonymous external reviewers provided a potent blend of critical and constructive feedback in the early and later stages of the book's development. Beyond the Press's reviews, I appreciate Jennifer Binis for providing thorough and constructive feedback to improve the book during the revision stage. Thanks to the National Academy of Education/Spencer Foundation Postdoctoral Fellowship program for giving me the time and resources to finish the revisions and edits for this book as I thought about and started researching the next book. Thanks to Abigail Michaud for managing the production process, Ben Shaw for indexing, and Dwight Ramsey for proofreading.

Finally, I appreciate the love and support my friends and family provided, especially during the last decade. Thanks to my parents, David and Julie, and my brother, Nate, and sister-in-law, Sam. Thanks to my in-laws Rick, Barb, Katie, Julie, Ryan, Oliver, and Asher. My wife and partner, Kristy, has consistently encouraged me throughout graduate school, writing and finishing my dissertation, and revising and publishing this book. She has supported me through this journey's many ups and downs and in-betweens. In the middle of this work, we created a beautiful family with two little people, Elodie and Lucia. I love you all to pieces.

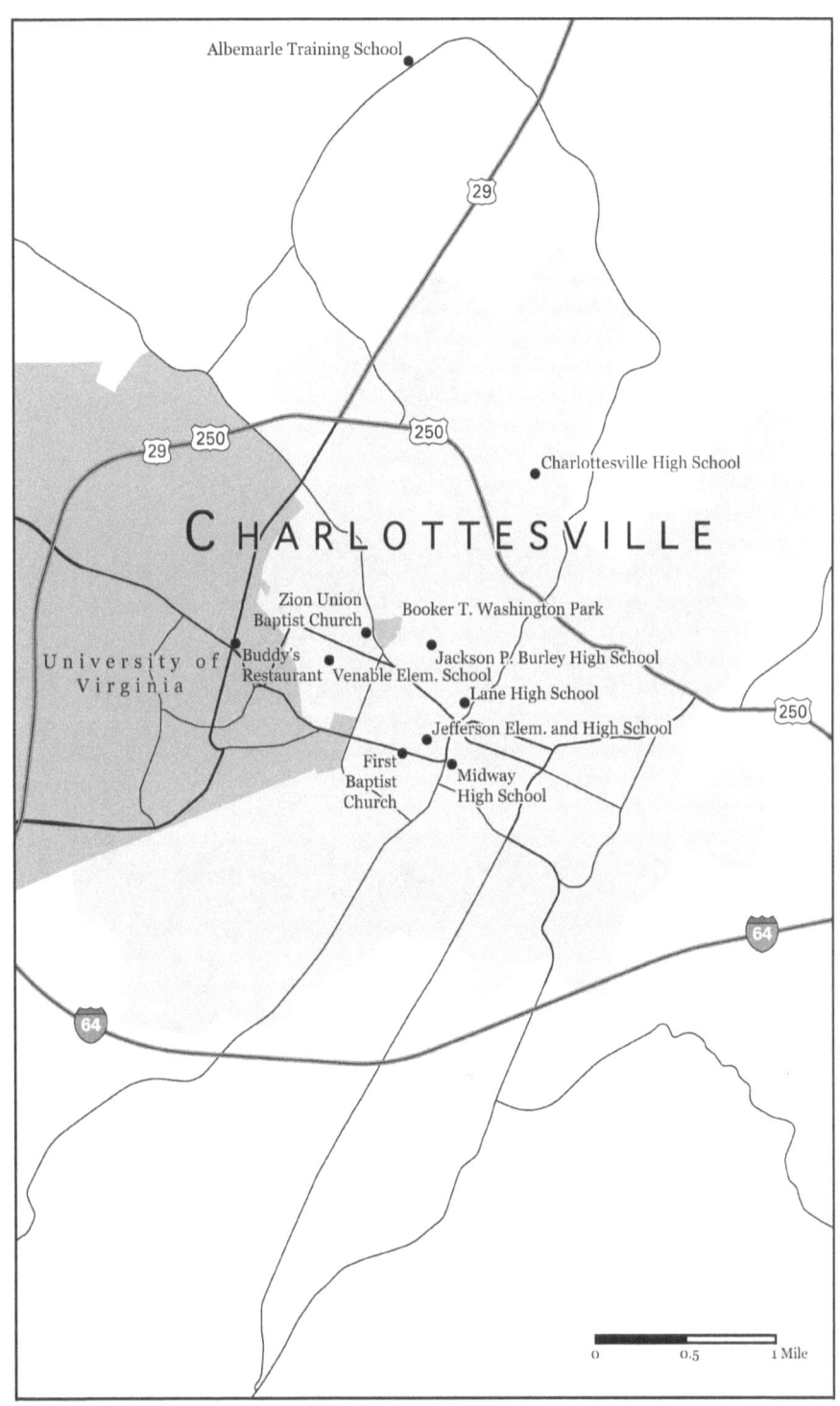

Map of Charlottesville. Courtesy of Glen Pawleski, Fitchburg, Wis., Mapping Specialists Limited, 2024.

TIMELINE

Pre-1600s The Monacan people lived on land today known as Charlottesville along the Rivanna River.
1600s First encounters between the Monacan people and English colonists.
1788 Virginia became a state in the newly formed United States of America.
1801 Virginia designated Charlottesville as a town.
1819 Thomas Jefferson founded the University of Virginia; the Virginia State Legislature passed an anti-literacy law prohibiting freed and enslaved African Americans from learning to read and write.
1831 The Virginia State Legislature passed an amended anti-literacy law prohibiting African Americans from learning to read and write and expanding punishments for white people caught teaching African Americans; Nat Turner led a rebellion in Southampton, Virginia, against white enslavers.
1861–1865 Duration of the Civil War.
1865 Jefferson Colored Graded/Elementary School, a segregated Black school, opened.
1870 The Commonwealth of Virginia ratified a new state constitution, and the Albemarle County Schools Division was formed, including schools in Albemarle County and Charlottesville.
1881 Midway Grammar School, a segregated white school, opened.
1888 Charlottesville became an incorporated city.
1890 Midway High School, a segregated white school, opened; African American residents held their first meeting to begin organizing for a Black high school.
1892 The Commonwealth of Virginia designated Charlottesville a city, and the Charlottesville City Schools Division formed, separating from the Albemarle County Schools Division.

1898 U.S. Supreme Court ruled in *Cumming v. Richmond County Board of Education*, asserting that school districts and divisions are not required to provide secondary schooling for African American students.

1902 The Commonwealth of Virginia ratified a new state constitution; the new constitution codified segregated schooling.

1916 McGuffey Elementary School, a segregated white school, opened.

1924 Midway High School became Lane High School; the Robert E. Lee statue was constructed in a downtown park and dedicated by UVA President Edwin Alderman.

1925 Venable Elementary School, a segregated white school, opened.

1926 Jefferson High School, a segregated Black school, opened.

1931 Clark Elementary School, a segregated white school, opened.

1940 Lane High School, a segregated white school, reopened in a new building.

1951 Jefferson High School closed; Jackson P. Burley High School, a segregated city and countywide Black school, opened.

1954 U.S. Supreme Court rules in *Brown v. Board of Education, I*, outlawing segregation in schools; Johnson Elementary School, a segregated white school, opened.

1955 U.S. Supreme Court ruled in *Brown v. Board of Education, II*, asserting that schools must comply with Brown with "all deliberate speed"; Burnley-Moran Elementary School, a segregated white school, opened.

1959 "The Charlottesville Twelve" desegregated Venable Elementary School and Lane High School.

1964 U.S. Congress passed the Civil Rights Act of 1964.

1965 U.S. Congress passed the Voting Rights Act of 1965.

1967 Jackson P. Burley High School closed; all Black high school students attended Lane High School.

1968 Black students at Lane High School organized two major protests and petitioned the school's administrators to enact reforms.

1974 Lane High School closed; Charlottesville High School opened.

1983 Black students protested a racist newspaper article in the Charlottesville High School newspaper, the *Knight Time Review*.

1984 U.S. Department of Education published *A Nation at Risk*.
2001 U.S. Congress passed the No Child Left Behind Act of 2001.
2016 Zyahna Bryant posted an online petition on Change.org to change the name of Lee Park and remove the Robert E. Lee Statue.
2017 White supremacist groups protested at UVA and in a downtown park against the removal of the Lee statue.
2019 Black students organized a protest after an online racial threat and petitioned the school's administrators to enact reforms.
2021 The City of Charlottesville removed the Lee statue.
2023 Charles Alexander unveiled the Black History Pathway in downtown Charlottesville.
2025 Zyahna Bryant announced a bid for a school board seat on the Charlottesville City School Board.

PROTEST AND PEDAGOGY

Introduction

During the twentieth century, Florence C. Bryant and Charles Alexander propelled and sustained the Black freedom struggle in Charlottesville, Virginia. Bryant came of age in rural Caroline County, Virginia during the Jim Crow era. As a student, she attended segregated Black schools, culminating in her graduation from Virginia State College in Petersburg. Bryant applied to the Charlottesville City Schools Division (CCS), seeking her first teaching job. She received an offer to teach at Charlottesville's Jefferson Elementary School, a segregated Black school, beginning in the 1940s. Originally known as the Jefferson Colored Graded/Elementary School, it opened during the Civil War era. After a year of teaching at the elementary school, Bryant moved to Jefferson High School (JHS)—the city's Black high school, which opened in 1926. She spent the rest of her career in education, over several decades, working at several different schools—segregated and desegregated—as Charlottesville experienced significant educational, political, social, and economic changes.[1]

Bryant's efforts within and beyond the classroom reveal a willingness to fight for justice, equity, and educational opportunity. At JHS and, later, Jackson P. Burley High School (BHS), the city's second Black high school, Bryant taught English and elementary French. During February, Bryant worked annually alongside her colleagues at the high school and elementary school to observe and celebrate Negro History Week. She facilitated a range of extracurricular activities, including creating the yearbook. Beyond the classroom, Bryant, a self-described "joiner," became involved in various social and political organizations, such as the local chapter of the National Association for the Advancement of Colored People (NAACP). As the death of Jim Crow neared, Bryant became part of the first wave of Black graduate students at the University of Virginia and Black educators to desegregate schools in the Charlottesville City Schools Division. Near the end of her career, Bryant became one of the few Black administrators before retiring from Charlottesville High School (CHS) during the 1980s. For the most part, Bryant's fight against racism, inequality, and white supremacy occurred in furtive and latent ways. Bryant's approach contrasted with Charles Alexander's approach, particularly as he entered high school.[2]

Around the same time Florence Bryant participated in desegregation efforts, Charles Alexander desegregated Venable Elementary School as a student. On September 8, 1959, when Alexander ascended the red brick steps and walked through a set of tall white columns of Venable Elementary School, he became the youngest of the twelve African American students desegregating the schools in Charlottesville. Alexander's entrance into Venable Elementary School, a historically white school, disrupted and challenged decades of segregation, inequality, and white supremacy in Charlottesville. Alexander did not decide, on his own, to desegregate the schools; his parents were approached by the NAACP about school desegregation following the Supreme Court's ruling in *Brown v. Board of Education* (1954). They agreed that Charles Alexander should be part of what would later become known as "The Charlottesville Twelve." He obliged his parents. Alexander attended desegregated schools for the remainder of his education in Charlottesville. Transgressing the boundaries between segregated public spaces marked the beginning of Alexander's experience as a student and, later, as an activist.[3]

As he entered high school, Alexander's approach shifted. Unlike Alexander's experience as a Black child at Venable Elementary, where he was one of the few Black children in classes full of white students, he entered Lane High School (LHS) alongside a greater number of Black youth. The passage and implementation of the Civil Rights Act of 1964 led to the acceleration of school desegregation, which included more Black students and, eventually, some Black educators at LHS. As a result, the Charlottesville City Schools Division desegregated across the school division and closed the city's segregated Black high school, BHS. Alexander, working with his peers and with the support of some Black educators during this era, participated in walkouts and petitioned school officials to reform policy, curriculum, and practice at historically white LHS. They called for a range of reforms, including hiring more Black teachers and counselors, and the integration of the Black experience in the high school's curriculum. Black students' protests led to changes at LHS, including creating a Black Studies elective course.[4]

Bryant, a Black woman educator, and Alexander, a Black male student, possessed different opportunities and faced different challenges in pursuing justice, liberation, and educational opportunities. At the same time, their lives and experiences elucidate the role African American high school educators and students played in the Black freedom struggle during the twentieth century. Furthermore, a closer examination of their experiences reveals the dynamic relationship between protest and pedagogy. Examining the experiences of Bryant, Alexander, and many other African American educators and students also illuminates the making of the American high school in Charlottesville, the South, and the United States.

Bryant and Alexander were just two of the many African Americans who fought for freedom, justice, and liberation within and beyond the high school classrooms of Charlottesville, Virginia. The existing historiography on the participation of African American students and educators in the Black freedom struggle tends to focus on either one group or the other. This singular focus on each group has yielded a deeper and more nuanced understanding of the experiences of African American youth and African American adults in these roles. However, such an emphasis on one group or the other obscures their influences on one another. Although some recent scholarship has explored the dynamic relationship between African American students and educators in specific eras, this book spotlights the perspectives of high school students *and* educators throughout the twentieth century. Focusing on both groups provides a more expansive portrait of the collaboration and contestation between teachers and students, tracing the long-term trajectory of African American youth and adults involved in education. Some of the students became teachers in Charlottesville, and some of the teachers remained in the school division and took on new roles as administrators. Youth and adults also participated in the Black freedom struggle beyond the school walls.[5]

African Americans' identities as students and educators intersected with their gender and class identities. The intersection of these identities shaped decisions about how—and whether—to participate in the fight for equity, justice, and educational opportunity. Their choices were also influenced by a particular era's broader political, economic, social, and educational context. However, neither identity nor context dictated the shape and course of

Charlottesville's Black freedom struggle. Instead, African American high school teachers and students, at times, created the context and, at other times, acted within the context created by others. The local Black freedom struggle shifted depending on the time and high school. Sometimes, Black educators and students collaborated in propelling and sustaining the fight for justice and equity; in other moments, they were in conflict about how to fight against white supremacy, racial oppression, and educational inequality. Indeed, Black educators and students did not move in lockstep collective groups. Within groups of African American teachers, and within groups of African American students, they did not agree about how—or whether— to protest. However, the protest of some Black students and teachers influenced all students' and teachers' lives and experiences.[6]

Protest and Pedagogy centers African American students' and educators' lives and experiences. At the same time, the book focuses on those individuals to illuminate the relationship between protest and pedagogy. Historians have tended to separate their examinations of protest and pedagogy. On the one hand, they have chronicled the protests of African American youth and educators. On the other hand, they have explored the changes and continuities of pedagogy in American schools. This book knits together these examinations, revealing how protest influenced pedagogy, and pedagogy influenced protest. In Charlottesville, the relationship between protest and pedagogy existed before the establishment of a Black high school in the city, and then, once opened, the relationship emerged and changed over time in the city's high schools: Jefferson High School (1926–1951), Jackson P. Burley High School (1951–1967), Lane High School (1959–1974), and Charlottesville High School (1974–present). This book engages with protest and pedagogy in broad terms. "Protest" at the city's high schools consisted of organizing, petitioning, desegregating, walking out, sitting in, and refusing. "Pedagogy" at the city's high schools consisted of how teachers taught, and students learned, but also what teachers taught and what students learned.[7]

The dynamic relationship between protest and pedagogy emerged and evolved within the high school space in four distinct ways. First, the relationship manifested as protest *for* pedagogy. Educators and students organized and agitated for expanded educational opportunities. For instance, following the Reconstruction era, African American educators helped organize for a Black high school, which led to the building of JHS for African American youth in Charlottesville. Second, it manifested in protest *as* pedagogy. For example, educators' and students' protests led to educational reforms at a particular moment and helped the broader Black community imagine and build a more just and equitable future. As Black students and teachers desegregated the historically white LHS, they transgressed the boundaries of segregation in Charlottesville. It was not just the legal cases that challenged white supremacy; it was also the individuals and groups who stepped foot in previously prohibited spaces. The students and teachers embodied progress, even as they faced white backlash during the school desegregation era.

Third, it manifested as pedagogy *as* protest. For instance, educators provided access to curriculum that challenged the status quo of anti-Blackness and white supremacy, while also centering Black people in the curriculum at JHS and BHS. Fourth, it manifested as pedagogy *for* protest. For instance, educators provided pedagogical approaches encouraging students to fight for justice within and beyond the schools. By illuminating the dynamic relationship between protest and pedagogy in Charlottesville, this book offers a framework for thinking about the intersection between education and the Black freedom struggle.

This book focuses on a specific part of the school system in the United States: the American high school. Historians of the American high school have focused on the institutional story. They have illuminated the unique nature of the high school within the school system of the United States and its place within American life. These accounts have concentrated on the high schools in the North and Midwest. In the South, historians have examined the rise and fall of segregated Black high schools and the rise of school desegregation. These accounts conclude with the closure of Black high schools as southern communities faced pressure from African American residents and the federal government to desegregate their schools.

Viewed from the perspectives of African American students and educators, the American high school was a paradoxical institution. On the one hand, high schools became a space that operated as a "movement center." The spaces within high schools—both segregated and desegregated contexts—became a place where the local Black freedom struggle incubated and expanded. On the other hand, the desegregated high school became a place where white people resisted the advancement of the Black freedom struggle in different ways, while also using the high school as their own "movement center." The paradox of the American high school does not fit neatly within a rise and fall narrative; instead, it oscillates across time and place. The high school provided a space to incubate and act out strategies for equity and justice in the Charlottesville City Schools Division *and* the broader community. While this book spotlights the high school as a space, it also examines the interactions between the high school and the wider community.[8]

Educational scholars have examined the circumstances leading to and the consequences of school closures. These works include historical and contemporary examinations, often showing the deleterious impacts of the closures on students, teachers, and communities. The opening and closing of schools in the city marked eras of the American high school. Examining the closures and openings of high schools in Charlottesville reveals a set of complicated and varied responses within the African American community.[9]

The opening of new high schools and desegregation of a historically white high school often meant, at least in theory, the expansion of justice, equity, and educational opportunity. The opening of JHS meant expanding job opportunities for African American educators and educational opportunities for African American students, both representing a victory for the local Black freedom struggle. The statewide equalization movement and local organizing led to the closure of JHS and the establishment of BHS—a high school with greater educational opportunities due to expanded facilities.

The closure of BHS meant the end of the Black high school, which elicited a range of responses from the city's African American community. Some questioned the quality of education at BHS and wanted greater access to the opportunities available at Lane High School. Others questioned whether African American educators and students would receive equitable opportunities at LHS. The closure of LHS represented the failure of the Charlottesville City Schools Division to adequately prepare for school desegregation. The opening of Charlottesville High School had the potential for a fresh start; however, African American students and educators faced similar issues at the new high school. Some of the problems became exacerbated by the school's location in the northern part of the city.

Protest and Pedagogy is a story of African American students and educators, the American high school, curriculum, activism, and the Black freedom struggle. But it is also a story about a place: Charlottesville, Virginia. Charlottesville has been associated with Thomas Jefferson or the University of

Table 1. Population of Charlottesville, 2020

Race and ethnicity	American Indian	Asian	Black or African American	Hispanic or Latino/a/x	Two or more races	White
Population	164	4,083	7,122	3,207	3,583	30,344

Source: "City of Charlottesville, Va.," Accessed on May 14, 2024. https://data.census.gov/profile/Charlottesville_city,_Virginia?g=050XX00US51540.

Virginia. However, as Zyahna Bryant, a young Black student observed in 2016, "there is more to this city that makes it great." Centering the lives and experiences of African American high school educators and students changes the story of Charlottesville.[10]

Today, Charlottesville has a population of 46,553, covering just over ten square miles. It forms an isosceles triangle with two nearby capital cities: Washington, DC, the capital of the United States government, and Richmond, the current capital of Virginia and former capital of the Confederacy during the Civil War. The city inhabits the Piedmont Region, with the Blue Ridge Mountains to the west and the Coastal Plain Region of Virginia to the east. The Rivanna River runs through the city and Albemarle County. The city's largest employer is the University of Virginia, and, as with other college towns, the university has been—and continues to be—entangled with the city's political, social, economic, and educational context. The Charlottesville City Schools Division, the city's public school system, consists of six elementary schools, one upper elementary school, a middle school, and a high school.[11]

Charlottesville's development has been inextricably linked with settler colonialism, white supremacy, and racism in the United States. Before the arrival of white English settlers, the Monacan Indians inhabited the area known as Charlottesville and nearby Albemarle County. After the arrival of white English settlers, the area became known as Charlottesville—named for Queen Charlotte, the wife of King George III. The white English settlers, throughout Virginia, brought enslaved Africans with them to establish and sustain the colony of Virginia during the seventeenth and eighteenth centuries. The English colonists in the area included Peter and Martha Jefferson. Thomas Jefferson, the son of Peter and Martha Jefferson and the third president of the United States, relied upon enslaved African

Americans to build the most enduring monuments associated with Jefferson and Charlottesville: Monticello and the University of Virginia.¹²

Monticello, a plantation designed by Jefferson and built and sustained by enslaved African Americans, overlooks the City of Charlottesville. In 1762, Charlottesville became part of Albemarle County; Monticello became Jefferson's primary residence a decade later. During Jefferson's time as President, Charlottesville became designated as a town. In Jefferson's absence and presence, during the late eighteenth and nineteenth centuries, African Americans built and maintained the plantation lands, including growing and harvesting tobacco and wheat crops. Down the mountain, in Charlottesville, enslaved African Americans built and maintained the University of Virginia, which was founded in 1819. While UVA depended on enslaved and, following the Civil War, freed African Americans to support the development of the institution, they were prohibited from enrolling there until the middle of the twentieth century. Beyond the university's grounds, though, African Americans in Charlottesville would push for access to educational opportunities in the local public schools.¹³

This book spotlights high schools as important institutions for the emergence of the Black freedom struggle during the twentieth century. At the same time, other institutions and organizations moved in parallel and, at times, intersecting ways to sustain the fight for educational opportunity, justice, and freedom in Charlottesville. Two of the city's Black churches, most notably, First Baptist Church and Mount Zion African Methodist Episcopal (AME) Church, provided space and sustenance for the Black community from the nineteenth century onward. Longtime pastor at the First Baptist Church, Reverend Benjamin F. Bunn, was involved in the establishment of the local branch of the NAACP. Bunn and the NAACP played a pivotal role in the local Black freedom struggle particularly around issues of education and housing. This book highlights the people, places, and institutions shaping Charlottesville. It is an imperfect city, but it is also a city where African Americans have led the charge to make it a more just and equitable place for all.¹⁴

Protest and Pedagogy is a social and political history. It employs an ecological approach to situate Black high school teachers and students in Charlottesville, Virginia's broader educational, social, political, and economic context during the twentieth century. As a result, the book dwells "in the specificity of the micro, the uncomfortable uncertainties that cannot be seen" at larger scales of inquiry. At the same time, it does not ignore the broader state and national contexts that intersect with Charlottesville. Instead, Charlottesville holds the center of the narrative while accounting for the city's entanglements with state and national contexts. Several different primary sources help illuminate the specificity, while the book also contextualizes, when possible and relevant, the specific to broader scales of place and time.[15]

The book is anchored by oral history interviews conducted during the late twentieth- and early twenty-first century to reveal the lives and experiences of African American high school educators and students. The interviews conducted for the TIM Project reveal the participation of African American educators during the Black freedom struggle in the South, emphasizing their lives and experiences within the classroom. The other oral history interviews and collections also help chronicle Black education's history in Charlottesville and the South.[16]

The book also relies on curriculum and pedagogical materials, teacher and student memoirs, newspapers, reports, and yearbooks to illuminate the relationship between protest and pedagogy within and beyond the city's high schools. In particular, the use of oral history interviews coupled with teacher- and student-generated documents, school newspapers and yearbooks, reveals how Black teachers and students helped make and remake the American high school in Charlottesville over time.[17]

Protest and Pedagogy unfolds over five chapters, employing a chronological and thematic approach. Chapter 1, "A Long, Hard Struggle and a Lot of Agitation," chronicles the fight for a Black high school education within and beyond the classroom in Charlottesville. This reveals the origins of pedagogy *as* protest through the life and work of educator Benjamin Tonsler and student Rebecca Fuller McGinness. The absence of a Black high school in the city led to covert efforts to provide an expanded curriculum in the classroom and, for families who could afford it, the need to send students outside of Charlottesville for greater educational opportunities. The chapter also illuminates the emergence of protest *for* pedagogy, which manifests the organizing for establishing a Black high school in Charlottesville.

Despite the rise of Jim Crow, the Black community agitated for expanded educational opportunities, which ultimately led to the establishment of Jefferson High School.

The following two chapters reveal the rise and fall of the Black high school in Charlottesville. Chapter 2, "Pillars of This Town," examines the development of Jefferson High School through the experiences of Black students like Booker Reaves and Black educators like Florence C. Bryant. It reveals the continuation and expansion of pedagogy *as* protest and protest *for* pedagogy amid the Great Depression and World War II. It also elucidates the statewide equalization movement by describing the circumstances that led to the closure of JHS, a citywide high school, and the establishment of Jackson P. Burley High School, a multicounty high school. Chapter 3, "To Take Their Place as Future Leaders," chronicles the fall of the Black high school at BHS due to the Charlottesville City Schools Division's response to the *Brown* decisions. It illuminates how BHS became a "movement center" with broader reach in Charlottesville and the surrounding counties. Black educators like Teresa Price and students like Berdell Fleming became involved in broader civil rights struggles at the same time as white resistance expanded. The experiences of Price and Fleming reveal the emergence of protest *as* pedagogy and pedagogy *for* protest. The chapter also chronicles the closure of BHS and its consequences for Black high school students and educators.

The final two chapters examine the desegregation of high schools in Charlottesville. Chapter 4, "A Little More Defiant, A Little More Militant," traces the rise of the desegregated high school at Lane High School. It spotlights the experiences of different waves of Black students like Charles Alexander and educators like Esther Vasser, emphasizing the emergence and evolution of protest *for* pedagogy, protest *as* pedagogy, and pedagogy *as* protest in a desegregated high school. As a result of African American students' and teachers' organizing and activism, LHS became an unwitting "movement center" space for the local Black freedom struggle. LHS closed in 1974. Chapter 5, "Because Racism Was So Deeply Ingrained," examines the limits of the desegregated high school through the story of Charlottesville High School. It reveals the changes and continuities in the relationship between protest and pedagogy through the events preceding and following a Black student protest in 1984. Finally, it illuminates the experiences of Black educators such as Florence C. Bryant and Diane Price as

A historical marker, placed in 2011, commemorates school desegregation in Charlottesville during the fall of 1959. Courtesy of the author.

they grappled with the enduring legacy of racism and resistance in the United States.

The conclusion, "The Statues Coming Down Is the Tip of the Iceberg," reveals the entanglements between the past, present, and future at the intersection between protest and pedagogy. It examines the recent wave of protest at Charlottesville High School through the experience of Zyahna Bryant and her peers during the past couple of years. Then, it turns toward future directions in examining the relationship between protest and pedagogy beyond the context of Charlottesville, Virginia.

Today, a historical marker stands outside of Venable Elementary School. An identical marker stands outside of the former Lane High School, which has been repurposed as the Albemarle County Office Building. The marker titled "Triumph of the Charlottesville Twelve," lists the twelve African American children and youth that desegregated Venable and Lane. It reads:

> On September 8, 1959, three African American children bravely entered Lane High School by order of U.S. District Court Judge John Paul. With the assistance of the National Association for the Advancement of Colored People—the children's parents sued the Charlottesville City School Board for equal access. Their fight began in 1955, following the Supreme Court decision of the 1954 case, Brown v. Board of Education. Parents took action to fulfill their civil rights by petitioning the Charlottesville School Board to transfer their children from the segregated Jefferson Elementary School and Jackson P. Burley High School. The School Board chose to take no-action on the petition request in 1956. Judge Paul ruled that Charlottesville must integrate Lane High School and Venable Elementary. The School Board filed several appeals contesting the decision to comply with integration. Using the strategy of "massive resistance," Governor James Lindsey Almond, Jr. ordered the closure of Lane and Venable on September 19, 1958 to prevent the integration of the Charlottesville City Schools. When schools reopened in February 1959, the School Board provided space in the Board office for students to take classes while they determined how to proceed with a plan for integration. On September 5, 1959, Judge Paul ordered the immediate transfer of twelve students who became known as "The Charlottesville Twelve."

In 2011, the City of Charlottesville placed these markers to memorialize the city's story of school desegregation and to contextualize the efforts of the African American students who enrolled at two of the city's historically white schools.[18]

Charles Alexander is one of the twelve names listed on the marker. The marker narrative focuses on the events between the Supreme Court's decision in *Brown v. Board of Education* (1954) and the first day of school desegregation in Charlottesville. On the one hand, the marker captures an essential event in the fight to end school segregation. It highlights how Alexander and his peers bore the burden of desegregating schools. On the other hand, the marker forgets much of the burden and work involved in seeking out justice, equity, and educational opportunity in Charlottesville. Focusing on the first day of school desegregation, the marker leaves out the continued struggle of African American male students like Alexander. Not only does the marker fail to remember the full extent of Alexander's experience in the Charlottesville City Schools Division, but it also forgets the experiences of African American educators like Florence Coleman Bryant. This is also true of African American students *and* educators beyond Alexander and Bryant.[19]

This book does what that marker does not. It aims to more fully remember the lives and experiences of African American educators and students in Charlottesville and the Black freedom struggle during the twentieth century. Remembering their contributions requires returning to the origins of the Black freedom struggle and the fight for a Black high school in the city during the nineteenth century.

PART ONE

The Rise and Fall of the Black High School

CHAPTER ONE

"A Long, Hard Struggle and a Lot of Agitation"
The Fight for a Black High School, 1890–1926

It took a long, hard struggle and a lot of agitation to finally get a high school for African Americans. It came too late for me to take advantage of it, but I was impressed with the dedication and persistence those who worked for it demonstrated.
—Rebecca Fuller McGinness, student at Jefferson Colored Graded/Elementary School and teacher at Jefferson Elementary School

Therefore, we the undersigned petitioners, citizens of Charlottesville, Va., do ask that you grant us a High School for the Colored Youth of said City. We are deeply grateful for the educational advantages which we have and pray that the time is ripe for giving us a High School.
—Petition for a Black high school in Charlottesville, circa 1920

In 1854, Benjamin Tonsler was born in Earlysville—a small town outside Charlottesville, Virginia. At the time of Tonsler's birth, it was illegal for him or any other African American, freed or enslaved, to attend a formal school or even seek literacy through informal means in Virginia. However, during his life, Tonsler would observe and participate in a significant expansion of educational opportunities in Charlottesville, Virginia, and across the South. This expansion, at the nexus between protest and pedagogy, would buttress the Black freedom struggle even amid a rising backlash against progress for African Americans.[1]

Before the Civil War, white politicians in Virginia's legislature passed two laws codifying the prohibition of African American education and schooling. In 1819, they outlawed education and schooling for all African Americans across Virginia. The law read, "That all meetings or assemblages of slaves, or free negroes or mulattoes mixing and associating with such slaves at any meeting-house or houses... in the night; or any school for teaching them reading or writing, either in the day or night, under whatsoever pretext, shall be deemed and considered unlawful assembly." Not only did this law make it illegal for African Americans to attend school, but the law also went a step further by making it illegal for them to even gather in groups. This law was passed during the same year that educational opportunities expanded for white men in the state, as Thomas Jefferson founded the University of Virginia in 1819.[2]

The Virginia legislature was not done with restricting African Americans' access to education. In 1831, before Nat Turner's rebellion in Southampton, Virginia, the legislature passed yet another law outlawing education and schooling for African Americans. The new law amended the previous one to punish anyone, particularly white people, who associated with and taught African Americans to read and write. Although the number of white people who would have even attempted to teach African Americans to read or write was small, this law aimed to create yet another obstacle for African Americans to become literate. White resistance to African American education is only part of the story. Despite the new legislation and enforcement, some African Americans in Virginia learned to read and write through creative and furtive means. As a result, approximately five percent of the state's African American population could read and write on the eve of the Civil War. During the Civil War, and in the decades following, though, that number would grow exponentially. African American children and youth enrolled at schools rather than learning in secret and through informal means.[3]

Benjamin Tonsler was one of those children. Tonsler, after his birth, remained in and around Charlottesville and Albemarle County. Tonsler attended the Jefferson Colored Graded/Elementary School in Charlottesville. The South's changing political, economic, and social terrain during the Civil War led to the creation of individual schools like the Jefferson Colored Graded/Elementary School for African American students. Accessing the school required great determination, time, and energy, as transportation would not have made it easy for Tonsler to attend a school located several miles away from where he lived. Depending on the local context, African Americans started schools in their local communities in the South, or African American and white northerners came to the region to expand educational opportunities.[4]

Some communities in the North possessed educational opportunities for African American and white students. However, for the most part, the South had lagged in developing individual schools and school systems for most people before the Civil War. In Virginia, Thomas Jefferson attempted to establish a public school system for white students; however, his efforts failed. The Civil War created an opportunity to expand educational opportunities. African American teachers from the North and South and white teachers, primarily from the North, established schools in the South with the support of philanthropic organizations. Teachers from the North, African American and white, and local African American teachers, would prove crucial to the education and development of students like Tonsler, who would take on several different roles in the post–Civil War world. Tonsler would not only become an educator but also one of the individuals who propelled the Black freedom struggle at the nexus between protest and pedagogy.[5]

During the Civil War, Isabella Gibbons started a school in Charlottesville for Black children and youth. Before starting a school, Gibbons, an African American woman, had been one of the enslaved people who labored and maintained the University of Virginia. Gibbons became free, and left UVA to start a new life and career as the war entered the waning stages. However, Gibbons was not the only one who opened a school for African American children and youth in the area around that time. Anne Gardner, a white Quaker and former resident of Nantucket, Massachusetts, relocated from New England and started another school in the city. Gardner named the school for Thomas Jefferson, affixing "colored" and "elementary" to denote the school's purposes. Gardner hoped that naming the school for Jefferson would help avoid the ire of local white residents. While her school—Jefferson Colored Graded/Elementary School—proved successful, Gibbons' school did not remain open for long. The circumstances leading to the closure of Gibbons's school are unclear. However, Gardner hired Gibbons within weeks to teach at the Jefferson Colored Graded/Elementary School. Gibbons also continued her education as a student at the school. Based on the surviving records of the school, Gibbons taught at the Jefferson Colored Graded/Elementary School for at least twenty years.[6]

When the Jefferson Colored Graded/Elementary School opened, Benjamin Tonsler became among the first wave of students to enroll there. As a student, Tonsler learned from Anne Gardner, Isabella Gibbons, and Philena Carkin, another white woman from New England. Carkin not only taught Tonsler, but she also advocated for him to receive education beyond the Jefferson Colored Graded/Elementary School. "Benjamin Tonsler was in my class for about two years," recalls Carkin. "[F]inding him a particularly bright and promising boy, I appealed to Gen[eral] Armstrong in his behalf, and succeeded in getting him into a position in the Hampton School where he could earn all the expenses of board tuition etc. while he remained there." Carkin's recommendation helped Tonsler secure a spot and a scholarship at the Hampton Institute. At the time, he had few options for pursuing secondary schooling. Since he could not attend high school or college in Charlottesville, Tonsler had to leave the city to seek further education. No local high school, college, or university, existed for African American students, as UVA only admitted white men at the time. So, Tonsler attended the Hampton Institute for his secondary and postsecondary education.[7]

The Hampton Institute, established by General Samuel Armstrong and funded by white philanthropic organizations, opened in 1868. Tonsler attended the school around the same time that the school's most famous alumnus, Booker T. Washington, worked there. Tonsler and Washington became friends during their time together at the Hampton Institute. When Tonsler attended Hampton, the curriculum and pedagogy aimed to prepare African American students to teach the South's first generation of African Americans during the Reconstruction era and beyond. Tonsler learned to teach from instructors' pedagogy, underpinned by what would become known as the "Hampton-Tuskegee idea." This ideological framework focused on developing African Americans' capacity for work in the Reconstruction era and beyond. By inculcating this idea into African American students at Hampton, many of whom would, in turn, become teachers across the South, Armstrong and other white philanthropists believed they could shape the future of African American education and, by extension, politics, and economics in the South. The reality was more complicated as students at the Hampton Institute went out into the world as educators and citizens. Tonsler, like many African American men and women of the time, earned a degree from Hampton and returned to their communities. He graduated in 1874.[8]

Beginning in 1867, a year before Hampton opened, the Commonwealth of Virginia held a constitutional convention. African American and white delegates from across the state met in Richmond, Virginia—the former capital of the Confederacy—until 1868, when the delegates had agreed upon the new state constitution. Several changes occurred because of the rewritten constitution, including the creation of a state-supported system of schools. Schools such as the Jefferson Colored Graded/Elementary School transitioned from stand-alone institutions to ones connected by larger city, county, and state systems. The Commonwealth of Virginia bucked the status quo of other states by not creating districts; instead, they called these individual units "divisions." The local divisions consisted of different sizes and shapes aligned with the counties and cities. In all the county and city school divisions, though, segregation became a reality not because of law at the time. Segregating schools by law did not pass; however, the schools in Charlottesville and around Virginia originated as segregated institutions during the Civil War, and they remained that way following the war. Only later would the segregation of schools become codified by state and federal law. At first, the Jefferson Colored Graded/Elementary School and the Midway School, the segregated white school, aligned with the surrounding schools in Albemarle County. In 1890, the schools in Charlottesville separated from the Albemarle County Schools Division to form the Charlottesville City Schools Division.[9]

Tonsler returned to teach at the Jefferson Colored Graded/Elementary School during the 1870s. Like many African American schools across the South, the Jefferson Colored Graded/Elementary School also transitioned away from having white educators and toward all-Black schools, including students, staff, and faculty. Besides owning a business or working for the city, teaching was among the few jobs offering greater economic security. While teaching provided some financial security, African American teachers like Isabella Gibbons and Benjamin Tonsler inhabited a precarious place during the Reconstruction and Jim Crow eras. Depending on where they were situated, African American teachers faced intimidation by paramilitary white supremacist groups, poor working conditions, unequal pay, and uncertain job security. It did not mean, however, that they were passive and acquiescent to white supremacy. Tonsler started as a teacher upon his initial return to the school. In 1897, he became the principal of the Jefferson Colored Graded/Elementary School. As principal, Tonsler not only led the school, but he continued teaching as Reconstruction ended and Jim Crow emerged in Charlottesville.[10]

During and after the Civil War, African Americans established schools, enrolled at the schools, and helped create school systems in Charlottesville and throughout Virginia and the South. The local work of Isabella Gibbons and Benjamin Tonsler led to expanding schooling and educational opportunities in Charlottesville. This work would become increasingly difficult as Jim Crow, a system of white supremacy and institutional racism, emerged in the city and across the state and region. But Tonsler would use his position to provide educational opportunities for African American students in the city amid increasing racial hostility and violence against African Americans during the late nineteenth and early twentieth century.

With the rise of Jim Crow, white people in Charlottesville—and across Virginia and the South—created and cultivated separate and unequal public spheres. White politicians and government officials used policy and violence to enact and maintain those separate public spheres. This process occurred over several decades in the twentieth century. But certain events revealed how the rise of white supremacy shaped the experiences of African Americans in Charlottesville. In 1898, white residents in Albemarle County—the county surrounding Charlottesville—accused John Henry James, an African American man, of assaulting a white woman, Julia Hotopp. James did not receive a trial—let alone a fair one, as the U.S. Constitution guaranteed. Instead, local white residents lynched James. White violence—and the threat of white violence—during the Jim Crow era combined with racist policymaking and the construction of white superiority myths.[11]

In 1902, Virginia held another constitutional convention to revisit and revise the one conducted during Reconstruction. While the constitutional convention of 1867–1868 included African American and white men, the 1902 convention included only wealthy, white males. African American and white women participated in neither of the constitutional conventions. The new constitution removed several past provisions, including those required for Virginia's readmittance to the United States following the Civil War. This removal signaled the legal codification of white supremacy and the minimization of the Civil War and its consequences. While the previous constitution relied on local custom to segregate schooling, the new constitution stipulated segregated schooling for Black and white children. While both public and private schools had been segregated on a de facto basis for several decades, the codification of such a reality manifested a shift in how the state viewed the purpose of African American schooling. African American youth could continue to pursue an elementary education. However, the state aimed to create a "separate" and, as would become more apparent over time, an "unequal" education.[12]

The new constitution represented just one shift in the political, social, economic, and educational landscape. The University of Virginia's Paul Barringer, a leader in the eugenics movement, believed that universal schooling "did not keep descendants of slaves from deteriorating into a savage and violent criminal class, their natural condition because the teachers in many of the schools were also black." It was not long before Barringer's beliefs and ideas would become the prevailing political and legal reality in Virginia. Barringer drew upon his mantle at the University of Virginia to propagate ideas of Black inferiority and criminality in the Commonwealth and beyond. The white supremacist logic espoused by Barringer would become dominant during the next few decades and influence the state's political consciousness. In turn, that political consciousness shaped how white people and African Americans viewed education. In 1924, state legislators passed the Racial Integrity Act. The new law "codified a two-tier racial hierarchy in which residents could only fit within the rigid racial categories of either White or colored." The combination of changes to the state constitution and laws during the early twentieth century dismantled the reality and, in many ways, the memory of Reconstruction.[13]

In Charlottesville, white politicians and residents enacted white supremacy in word and deed. The University of Virginia named their newly formed School of Education for Jabez Lamar Monroe Curry—a former slaveholder, member of the Confederacy, and "white architect" of African American education. Before his death, Curry lacked any substantive connection to the university besides a personal relationship with the university's president, Edwin Alderman. Affixing Curry's name to the University of Virginia's School of Education symbolized the university's complicity in undermining African American liberation and freedom using education both locally and statewide. Beyond the university, Charlottesville built a statue honoring Confederate General Robert E. Lee. The statue's presence

Table 2. Population of Charlottesville, 1890–1920

Year	Black	White	Total
1890	2,528	3,063	5,591
1900	2,613	3,836	6,449
1910	2,524	4,241	6,765
1920	2,947	7,741	10,688

Source: Barksdale, "A Comparative Study of Contemporary White and Negro Standards in Health, Education, and Welfare," 11.

served as a reminder of white supremacy's grip on Charlottesville and the need for white people to keep the African American communities in their place.[14]

African American residents in Charlottesville challenged Jim Crow by employing a variety of tactics and strategies. During and after the Civil War, the city's African American population grew significantly, which bolstered their capacity for fighting against white supremacy. Rather than stay on or near the plantations, many African Americans migrated to urban spaces throughout Virginia. While not a significant population center then, Charlottesville offered African Americans the chance to start anew in nearby counties. Following the Emancipation Proclamation, African American residents in counties surrounding Charlottesville moved into the city, seeking greater economic and educational opportunities. As African Americans migrated to Charlottesville, the Vinegar Hill neighborhood became one of the city's prime areas of Black life. The rise of Jim Crow meant that housing, businesses, and other aspects of public life were segregated. Black businesses provided goods and services for the city's African American community. Vinegar Hill was not just the center of African American life in Charlottesville. Eventually, it became home to Jefferson High School and the many individuals who attended, worked at, and supported it.[15]

African Americans possessed few job options during the Jim Crow era in Charlottesville. "I took care of people, and babysitter, and helped people out in doing housework. I really loved what I was doing because I didn't have education to do nothing else," Drusilla Hutchinson, a lifelong resident of the Vinegar Hill neighborhood, recalls. "Back then, there wasn't anything for you to do but maybe work in somebody's kitchen or restaurants, you know, movies and things like that." Hutchinson's employment options were circumscribed both by the lack of access to education and white discrimination within Charlottesville. Her experience mirrors others with similar qualifications at the time.[16]

Despite having few job opportunities, many African American residents made the most of the economic opportunities available. Mattie Thompkins, another resident of Vinegar Hill who became a telephone operator, remembers her parents' experiences. Her father worked at Leggett as a janitor and "he wasn't making anything but like seven dollars a week." He eventually secured a position at Chancellor's Drugstore, where he stayed for twenty-seven years. Thompkins's mother was "doing like maid work, going from house to house, cleaning houses. That's about it—domestic work or whatever." Most African American people in the city were subject to the labor market's ebbs and flows.[17]

Some African Americans possessed the means to create their own businesses. George Inge started a grocery store. J. F. Bell opened a funeral home during the early twentieth century. Both businesses served the city's African American community and, to a lesser extent, its white residents. The City of Charlottesville and the University of Virginia were also major employers. Raymond Bell, the son of J. F. Bell, remembers, "People on Williams Street, most of them worked at the City Yard, trash collecting. Years ago when there were not indoor toilets, they had a truck that went around and would empty the outhouses. And blacks worked in those jobs—street repair, excavations, all kinds of work. At one time there was an incinerator right in the City Yard . . . all the trash in Charlottesville would be burned in that incinerator. The other place they worked was at the university hospital. They worked at the school, doing domestic chores." As the university modernized and expanded during the early twentieth century, jobs for the city and university multiplied. However, access to the highest-paying jobs with both employers remained elusive for Black people.[18]

Working at the Jefferson Colored Graded/Elementary School as a teacher remained one of the better jobs for African Americans during the Jim Crow era. While the school was important for African American students to learn, it also provided jobs for African American adults living in the city. So, the push to expand the Jefferson Colored Graded/Elementary School would not only offer more educational opportunities for African American students but also greater job opportunities for African American adults who arrived in Charlottesville to teach at the Jefferson Colored Graded/Elementary School.

During the post-Reconstruction and Jim Crow eras, Benjamin Tonsler taught several students at the Jefferson Colored Graded/Elementary School. Rebecca Fuller was one of those students. In 1892, Rebecca Fuller was born in Charlottesville. She recalls growing up at a time when the city was growing and modernizing. During the same year of Fuller's birth, Charlottesville became an incorporated city. *The Daily Progress*, the city's newspaper, opened and started circulating. Fuller's family lived in the Starr Hill neighborhood. At the beginning of Fuller's life, the city was less segregated than during the Jim Crow era; however, Black people lived primarily in the neighborhoods of Starr Hill, Gospel Hill, Ridge Street, and Vinegar Hill. Jefferson Colored Graded/Elementary School was in the Vinegar Hill neighborhood.[19]

For most of her life, Julia Shelton Fuller, Rebecca Fuller's mother, worked as a laundress, while Charles Fuller, her father, worked as a waiter and a butler. Her parents, particularly her father, influenced her approach to education and schooling. Despite being denied formal education as a formerly enslaved person, Charles Fuller ensured his children were well-educated and learned Black history. For Rebecca Fuller, learning about Black history resonated deeply. "I'll never forget reading about the Underground Railroad," Fuller recalls, "That book made me hungry to learn more about slavery in the United States and how African Americans had survived slavery. I became an avid reader then and still am today."[20]

Rebecca Fuller's education extended beyond her household, too. She attended the Jefferson Colored/Graded Elementary School for elementary school. "It taught grades one through eight," recalled Fuller, "The school was a large two-story building with four big rooms separated by a wide hallway on each floor. The faculty consisted of seven teachers." At a time when one-room schoolhouses still dotted the South and other regions of the United States, the Jefferson Colored Graded/Elementary School offered substantial educational space. Despite all the space, the school had to run a double-shift schedule to accommodate all the city's Black students. The first four-hour shift started at 8 a.m., while the other started at noon. Each class consisted of between "thirty-five to forty students." The demand for an elementary education far exceeded what the Jefferson Colored Graded/Elementary School could provide. As was the case among other elementary schools for African American students throughout the South, this reality was more common than not.[21]

"We received a quality education at Jefferson School," asserts McGinness. Students were taught using "rote" pedagogy; however, according to McGinness, such pedagogy was a "very valuable technique for learning oral expression and developing self-confidence and poise." Discipline at the elementary school was "very strict." On the one hand, African American residents gained significant educational opportunities at the Jefferson Colored Graded/Elementary School and greater job opportunities. On the other hand, white people retained control over the administration of the Charlottesville City Schools Division. This reality required a creative and pragmatic approach from African American educators to provide students like Fuller with the opportunity to reach "their highest potential."[22]

Despite white oversight from the Charlottesville City Schools Division, Tonsler provided furtive access to an advanced curriculum. Even though Tonsler held the role of principal, he still taught classes. "Professor Tonsler taught accelerated courses along with the regular curriculum," remembers Fuller. "He taught us ancient history, Emerson and Bender Language, and high mathematics." The courses themselves would not have been considered radical at the time. Tonsler, at least according to Fuller, was not teaching a course in Black history. However, Tonsler's classes would have been considered part of a high school curriculum. Given the position of the local division that African American students should not be provided an education beyond eighth grade, providing these pedagogical opportunities to students was a radical act. Fuller describes not just the courses Tonsler taught her and others, but how they were administered and placed out of white sight.[23]

Tonsler could not use school funds to purchase the books for these courses. So, he had to rely on the students and their families to support his aims of providing an expanded curriculum. Fuller recalls, "Our parents bought us extra textbooks, as well as those required by the Charlottesville [City] School[s] [Division] Board." It was normal for students to buy their books from the Charlottesville City Schools Division at the time. African American students and their families not only bore the burden of paying for their books but also paid additional funds to receive the necessary materials to access Tonsler's courses. African American educators and students kept their books and pedagogy out of the sight and mind of the Schools Division officials. Fuller recalls, "[Tonsler] put the extra books out of sight whenever the superintendent visited the school." The general lack of support and attention from white administrators at CCS meant that Black students and families were "double-taxed" in their curricular offerings. At the same time, this lack of attention and presence provided openings for Black educators like Tonsler to engage in pedagogy *as* protest.[24]

Students could become teachers after completing the program through eighth grade at Jefferson. To become a teacher, they had to pass an exam. Several small one- or two-room schoolhouses in Albemarle County needed teachers. So, if potential teachers passed the exam, then they did not have far to go to locate a teaching position. While some students from the Jefferson Colored Graded/Elementary School became teachers via that route, others opted to attend college and earn a teaching certificate. McGinness opted for the latter path. She was inspired by her uncle, John Shelton. Shelton lived next door to McGinness and her family, was an educator, a graduate of the Hampton Institute, and the publisher of the *Charlottesville Messenger*—the first newspaper for African Americans in Charlottesville. Most students could not afford education beyond the eighth grade. "It was not because they didn't want to, as many books would lead one to believe. A college education was as precious as it is now. I was one of the lucky ones to have been able to further my education."[25]

After completing her studies at the Jefferson Colored Graded/Elementary School, Rebecca Fuller left Charlottesville to pursue further educational opportunities. Rebecca's father, Charles Fuller, encouraged all his children to attend the Hampton Institute because his "idol, Booker T. Washington, had attended" college there. Charles Fuller met Washington during a visit to Charlottesville. So, like Tonsler and many other African American students in Virginia at the time, Fuller attended high school and college at the Hampton Institute. She earned a degree in education and, like Tonsler, returned to Charlottesville. Rebecca Fuller married Melvin McGinness and, as a result, became Rebecca Fuller McGinness. As McGinness, she taught at the Jefferson Colored/Graded Elementary School until the eve of school desegregation in the city and across the South. Between the start and end of her career, African American residents would fight for and gain expanded educational opportunities in the city, and, in the process, more African Americans would gain access to better-paying jobs in a community through the establishment of a Black high school.[26]

Although universal elementary schooling became widespread during the Civil War and Reconstruction, high schools in the South were few and far between. As an institution, like universal elementary schooling, the high school originated in the North. During the nineteenth century, the American high school became a prominent institution. The triumph of the public high school in the North did not spill over to the South—at least, not at first. In the South, white and affluent students attended academies or received private tutoring in high school subjects. For most students—African American or white—a high school education would not be accessible until the twentieth century, though. For African American students, gaining access to a high school education would require persistent protest. They could not wait for the state to act. White youth benefited from the collaboration between local school divisions and philanthropic organizations to establish high schools throughout the South.[27]

The establishment of high schools for white youth occurred at a rapid rate. A combination of state attention and resources from the General Education Board, a white philanthropic organization, led to the establishment of high schools. The support of the General Education Board led to the development of high schools in urban *and* rural areas throughout the South. Such an expansion of secondary schooling for white students occurred because of the attention of southern states and the resources from the General Education Board. "As late as 1888, the United States commissioner of education reported only 67 public high schools in the southern states, and in 1898 only 796," asserts James Anderson. Nevertheless, "Over the next two decades southern states, in partnership with the General Education Board laid a solid foundation for universalizing white public secondary education." In this context, the high school moved from only serving a select group of white male students to becoming accessible to a broader swath of Southern white youth.[28]

For the Charlottesville City Schools Division, the first attempt at a segregated high school for white students failed. The high school opened in 1877 and closed just five years later. The second attempt succeeded in both the short- and long-term. In 1890, the Midway School expanded to include a high school curriculum. The curriculum included Latin, French, history, mathematics, natural philosophy, and chemistry. Students living within the city limits were charged three dollars per month. If students had parents who paid an annual property tax valued at least $1,000, then the monthly fee was waived. The expanded course offerings in high school subjects quickly led to overcrowding at the Midway School.[29]

As a result, three years after a high school curriculum appeared, the Charlottesville City Schools Division Board passed three resolutions. First, the Board observed the limitations of using a converted hotel to house the school for white students. Rather than remodeling and expanding the hotel, the board contended, "The old building should be torn down and a new one erected." Second, they resolved that the new building should have a capacity of no less than 800 students due to an increase in Charlottesville's school-age population. Third, the board decided that the Jefferson Colored Graded/Elementary School building needed to be replaced and that they would do so "without delay." However, there was a delay concerning the Jefferson Colored Graded/Elementary School building. In fact, a long one. The Jefferson School building did not receive significant attention for another decade.[30]

African American students in Charlottesville and throughout Virginia faced several barriers to receiving a high school education. In 1898, the U.S. Supreme Court decided *Cumming v. Richmond County Board of Education*. The *Cumming* decision had significant implications for the future of Black secondary schooling in the South. It created substantial obstacles for the expansion of Black high schools and, according to historian James Anderson, "meant that southern school boards did not have to offer public secondary schooling for black youth." Despite this case and its implications, though, Black high schools were still established throughout the South despite the emergence of Jim Crow. By 1916, there were sixty-four public high schools for African American students in the South. Of those high schools, Virginia had eleven Black high schools. Charlottesville took longer than other communities in Virginia and the South, but the Charlottesville case reveals how high schools emerged and evolved during the rise and fall of Jim Crow in the region.[31]

The fight to expand high school education to African Americans occurred throughout the South. These organizing efforts not only led to the establishment of Black high schools, but also created an infrastructure for future organizing, which led to the Black freedom struggles throughout the twentieth century. In Atlanta, Georgia, African American residents organized for the establishment of Booker T. Washington High School. Before the *Cumming* decision, Charlottesville's African American community started organizing for the expansion of educational opportunities in the city. The first recorded meeting of community leaders discussing a Black high school occurred at First Baptist Church in 1891. Just a single newspaper article is surviving as a reference to this meeting. Although nothing tangible resulted from that initial meeting, the church would be a key site of the struggle for the high school.[32]

Neither Tonsler nor Fuller could attend high school in Charlottesville. They, along with any other African American students who wanted to pursue a high school education or college education, had to leave the city. And both did. But their decision to leave was unique. Few had the means to make that decision. George Ferguson describes the costs of seeking high school and college education elsewhere. Ferguson was born in 1911, and his father was one of Charlottesville's two Black doctors. He asserts, "I can recall when my sister finished the eighth grade, my father had to make arrangements for her to go to high school in Washington[, D.C.]." Ferguson also relayed the story of his friend, Tom Inge, and how Tom's father discussed the short-term and long-term costs of not having access to a high school in the city. There were nine kids in the Inge family. As Ferguson claims, "if he [Tom's father] had been able to send his children to high school here and the University of Virginia, he could have left his children a much larger estate than he did. But he had to spend this money to send all of them away to high school."[33]

Based on the limited accounts of African American students from the turn of the century, they either attended a high school in Washington, D.C., or participated in a high school program at one of the state's segregated Black colleges. Attending high school in Washington, D.C., required a significant sacrifice for the students and their families. Washington, D.C., is located more than one hundred miles northwest of Charlottesville. So, students could not go back and forth to their homes and school each day. Families had to make living arrangements with a relative or local family member. At the same time, students also had to leave the comfort of their homes and immediate families. The other option, attending a high school program at a college, did not require students to travel as far, but it still included challenges of its own. Laura Franklin's experience reveals one such challenge. Franklin finished eighth grade at the Jefferson Graded School, during the early 1920s, and left to attend the Hampton Institute for high school. Due to financial challenges, Franklin did not complete high school, though.[34]

Ruth Coles had a different outcome in following a similar path to a high school education. "Then when I finished eighth grade here [in Charlottesville]," Coles recalls, "I went to Petersburg to what was then known as Virginia Normal and Industrial Institute, having changed hands from Virginia Collegiate.... I finished Normal School there in [19]21." While Coles completed enough secondary schooling to become a teacher then, she did not earn a bachelor's degree. After teaching for four years, Coles left the classroom for nine years to raise her four children. She later returned to teaching and earned a bachelor's degree with her daughter at Virginia State College. Her path to teaching and earning her degree was circuitous, which says more about the lack of access to educational opportunities than Coles as an individual.[35]

The experiences of Benjamin Tonsler, Rebecca Fuller McGinness, the Inge family, Laura Franklin, and Ruth Coles reveal the landscape of educational opportunities at the turn of the century. On the one hand, these African American students completed schooling through eighth grade in Charlottesville. If they had experiences like McGinness, then these students might have been exposed to an advanced curriculum, too. No other surviving record of pedagogy *as* protest beyond McGinness's account of Tonsler exists. But the lack of record does not negate the possibility of others following—or even preceding—Tonsler's pedagogical footsteps. On the other hand, they bore the burden and costs of being educated elsewhere, including in colleges far from Charlottesville, particularly when they had fewer options for traveling those distances. They earned credentials, which provided them with an opportunity to teach. They received educational opportunities that fit within contemporary conceptions of secondary education.

Reverend Clarence M. Long, the pastor at First Baptist Church, helped revive the struggle for a Black high school following World War I. Reverend Long used his platform as a preacher and the physical space available to advocate for a Black high school. He started the fight for a high school by organizing a Parent Teacher Association. The group consisted of the community's Black teachers and parents who met in the basement of First Baptist Church. He also advocated for the founding of a high school regularly from the pulpit. Long recalls, "I never missed an opportunity to plead the cause of the Negro. I urged them to build homes and to educate their children. . . . I always had the courage to speak my convictions." While speaking his convictions led to his ouster from serving as the pastor to First Baptist Church, Long's organizing and speaking helped Charlottesville's Black community imagine a future that included more comprehensive educational programming for their children.[36]

Reverend Long's use of the pulpit led to direct action on several occasions. For example, in 1914, Black residents protested the requirement that all males take industrial training courses. Several African American pastors in the city "protested the Charlottesville School Board's requirement of manual training in industrial arts for boys enrolled at Jefferson Grade School." After the church services on Sunday, Superintendent James G. Johnson heard from several members of that African American community that they wanted their boys to be educated to do more than "to work with their hands." As a result of the protest, "the superintendent and board eliminated the Carpenter Shop at Jefferson School—a measure that could be interpreted as both palliative and mean-spiritedly punitive." In other words, Johnson gave the African American community what they wanted, but such an act should not be interpreted as an act of good faith.[37]

Reverend Long's words and organizing affected him and the city's Black community. He helped auger the rise of protest *for* pedagogy in Charlottesville. On the one hand, Rebecca Fuller McGinness recalls how Reverend Long "stirred up the white people so much that they thought it better to concede to the African American community's demand for a high school than to allow him [Reverend Long] to stir up the African-American community any further." On the other hand, Long was run out of town by the city's white elites, including individuals involved with the Charlottesville City Schools Division. Before he left Charlottesville, though, he laid the foundation for continued organizing and activism.[38]

Others filled the leadership vacuum when Reverend Long left the city, including Thomas J. Inge and Jackson P. Burley. Inge inherited the grocery store in Vinegar Hill from his father. Burley worked as an educator in

Charlottesville and Albemarle County. Both continued to engage with the Parent Teacher Association founded by Long and organized the larger African American community on several occasions to push for the high school. Long, Inge, and Burley may have been leaders in the struggle for a high school, but they were not alone. As mentioned in the opening of this chapter, Black residents petitioned James G. Johnson to build the high school, and Johnson acted on the petition. He appealed to white residents, particularly those in power, to improve and expand educational opportunities for African American students in Charlottesville.[39]

In the early 1920s, eighty-five African American residents petitioned James G. Johnson, the CCS superintendent, for a new high school in the city. White students already had access to a high school in the city. Like school divisions all over the Commonwealth of Virginia, the Charlottesville City Schools Division was segregated by race. Although segregation in the other areas of public life emerged during the Jim Crow era, schools were segregated from the outset of their establishment during the Civil War. In the 1890s, the Charlottesville City Schools Division expanded opportunities for white students at the Midway School—the city's white elementary school—by offering a high school curriculum. At the same time, Black residents started organizing an effort for a local high school of their own. These organizing efforts reached a crescendo with the petition to build a high school—thirty years after the Midway School opened its doors to only white students. There is little evidence of Black residents' petition efforts besides the document itself and references from Superintendent Johnson; however, we can imagine the work and danger involved in such an endeavor.[40]

Amid Jim Crow and its consequences, Charlottesville's African American residents organized for expanded educational opportunities. They met and composed a petition. They gathered the signatures of Black residents in the city. They addressed the petition to the Charlottesville City Schools Division and Superintendent Johnson. The petition read,

> Whereas, since the City of Charlottesville offers nothing higher to the Negro Youth to the Eighth Grade at the Jefferson School, and whereas, each year we have large classes to graduate who must go from home at such an early age to pursue higher courses, and since sending our

children away at the age of fourteen years, which is the average age at which they graduate, we incur a great expense besides depriving them of the home training and influences; Therefore, we the undersigned petitioners, citizens of Charlottesville, Va., do ask that you grant us a High School for the Colored Youth of said City. We are deeply grateful for the educational advantages which we have and pray that the time is ripe for giving us a High School.[41]

The petition noted the lack of educational opportunities beyond eighth grade for African American youth in the city and the consequences. On the one hand, the city boasted a segregated high school for white youth—the Midway High School—and an institution of higher education for white, Protestant men—the University of Virginia. White male youth could walk to the Midway High School and the University of Virginia and be granted access to those institutions. Despite the onset of Jim Crow in all facets of city life including housing, Black youth—young men and young women—could also walk to the Midway High School and the University of Virginia. Still, the policies and practices of white people denied African Americans the same educational opportunities at those institutions. The inequality of opportunity at the high school level existed for nearly three decades. The inequality of opportunity at the University of Virginia would continue well into the middle of the twentieth century for white women; the same was true for Black men and women, too.[42]

The petition was only the beginning. There's no record of Johnson responding directly, in writing or otherwise, to the petitioners. However, following the creation and submission of the petition, Johnson's actions suggested that the African American community's organizing spurred him toward establishing a Black high school. Johnson started to make the case to the city's white residents. On March 16, 1922, Johnson addressed the Young Men's Business Club to provide an analysis of the Charlottesville City Schools Division as a whole. On the state of the Jefferson School building, Johnson argued, "[I]t is a good building and has very good equipment; it is fairly well adapted to school work [sic] according to the needs of present conditions, but it is totally inadequate in capacity to accommodate the enrollment that is to be cared for each session. Changes entailing a moderate cost would make it a splendid plant for upper grade academic work with some added industrial features." Overcrowding was a significant problem at the school. Johnson asserted, "The building for colored pupils would comfortably care for 400 pupils but has to serve about 700; the result is that almost every school there has to run a half-day or three-fourth-day basis ... added to this serious handicap in the limited amount of time any child may be in school each day is the additional drawback of a heavy load in enrollment for every teacher."[43]

Johnson wrote editorials to *The Daily Progress* seeking improvements to the city's educational facilities, including a Black high school. These editorials called for improvements in Charlottesville to expand the Jefferson School into a high school. Historian Scot French observes, "Johnson stressed the benefits of the project—including the plans for a two-year high school—to 'the larger citizenship of the present and future.' He urged skeptics, presumably white, to take a 'sympathetic' view of matters and do 'the right thing to give us a more intelligent and a happier population.'" Building the new high school not only required the acceptance of the city's white community. It also required passing a bond to cover the cost of building and opening a new school.[44]

Johnson's appeal for a new building to serve African American students was heard by other political leaders in Charlottesville. On March 26, 1923, Mayor John R. Morris announced a bond election for April 10, 1923. The bond was to meet several needs within the city, including expanding and improving the Charlottesville City Schools Division. In addition to purchasing land to build another white elementary school in the city, the bond also called for funds to "enlarge the present Jefferson Colored School Building by the addition of certain rooms and to make such other necessary improvements to the present building and grounds at said Jefferson Colored School as necessary to meet the needs of properly housing the colored school children of the City."[45]

Johnson sought support from local civic organizations to bolster the chances that the bond would pass. These organizations included the League of Women Voters, the Kiwanis Club, and the Young Men's Business Club. The combination of the petition and efforts by Superintendent Johnson yielded the necessary support for the bond even though Black voters could not vote in the bond election. White politicians had restricted their right to vote through poll taxes and literacy tests. White voters of the city passed a bond of $290,000. The bond paid for the Jefferson School to be enlarged from eight to sixteen classrooms. While the efforts of the African

American community and Johnson were key to the bond's passage, those reasons weren't the only ones. Not only did the bond support the expansion of the Jefferson School, but it also supported the construction and opening of Venable Elementary School, a new all-white school.[46]

Without allocating funds for a new white elementary school, it's difficult to imagine that the bond would have passed. The interest convergence of African American and white residents—particularly elites and politicians in the city—ultimately led to the establishment of a Black high school. The original plan only included expanding the high school within the Jefferson Elementary School building. However, during the development of plans for the new Black high school, the construction company discovered issues with the nearby heating plant. So, rather than expand the current school into a comprehensive building, Johnson and the Charlottesville City Schools Division decided to construct a new building for the high school. After receiving approval from the Virginia Superintendent of Public Instruction, Johnson and the Charlottesville City Schools Division moved to develop and construct a new building, whose main entrance would be on Commerce Street.[47]

In 1926, Jefferson High School opened and became the first Black high school in the city. Though Benjamin Tonsler did not live long enough to see the development of formalized high school education for African American students in the city, the African American community's organizing for a high school resulted in tangible results. The new high school and its descendant spaces would become a critical space for incubating the development of protest *and* pedagogy.

CHAPTER TWO

"Pillars of This Town"

Jefferson High School, 1926–1951

The people who are basically pillars of this town would not have been had it not been for a school like Jefferson [High School]. Jefferson [High School] has put out some people that have contributed a lot not only to Charlottesville but a lot of people around the world.
—William Gilmore, a student at Jefferson High School

Therefore, as we begin school work [sic] this year, let us resume the march toward freedom and peace. Let us enter our classes with a purpose, and let that purpose be to carry on in the path of Pasteur, Edison, Carver, of Jefferson, Lincoln and Roosevelt in curing the ills of mankind through science and government.... If you are to win your peace, it must be through school. I welcome back to this march towards peace and freedom. I implore you to be a good soldier.
—Owen Duncan, principal of Jefferson High School, 1945

Booker Reaves was among the first students to attend and graduate from Jefferson High School (JHS). In 1915, Reaves was born in Free Union, Virginia—a community outside Charlottesville. His parents, Lewis and Lottie Reaves, moved their family from Free Union to Buffalo, New York, briefly after Booker Reaves was born. However, Reaves recalls that his "mother didn't like it there" in Buffalo, and the family returned to Charlottesville during the mid-1920s. The ability to even contemplate, let alone move at the time, reveals the socioeconomic standing of the Reaves family: They had the means to leave Charlottesville and then return to the city after deciding not to live in Buffalo. After returning from Buffalo, the Reaveses remained in Charlottesville and put down roots.[1]

The Reaves family lived all over Charlottesville before settling into a house on Ridge Street. Living on Ridge Street meant they had proximity to the Jefferson Elementary School and Lewis Reaves's job. Reaves's father

Table 3. Population of Charlottesville, 1930–1950

Year	Black	White	Total
1930	4,083	11,579	15,242
1940	4,152	15,246	19,378
1950	4,720	21,249	25,969

Sources: Barksdale, "A Comparative Study of Contemporary White and Negro Standards in Health, Education, and Welfare," 11; "1950 Census," prepared by Social Explorer from the U.S. Census Bureau, Haines, *Historical, Demographic, Economic, and Social Data.*

worked at the University of Virginia hospital for forty-five years, and his mother stayed home to raise him, his brother, and four sisters. Reaves and his siblings attended the Jefferson Colored/Graded Elementary School before they continued their education at the city's new Black high school, Jefferson High School. Unlike many other African American students before him, such as Rebecca Fuller McGinness, Reaves did not have to leave the city to receive a high school education.[2]

Compared to most other African American students across Virginia and the South, Reaves and his classmates had greater access to educational opportunities. By 1934, Jefferson High School was just one of six accredited Black high schools in Virginia. Particularly during the first few years, the school building did not possess the facilities or resources of a comprehensive high school in other parts of the United States. The curriculum at the high school consisted of a combination of vocational and a liberal arts education. While the curriculum was limited during the initial years of the school's existence, the school did prepare graduates for higher education. For example, in the graduating class of 1934, "more than twenty-five percent of Jefferson High School graduates are attending, at present, institutes of higher learning." This number does not specify higher education institutions, but since higher education remained segregated then, we know that these graduates attended historically Black colleges and universities.[3]

Booker Reaves left Charlottesville for college. But he eventually returned to the city as an educator. Returning to Charlottesville, Reaves became one of the first African Americans to attend *and* teach at Jefferson High School. Much like Benjamin Tonsler and Rebecca Fuller McGinness, Reaves continued the work of propelling and sustaining the Black freedom struggle as students and educators in Charlottesville. Reaves would participate in and observe the evolution of pedagogy *as* protest and the seeds of other forms of the relationship between protest and pedagogy as they began to sprout at JHS.

Since the end of the Civil War, educational opportunities had expanded for most African Americans in Charlottesville and throughout the South. Rates of literacy grew in Charlottesville. With the establishment of Jefferson High School, the city boasted one of the few Black high schools in Virginia. However, illiteracy among African Americans remained an issue in the city. Undoubtedly, the Jefferson Elementary School's presence made a difference following the Civil War. By 1930, ninety-one percent of African Americans over ten years old were literate. However, that meant nine percent were illiterate, which was double the number of illiterate whites in the city. *The Reflector* observed, "It sounds incredible at a time like this, that there are so many right in our midst who can neither read nor write, to whom the printed page means nothing." To solve the issue, it urged "the professional men and women of our city would organize themselves into a sort of 'Help the Intellectually Meager' club and devote a couple hours a week to training adults in night school, think of the great amount of oil that may be produced to help make the well of progress move more smoothly."[4]

Access to Jefferson High School did not mean that all or even most African American students in Charlottesville pursued a secondary education or higher education, though. On the one hand, access to high school provided more opportunities for secondary education. The proximity between the elementary and high schools lowered the bar for receiving a secondary education. On the other hand, as the Great Depression unfolded, the choice to attend high school or enter the workforce depended on several contextual factors. The Reaves family could afford Booker Reaves the opportunity to receive a high school education and, later, higher education; however, this was not a reality for many African American families during the early years of JHS.[5]

When Reaves and the first African American students enrolled at Jefferson High School, the African American community continued to organize and agitate for justice. African American residents used a multitude of methods to raise awareness and to organize around political, social, economic, and educational issues. *The Reflector*, a Black newspaper in the city mentioned earlier, aimed to inform and create change in the local community. Thomas J. Sellers edited and owned the newspaper. The newspaper was created in response to the segregation in the city's daily newspaper, *The Daily Progress*. Unlike *The Daily Progress*, which only reported on events and issues related to white people's lives in the city, state, and country, *The Reflector* focused on the African American experience in the city.[6]

African American educators or students did not contribute to the newspaper. However, some educators and students at Jefferson High School likely read it, mainly as the newspaper focused on issues affecting youth, education, and civil rights. In 1933, as the story and subsequent trial of the Scottsboro Boys unfolded in Scottsboro, Alabama, the newspaper exhorted local African American citizens to think not just about the youth in Alabama but also the African American youth of Charlottesville. Of the African American community in Charlottesville, one article asserted, "We have in our midst, hundreds of young men and women, growing into manhood and womanhood, without the slightest idea of their civil rights. We have also, hundreds and hundreds of matured citizens, who have lived these many years without putting forth the least show of effort to demand certain rights as American Citizens." The article used the situation in Alabama to highlight the need for African American youth and adults to learn about their civil rights. It also highlighted the material needs of Charlottesville's African American residents, including clothing, food, and money.[7]

Protest *for* pedagogy manifested within and beyond the walls of Jefferson High School. Some of the African American community's organizing centered on improving the city's existing educational opportunities. Indeed, it was related to improving the experiences of African American students at the city's schools. For several years, the African American community battled with the city council over the resurrection of the Booker T. Washington Park Recreational Center. Jefferson High School used the park for extracurricular activities, including football. On February 17, 1934, *The Reflector* ran an article about the situation. The staff observed, "Over five years ago ... Mr. McIntire gave a large tract of land, located on Preston Avenue, for the building of a Negro Recreational Center. A Negro committee was formed, the ground named, some funds obtained, and then activity ceased." The article also notes that African Americans are not the ones at fault for the cessation. Instead, there are "hundreds and hundreds of Negro citizens and many white friends" who are ready "to follow a logical procedure that will put into practical use Mr. McIntire's gift of five year's [sic] standing."⁸

During the Jim Crow era, local white politicians implemented policies that calcified segregated housing in Charlottesville. African American residents were forced into neighborhoods surrounding the city's segregated Black schools—Jefferson Colored Graded/Elementary School and Jefferson High School. Helen Camp de Corse, a graduate student at the University of Virginia and a Phelps-Stokes fellow, wrote a thesis about the housing situation for the city's African American community. She wrote, "The areas occupied by Negroes in Charlottesville are clearly defined—their homes and businesses set apart from white occupation, hence there is little racial friction." De Corse's observation about the segregation of Black homes and businesses revealed the local consequences of Jim Crow in Charlottesville.⁹

The condition of housing for Charlottesville's African Americans varied widely. Most African Americans rented their homes from whites in the city. Due to negligent white landlords, the rental properties were not well-maintained. The conditions surrounding these areas also illustrated a lack of concern for the city's African Americans. Houses near the gas house were near "a stream carrying refuse" from the building. While the stream usually just ran alongside the rental homes, there were times when the combination of rain and refuse overwhelmed the stream.

Nevertheless, not all the areas inhabited by African Americans faced negligent and environmental racism. De Corse reported, "The west end of Preston Avenue, to Rugby Road is occupied by Negro home owners [sic], whose houses are good and yards attractive." She also spotlights the Vinegar Hill and Ridge Street neighborhoods as places of "education and prosperity." Overall, the neighborhood descriptions demonstrate the stratification by race and class in Charlottesville during the 1920s and 1930s. The stratification along class lines depended on how and the extent to which one's job was connected to the University of Virginia.¹⁰

In certain parts of Charlottesville, the living conditions for African Americans revealed how the city had created inequality. On November 18, 1933, *The Reflector* called for a "City Improvement Plan": "There are sections of our city where the residents have been paying taxes either directly or indirectly, yet each rainy day they find themselves knee-deep in mud and cinder paths." The newspaper proposed that to deal with these conditions, "A loan could be secured from the public works fund, and streets and sidewalks could be constructed. The cost of the work could be paid by the property owners over a certain term of years with a removable interest." Not only would such a plan have improved the overall conditions within the city, but, according to the newspaper, "it would give our many idle men work to do" and "make various Negro rental sections in Charlottesville modern, sanitary places in which to live and in turn produce citizens proud of and helpful to their country." Despite such housing disadvantages, proximity to Black schools was not an issue for most African American residents. The high school, like the elementary school, sat near the segregated African American neighborhoods.[11]

Ruth Coles, a student at Jefferson High School, remembers, "Yeah, very convenient. Sometimes, it wasn't too convenient when you wanted to stroll home with your friends and stay out a long time, because you were expected to be in the house after school within five minutes of the time school let out. So, you couldn't play very long." Whereas previous generations of Black students had traveled to Washington, D.C., and to the other side of the state to attend high school, this generation of Black students could walk to school. The proximity between housing and schooling meant students' home and school lives intersected significantly.[12]

Although most JHS students lived in Charlottesville, a few lived outside the city and commuted to the school. For example, Braxton Coles resided in Albemarle County alongside thirteen other siblings. Although he lived in the county, he invested substantial time and energy to secure a high school education. He left the house early in the morning because the trip took at least an hour and a half, sometimes two hours. Although Coles attended the schools in the city, only one of his thirteen siblings joined him. Coles and his sister Carrie decided against attending the county school, Albemarle Training School. The Albemarle Training School opened in 1893. While Coles never mentions a reason for his other siblings' decisions to stay at the county school, it is not hard to see that the distance would be a significant obstacle.[13]

Eventually, Coles moved to Charlottesville. Moving to Charlottesville presented a series of other challenges. "I had no social life connected to the high school because after the first two years, I got a job at a boardinghouse, and they gave me room and board [in Charlottesville]," recalls Coles. Working at the boardinghouse meant Coles had to sacrifice involvement in extracurricular activities. "No, I couldn't even attend sporting events because I had to go to school and rush to the boardinghouse and start getting ready to take in the guests and I even started helping her cook." The sacrifice was worth it to Coles because he became the only one of his brothers to graduate high school and attend college. His brothers ended their schooling and started working in various jobs. In contrast, after graduating from Jefferson High School, Coles attended and graduated from the Hampton Institute and studied to become a doctor.[14]

Coles's many brothers and sisters were not alone. Inside the walls and classrooms of Jefferson High School, few students enrolled in the early years of the Depression era. In fact, not even all eligible Black youth who attended Jefferson Elementary continued through to JHS. On the one hand, the existence of the high school meant Black youth could access greater educational opportunities in the city. On the other hand, the existence of JHS did not ensure that all students would seek a secondary education. There were other factors involved. During the Great Depression, attending high school meant forgoing the opportunity to work full-time. The Reaves family could afford Booker Reaves the chance to attend high school and college; however, this was not a reality for many Depression-era families. Only as the United States left the Great Depression behind and entered World War II did the number of students attending high school in the city grow. Some young people returning from World War II enrolled at Jefferson High School. These trends mirrored towns and communities throughout the United States.[15]

Of course, not everything about the school's location was ideal. The high school sat next to a gas plant. "Yes, the number one thing I remember is that the gas house was right next to the school and the noxious odors and the gasoline, not gas but cooking gas, and that type of thing," Rudolph Goffney remembered. "There was no EPA [Environmental Protection Agency] or any pollution laws at that time, so the fumes were just released into the air and the school was right next to it, or just about." While there is not any definitive evidence that Black students and educators faced health problems because of the gas plant, the placement of the plant next to the school shows a lack of respect for the city's African American residents. Whether regarding housing or schooling, this lack of respect and underdevelopment of Black life was omnipresent.[16]

Booker Reaves graduated from Jefferson High School in 1935. While Reaves could access secondary schooling in Charlottesville, he did not have the same access to a postsecondary education. No Black college or university had been established—nor would ever be established—in the city, and the University of Virginia only allowed white men to enroll. Even if the University of Virginia had allowed Reaves to enroll, there is no guarantee that he would have wanted to attend the university then. So, like Benjamin Tonsler and Rebecca Fuller McGinness before him, Booker Reaves left the city to attend the Hampton Institute. Reaves earned a degree at Hampton and started his teaching career in Fluvanna County. However, after a brief stint there, he returned to teach at Jefferson High School in 1939. Reaves taught social studies and facilitated extracurricular activities at the high school. Reaves continued the Black educational tradition started by Tonsler and McGinness by returning to the city and serving in the Charlottesville City Schools Division. Reaves knew not only the students and their families but also the city.[17]

Without a previous connection to Charlottesville, African American teachers also arrived to teach at Jefferson High School during this era. Florence Coleman Bryant grew up in Caroline County, Virginia. Bryant's church, community, family, and schools significantly influenced her choice to enter the teaching profession and how she approached teaching. Bryant attended segregated Black schools in Caroline County, including Union High School. After spending about a year working as a maid in Philadelphia, Bryant returned to Virginia and attended Virginia Union College. She was involved in extracurricular activities in college and earned a degree in English. She learned of a teaching job at the Jefferson Graded School from her roommate and applied for the job. Bryant received a job offer from James G. Johnson and Owen Duncan.[18]

Bryant's experience as a young person and student in segregated schools influenced her approach to teaching in Charlottesville. Formalized schooling in Caroline County for Black residents emerged amid the Civil War. A mixture of public and private schools for Black residents opened in the county during and after the war, with elementary schools appearing first and, later, high schools. Alongside the other neighborhood children, Bryant attended St. John Elementary School. St. John sat approximately two miles from her childhood home. The school consisted of two rooms with a porch running across the entirety of the building. Within the classrooms, which were similarly sized, there were large windows and a wall-length blackboard on the opposite side. Bolted wooden desks ran in two rows—all turned toward the blackboard. One room held students in grades one to three, while the other held students in grades four to seven. "It epitomized the neighborhood school concept, in that the parents and teachers worked together, not only in school activities, but in church and community activities as well," recalls Bryant. "Working as a unit, the school, home, and church fostered the development of the whole child." The experience at St. John Elementary and other community institutions, including the church, built a strong foundation for Bryant as she moved on to the next steps in her formal education.[19]

Bryant's time at St. John Elementary ended earlier than her peers. Halfway through seventh grade, she transferred to Union High School. "I missed my chance to be one of the honored participants at seventh grade commencement, which was an important event, but having the opportunity to become acclimated to the high school environment to ease my transition there was worth it," remembers Bryant. She observed stark differences between the two schools. While St. John Elementary consisted of students from the nearby community, Union High School was larger, drawing students from throughout the county. Union High School proved to be more challenging than St. John Elementary. "The classwork was much more concentrated and competitive," Bryant recalls. "My best friend had already transferred to Union High, so I didn't feel entirely alone. The class of forty-plus students remained largely intact throughout high school." Bryant's entry into secondary schooling coincided with more and more Black students in Virginia and across the South gaining greater access to education beyond elementary school. Access to secondary schooling for Black students still lagged behind access for white students in Virginia as a whole, though.[20]

Like some other areas in Virginia, including Charlottesville, Lynchburg, and Richmond, the Caroline County Public Schools Division expanded to include a Black high school during the first half of the twentieth century. In 1903, Bowling Green Industrial Academy opened; Caroline County Training School replaced it in 1914, which, in turn, was replaced by Union High School in 1929, serving all the Black students seeking a secondary education in Caroline County. When Bryant attended Union High School, the teachers lived primarily in Richmond. Some of the teachers lived in Union's dormitory during the week, and they returned to the capital city on the weekends. The school's teachers possessed degrees aligned with their expertise, and few left them. There was a single curriculum track at the school: college preparation. The course offerings included English, mathematics, social studies, science, foreign language, health and physical education, and agriculture or industrial arts for the boys and home economics for the girls. Union High School's extracurricular activities included baseball, softball, basketball, and choir. Bryant sang in the choir throughout high school, but she did not participate in any sports or other activities beyond the classroom. "Our tight schedules allowed no flexible or free time," recalls Bryant.[21]

Bryant has fond memories of her teachers at Union High School. Mrs. Virginia Scott Jackson and Mrs. Louise B. Carter left an indelible mark on Bryant's education and future career as an educator herself. Mrs. Jackson taught both math and science. While Bryant struggled a bit more in math and science than in other courses, she still enjoyed the coursework, especially in science, where she was "enthralled by the use of Bunsen burners and test tubes, studying microbes, and writing up analyses of the experiments." Bryant's favorite subjects were English and French. Mrs. Carter taught both classes, and Bryant viewed her as a role model. "I regarded Mrs. Carter as the epitome of what a school teacher [sic] should be: intelligent, articulate, interesting, and friendly," remembers Bryant. "I especially loved the literary selections we studied. Vicariously, I shared the romance, intrigue, and adventure in which the characters were involved." Witnessing the work of her teachers in the segregated Black schools of Caroline County provided Bryant with models of how to engage students and make the most of the available curriculum and pedagogy materials.[22]

After one year, Bryant moved from Jefferson Elementary to Jefferson High School. Bryant relished the opportunity to work with high school students. When Principal Duncan approached Bryant about moving from elementary to high school, she embraced the idea because "The new assignment was more in keeping with my training, my student teaching experience, and my personal preference. The students were older, and therefore, more mature. They were, in addition, more self-directed and goal-oriented [sic]. It was easier for me to adapt my instructional program and teaching methods to their needs." She also enjoyed the opportunity to know students beyond the classroom setting. She helped with several clubs and extracurricular activities, including creating the school yearbook. The proximity between housing and schooling in the city supported Bryant's work in the classroom and during extracurricular activities.[23]

Reaves and Bryant worked alongside many other African American educators who developed a school culture and community. Rudolph Goffney graduated from Jefferson High School in 1941. Goffney remembers, "The churches and the schools were basically the center of the community, the heart of the community. That's where you saw people, that's where you did things, and you interacted. And, as I said earlier, most people knew everybody else. It was pleasant. Remarkably pleasant for the times and conditions." Jefferson High School, according to Teresa Price, "meant everything to the African American community. It was full of people here servicing those students." Price remembers, "We had some great teachers. And in order to give you things so that the school was accredited, and so you could get into most colleges, she was one of the people willing to go to summer school or do something to make herself accredited so that she could teach. She taught French, she did the music program, you know, the chorus, along with Pauline Garrett's mother." She also asserts, "It's people like this that made such a difference and made that school like a home and also a symbol at the same time."[24]

During and after World War II, it was common for students to work and attend school. Goffney contends, "Most kids who could get a job after school, got a job. Because it was during the Depression years. And funds were limited. At that time, blacks were at the bottom of the economic pole. In a way, if you wanted to move up, you had to get a job, you had to do something to beat the rest. That was necessary. So most of the people who did that, most of the people who aspired to move up, had to do something differently." Students worked a variety of jobs in the city. Priscilla Whiting remembers, "I went to work when I was a senior. It was a dress shop downtown called Smart and Thrifty." Grafton Payne, another student a year behind Whiting, also worked at the store. "We'd unpack the clothes, and put them on the hangers," recalls Whiting. "Most of them you had to put the tags on, and that's the kind of stuff you'd do if you went to work after school." William Gilmore claims, "Most other kids I knew worked while they went to school. Cubbie Anderson worked, Baker worked downtown. Most of them are deceased. Bill Chapman, who used to play football, there were a lot of guys working and going to school."[25]

Students and faculty participated in extracurricular activities. Sports were a prominent part of that programming. Sports were not only a community-building activity for those playing the sports, but also for the African American community in the city. Rudolph Goffney recalls, "If there was a football game or a basketball game or what not, then all of the community would participate in it because that was probably the only thing happening at that particular time. So it was a real wholesome time at that time in history." All the sports were played against other segregated Black high schools, the number of which was growing at the time. JHS had a range of extracurricular activities beyond athletics, too.[26]

The Deluxe Glee Club was a prominent extracurricular activity. In 1933, Mr. J. Franklin Brown organized and led the group of twenty male students. The club's first performance was held on April 30 in the Jefferson High School auditorium. The organization's purpose was "the presentation of Negro Spirituals and Melodies in the original manner." The performance was slated to include "a group of best known and most beautiful songs rendered with the same rhythm and deep feeling that placed them on a pinnacle in the world of music and caused them to be considered as one of the outstanding contributions of our race." The songs were "expressive of the slave in the field, the patient christian [sic], who had still faith in deliverance or the jolly, carefree stevedore, strumming his cares away" because the Glee Club aimed, "to preserve all of the original sincerity of purpose depicted in the Negro's most valuable contribution to the world."[27]

Students, supported by the school's faculty, created a yearbook, *The Crimson*, and a school newspaper, *The Jeffersonian*. To create the yearbook, Teresa Price recalls, "We prepared our own yearbook in that classroom, you know typing stencils and duplicating, and we had students—Walter Johnson—who was great in art, who did all our artwork. And my brother did all the ads." Both Black and white businesses within the city contributed advertisements to the yearbook. Those advertisements helped pay for the costs of creating the yearbooks for the students. Rather than being made in a class, students worked on the yearbook as part of a club. The club had several community aims, including "To educate the community as to the work of the school" and "to promote co-operation [sic] between parents and the school." The club also had specific aims for students. It aimed to "develop students' power of observation and discrimination concerning the relative merits of news articles" and to "develop qualities of co-operation; tact, accuracy, tolerance, responsibility, initiative, and leadership." Clubs provided an opportunity for students to develop their interests and bolster the ties of the community. Based on an analysis of the existing yearbooks from Jefferson High School, all senior students were involved in one or more clubs during their time at the school.[28]

African American educators and students continued to engage in pedagogy *as* protest at JHS. Like African American students in previous generations, students at JHS were required to purchase their books. "We had to buy them," remembers Rudolph Goffney. As a result of having to purchase their books, some students did not have books of their own. Rather than go without books, students would share their books and work together on homework assignments. Sharing books had some positive consequences. Because students had to share their books, they were more likely to study together. Goffney recalls, "[w]hen you were assigned a project or something to do, you worked together with someone else. If you didn't have the books that you needed for yourself, then you worked with other kids, that was a lot of fun."[29]

Throughout its existence, JHS aimed to cultivate a consciousness of students' immediate surroundings. In the fall of 1934, Mrs. C. B. Duke settled on a theme for the Patron's Day Exhibit. Duke declared that the theme would be "a Century of Progress." In response, the senior class focused on the evolution of "Negro Education in Charlottesville" by collecting "pictures and data from the venerable residents of the city" and "wrote themes and posters to that effect." The junior class focused on politics within Charlottesville. The class visited Charlottesville City Hall to access statistics about the city and learn about the "evolution of the voter's interest[s]." The sophomore class had two projects: one in history and the other in English. In history, they focused on the Civil War and the Great War. Students reconstructed battle scenes from the wars. In English, they focused on the evolution of newspapers. Students collected and analyzed newspapers from 1834 to 1934. These projects reveal that students were learning about local, regional, and global issues and how to approach learning about them.[30]

Within the formal curriculum, African American students did not spend as much time in high school as their white peers. On the curriculum at the school Laura Robinson asserts, "All of the classes that were taught at Jefferson were not the same as what was taught in the White school system. We did not have as many classes to do as they had to do. We completed eleven years of schooling at Jefferson because we had to take off to college." Despite having different classes than the white high school, Robinson recalls, "Yes, I had science classes, I had math classes. I had history class, English, and what else did I have? Geometry. Algebra. French." While Robinson and her peers at Jefferson spent fewer years in high school, they were still receiving a vocational and liberal arts education, which prepared them for higher education and life within and beyond Charlottesville.[31]

JHS's teachers prepared students for the world beyond the classroom. Goffney contends, "It was demanding, because the teachers were trying to prepare . . . they were telling you what the situation was and preparing you for a better life. So, they were demanding. They asked you to take advantage of what you had. To prepare yourself for the future. If you wanted to aspire for more." Frances Wood remembers, "All my teachers were my favorites. They were all wonderful people. We had great teachers. Dedicated teachers. Hard-working teachers." Mrs. Rosemary Byers had a memorable influence on Wood. "I can think of Mrs. Rosemary Byers, who was my French teacher. And we used to have the French Club, and we used to meet at her house. That was one good opportunity to be able to go somewhere. Away from home. And Mrs. Florence Bryant, who is here with us today. I had her in English. All of my teachers, as we said, were favorites. I could just go back and name most of them."[32]

During this era, there was less direction about what and how teachers were expected to teach. In terms of pedagogy, Florence C. Bryant remembers, "Conducting classes was different then. Now there's so much more interaction with the students. When I came out, it was almost rote. You had your lesson plans. Nobody told me what to teach. There were no curriculum guides." Despite having secured a building, JHS still struggled to receive the necessary resources and ones that reflected the African American experience. Teachers and students had to make the most with what they had. Bryant recalls, "We had the same books as the other schools. We didn't see any black faces in those books. They were state textbooks . . . we had *Uncle Tom's Cabin*; that was about it. We didn't have a lot of outside reading." Bryant's observation about the lack of Black people in the curriculum would be mitigated by the work of Carter G. Woodson, but would also recur as an issue throughout the history of high schools in Charlottesville.[33]

Teaching African American history at the school occurred from the school's inception. This effort was supported by the work of Carter G. Woodson and the Association for the Study of Negro Life and History (ASNLH). In the same year that Jefferson High School opened, 1926, Woodson established Negro History Week. Woodson, the founder of the ASNLH, provided materials to African American teachers throughout the South and offered what Jarvis Givens calls "abroad mentorship." The materials provided by ASNLH helped to supplement and challenge the existing curriculum available to students at Jefferson High School. Thus, the creation and continued observance of Negro History Week not only provided a means of learning about African American history and Black experiences in the United States, but it also challenged the narratives of white supremacy and anti-Blackness prevalent in the curriculum of American schools at the time. This effort by the teachers at JHS manifested a continuation of Benjamin Tonsler's pedagogy *as* a protest.[34]

Recollections of African American teachers and students at JHS reveal the observance of Negro History Week inside and outside of the school. For example, in 1934, the Jefferson High School choir performed at the school *and* on the radio. The program at the school included the singing of "Lift Every Voice and Sing," also known as the "Negro National Anthem." Teachers and students also participated in programming at a local church, Ebenezer Baptist. At the church, congregants sang the "Negro National Anthem," and there were presentations on "Negro History" by T. J. Sellers, "The Life of Frederick Douglass" by Miss Eva Powell, and "The Life of Booker T. Washington." Interspersed with the presentations, congregants recited poems and sang spirituals. The combined celebrations at school and in the community would continue throughout the history of segregated schooling in Charlottesville and, eventually, at desegregated schools, too.[35]

Jefferson High School closed in the spring of 1951. The equalization movement spawned at the nexus between the NAACP and local African American activists, which led to the closure. The equalization movement consisted of two separate, but related fights for better pay among African American educators and better educational facilities for African American educators, students, and communities across Virginia. In Charlottesville, during the existence of Jefferson High School, African American educators, including Rebecca Fuller McGinness and Booker Reaves, pushed Superintendent James G. Johnson to increase the salaries of Black educators in the city to equalize them with white educators. As a result of their organizing, African American educators received higher salaries, and unlike other African American educators of the era, McGinness and Reaves did not lose their jobs. Reaves and McGinness fought for justice in the Charlottesville City Schools Division and the community long after the equalization movement.[36]

The equalization movement, led by local African American educators and supported by the NAACP, also pushed for better facilities throughout Virginia. Schools and school divisions across Virginia remained segregated and operated under the "separate but equal" precedent set in *Plessy v. Ferguson* (1896). As school divisions, including Charlottesville, built new facilities for white students, African American communities organized in response. The Charlottesville City Schools Division, using funds from the Works Progress Administration and on lands where they displaced African American families, built a new building for Lane High School. Although the Supreme Court's ruling in *Cumming v. Richmond County* (1898) meant that school divisions did not have to provide secondary schooling for African American students, this did not stop African American communities from forcing their hand. Charlottesville's Black community had been successful in a more challenging political environment in their pursuit of establishing JHS. They built on that success, which expanded educational opportunities at another high school less than a mile away. The new high school would be more than just an expanded version of JHS; it was an upgraded facility meant to at least superficially meet the standard of "separate, but equal."[37]

In the late 1940s, Charlottesville City Schools Division made plans to replace JHS. To replace the high school, though, CCS collaborated with the nearby Albemarle County Schools Division (ACS) to build a larger and regional high school building. CCS and ACS built the new high school and named it after a familiar African American educator in the area: Jackson Price Burley. The new high school had a name that better reflected the hope for education and a physical plant that provided more educational opportunities, including higher education. Rather than appease the city's African American community, as the white establishment may have hoped, the establishment of Jackson P. Burley High School provided yet another tangible example that organizing and activism could yield results. This effort represented a continuation and evolution of protest *for* pedagogy.[38]

The effort to build a new high school meant providing more educational opportunities for African American students. For African American educators, this would mean greater job opportunities at a school with more students and more space to accommodate those students. The new high school would build on the tradition established at JHS and become a "movement center" for the local Black freedom struggle.

Several decades after the closure of JHS, William Gilmore reflected on the long-term impact of the high school. In 1945, William Gilmore moved from Nelson County, Virginia, to Charlottesville for better job and educational opportunities. By the time Gilmore arrived, Jefferson High School had been open for nearly two decades, and the city had endured the Great Depression and World War II.

Shortly after his arrival, Gilmore enrolled at JHS. Before heading to school each day, he worked at the Albemarle Hotel or the University of Virginia cafeteria. When he finished working in the morning, Gilmore took a short walk, from the hotel, or a longer walk, from the university, along West Main Street to the high school. Since several of Gilmore's classmates also worked at the hotel and university, Gilmore would have likely been accompanied by peers on the walk to school. A trolley car traveling between the university and the C & O station would have followed his route, too. Instead of an asphalt road, his path from the university to JHS's red brick building is located on the corner of Fourth Avenue and Commerce Street. After two years of this morning routine, Gilmore graduated from JHS in 1948.[39]

After graduating from Jefferson High School, Gilmore served in the military. Gilmore then enrolled at North Carolina Agricultural and Technical College in Greensboro, North Carolina. He secured a job at a hotel in Greensboro through a connection between a white hotel owner in Charlottesville and another white hotel owner in Greensboro. He combined funds from the hotel job and the GI Bill to pay for tuition and living expenses at North Carolina A&T. He graduated with a degree in criminal justice and worked in the criminal justice system.

Gilmore credited success in his life to the foundation built during the time he spent at JHS. Of the school's impact, Gilmore remarked, "The people who are basically pillars of this town would not have been had it not been for a school like Jefferson [High School]. Jefferson has put out some people that have contributed a lot not only to Charlottesville but many people around the world." In 1926, when JHS opened, few could have known the school's influence on William Gilmore, his classmates, his educators, and Charlottesville's African American community.[40]

CHAPTER THREE

"To Take Their Places as Future Leaders"

Jackson P. Burley High School, 1951–1967

So that they might be prepared to take their places as future leaders of this "Great Society," the seniors became thoroughly grounded in the Constitution.
—*Jay Pee Bee*, Jackson P. Burley High School Yearbook, 1965

Burley was not just a school—it was the center of our culture. A lot of community events were going on at Burley.
—Berdell McCoy Fleming, a student at Jackson P. Burley High School

*B*rown v. Board of Education would soon arrive. So, as the potential for a case challenging segregation in public schools increased, several communities across Virginia participated in a massive school-building campaign during the 1940s and 1950s. This policy framework became known as "equalization." In other words, Virginia—alongside other southern states, including nearby North Carolina—attempted to uphold the facade of "separate and equal." This idea originated and aligned with the Supreme Court's decision in *Plessy v. Ferguson* (1896). The policy of equalization in Virginia occurred in segregated elementary and high schools. Charlottesville joined the efforts during the late 1940s, but the city and the school division uniquely approached the issue. Instead of working independently to replace Jefferson High School, the Charlottesville City Schools Division collaborated with nearby cities and counties.[1]

In 1949, two significant events occurred that led to Jackson P. Burley High School. First, the Charlottesville City School Board voted to merge Jefferson High School with nearby Esmont High School and Albemarle Training School. Second, the City of Charlottesville and Albemarle County voters approved a $1,000,000 bond. Rather than having three separate high schools, the new high school would merge into a single school building for all Black students and teachers in the city and county. A year later, the

Charlottesville City Schools Division and the Albemarle County Schools Division purchased a seventeen-acre tract of land from Jackson Price Burley's family. Burley, a former teacher in the Albemarle County Schools Division, retired in 1935, and passed away ten years later. As chronicled earlier, Jackson Burley played a pivotal role in organizing for the city's first Black high school. Mrs. Maggie P. Burley, who also worked in the county schools as a supervisor, oversaw the sale of the land tract. The Burley family had lived on the land for several decades. But with her husband's passing, Mrs. Burley decided to sell the land and relocate to Atlanta, where their daughter lived. To memorialize his work as a teacher and community leader, the Charlottesville School Board named the new school for Mr. Jackson Price Burley.[2]

After purchasing the land near Rose Hill Drive, the school district hired the J. W. Daniels Construction company to build the school. Pendleton S. Clarke of Lynchburg and Baker, Hayward, and Lorens of Charlottesville, two white-owned architectural firms, collaborated on the school's design. The school's design included an auditorium enhanced by a stage with light facilities for drama presentations. The auditorium opened to a large lobby area. The gymnasium sat opposite the auditorium, forming two bookends for the school. The gymnasium held 720 seats and came equipped with a motorized dividing wall to create two basketball courts—one for the boys and one for the girls. Downstairs from the gym was the cafeteria, which included both a large ice box and a refrigerated garbage room. The vocational shops sat in a separate building behind the main school building. Compared to JHS, the new building possessed a greater capacity for various courses and extracurricular activities.[3]

In 1950, the construction process commenced. Between the Charlottesville City Schools Division and the Albemarle County Schools Division, the Burley High School's estimated costs ran to $732,000 for the building and over $100,000 for classroom equipment and surrounding campus structures. However, by the time the school opened, the total cost was $1,400,000. Not only was the building more expensive than estimated, but it was also unfinished when the school opened. On the one hand, the exterior was finished. The squat brown building was constructed using dark brick, including several large windows and a grand entrance. On the other hand, the interior left much to be desired. Although the classrooms and gymnasium were finished, the auditorium, cafeteria, athletic fields,

The entrance to Jackson P. Burley High School, which operated as a city and countywide high school for Black students from 1951–1967. Courtesy of the author.

basement, and vocational shops had been completed to varying degrees. The school would remain open for more than fifteen years as a segregated Black high school.⁴

Jackson P. Burley High School opened in the fall of 1951. Despite the unfinished interior, 26 African American teachers and 543 African American students from Charlottesville, Albemarle County, and Scottsville started classes in September 1951. Black students and teachers entered and occupied an unfinished building, and the dedication occurred during the latter half of the school year. In March 1952, the city and county held a dedication ceremony for the new consolidated high school for African American students in Charlottesville, Albemarle County, and Scottsville.⁵

The dedication was held in BHS's new—and now complete—nine-hundred-seat auditorium. Joseph T. Henley, the Albemarle County School Board chairman, led the proceedings. BHS's band played, and the choir sang; Dr. E. D. McCreary offered an invocation, and Reverend Waddell Ward gave the benediction. The executive secretary of the Virginia Teachers Association, the state's Black teacher association, Dr. J. Rupert Picott, attended the ceremony. Several local and state white officials with connections to African American education in the state participated in the ceremony and, in some cases, offered comments. The officials included University of Virginia President Colgate W. Darden, Jr., State Superintendent of Public Instruction Dowel J. Howard, and Virginia Governor John S. Battle. The presence of so many local and statewide white politicians and policymakers signaled the importance of the school's establishment as a physical building for the city and county's Black communities and marked a shift in white resistance.⁶

Governor John S. Battle, a native of Charlottesville, attended the event as the guest of honor. His presence at the ceremony had less to do with his connection to Charlottesville and more to do with making a political statement about segregated schooling for African Americans in Virginia. During his remarks at the dedication, Battle lauded the cooperation between the city and county schools in building the school as an educational plant. Regarding the school's larger political and economic significance, Battle declared, "[W]e must have just as good schools for our Negro citizens as we have for our white citizens... and that must be done not because of any impelling force from the federal courts but because it's right." In a mixed-racial company, Battle's remarks earned mixed reviews. A few people offered affirmation; however, according to a newspaper account of the event, African American community members sat silently.[7]

Human W. Walsh, Chairman of the Charlottesville City Schools Division, spoke next at the high school's dedication. Walsh contended that Burley High School was now one of the best segregated Black schools in Virginia. Walsh punctuated his speech by sharing his views about the relationship between schooling and democracy. Walsh observed, "Here is evidence of the functioning of a fundamental tenet of democracy, of American democracy. In dedicating this property to the education of Negroes, so that they may enjoy these fundamental rights of man, the obligation inherent in the rights of majority is thus recognized and fulfilled." The building may have supported Black education in the city and county. But, more than anything, the building foreshadowed one of the many ways and lengths that Southern locales would evade and resist the impending *Brown v. Board of Education* decision.[8]

BHS emerged during a time of significant transition in Charlottesville, the South, and the United States. During the same year BHS opened, Moton High School students began their protest approximately sixty miles south. As had been done in Charlottesville, in 1951, Barbara Johns and her classmates engaged in protest *for* pedagogy and protest *as* pedagogy. Johns and the other students at Moton protested the inequitable conditions at Russo R. Moton High School in Farmville, Virginia. Their protest also taught adults in Farmville what could be accomplished through organizing and activism. The story of Johns and her classmates at Farmville's Moton High School is familiar within the history of high school student activism and the Black freedom struggle in Virginia. That year, Johns and her classmates walked out of school, which sparked significant political, social, and economic changes that reverberated throughout Prince Edward County and the United States. After the walkout, the NAACP filed a lawsuit against the local school division. This lawsuit became one of the five cases consolidated under *Brown v. Board of Education* (1954). However, unlike the situation in Farmville, there was not a single pivotal moment that yielded a new Black high school in Charlottesville. However, like the situation in the

Prince Edward County Schools, the impending consequences of legal actions coordinated by the NAACP did help yield improved facilities for segregated Black schools throughout the Commonwealth of Virginia.[9]

Even as the Charlottesville City Schools Division built BHS, the city's Black community continued to press for educational equity in other ways including school desegregation. African American teachers and, for the most part, students remained at BHS throughout the late 1950s as the policy of "Massive Resistance" emerged at the state levels. The Massive Resistance campaign orchestrated by white politicians and policymakers included a range of strategies to delay school desegregation. The most notable strategy—and one that had local consequences for Charlottesville—was closing schools identified for school desegregation. In 1958, Governor J. Lindsey Almond ordered the closure of schools in Charlottesville, Norfolk, Prince Edward County, and Warren County. Venable Elementary School and Lane High School closed during the fall in Charlottesville. These school closures impacted the twelve Black students who were slated to desegregate Venable and Lane alongside the white students who had previously attended those schools.[10]

Although a handful of African American students desegregated LHS during the late 1950s and 1960s, most African American students stayed at BHS in the city and surrounding counties. Some students who initially desegregated LHS changed their minds. That handful of students, who changed their minds, petitioned the Charlottesville City School Board to leave LHS and return to BHS. Garwin DeBerry, Vernetta Lewis, Diane Gardner, Deborah Charlene Brown, and Clyde Melvin all returned to Burley due to, in most cases, a feeling of exclusion at Lane. Garwin DeBerry's experience reveals the limitations of school desegregation efforts. In the fall of 1962, DeBerry enrolled at Lane High School. Although DeBerry was allowed to attend classes, he could not play football. "We were told you can go to school, you can go to class, but that's about all you can do, you can't do any extracurricular activities because no one would participate against us," recalled DeBerry. "I decided to ask mom is it okay if I could go to Burley, I hadn't gone to Burley yet, but she said, look it was a pretty tough situation getting you into Lane [High School], I will see if we talk to somebody who will let you play." DeBerry never played for LHS. After making several attempts to play at LHS, DeBerry transferred to BHS. After graduating from BHS, he enrolled and played football at Virginia State University.[11]

Patricia Edwards also attended BHS as a student during the era of school desegregation. Before she enrolled at BHS, the local chapter of the NAACP approached Edwards and her family about becoming one of the students who would desegregate the Charlottesville City Schools Division. Initially, Edwards wanted to be part of the initial desegregation efforts at LHS. Her parents believed she would be better off staying at BHS. Edwards and her family ultimately decided to forgo desegregating the city's historically white schools and instead ended up attending and graduating from BHS.[12]

During the initial years of BHS's existence, white politicians and policymakers in Charlottesville and across Virginia used the school as an example of equalization. When the Supreme Court ruling prohibited segregation in public schooling, BHS continued to operate and enrolled most Black youth in the area. Black educators remained at the school, too. School desegregation at LHS consisted of only a few Black students, and only a few remained at LHS until graduation. As the local Black freedom struggle reached a different phase with the desegregation of schools and other public places, white politicians and policymakers resisted African American progress not just in the city's school buildings but beyond them, too.

As the fight for equitable education intensified and school desegregation became the central area of that fight, there was another fight over housing and development brewing in the city. Following the initial desegregation efforts at LHS, the City of Charlottesville held a referendum on urban renewal in 1960. Over the next five years, removal and "renewal" caused significant disruption in the Vinegar Hill neighborhood. Hundreds of Black residents were displaced. The Charlottesville Housing Authority provided housing to displaced residents at the Westhaven Housing project. African American businesses were also disrupted and displaced. Over a hundred Black businesses lost revenue and their physical buildings with only modest reimbursement from the government's urban renewal funds. So, while Black high school students were receiving a seemingly more equitable schooling experience at BHS and LHS, the city's white elites were disrupting Black life and community beyond the classroom. And that disruption would continue as full-scale desegregation took hold in the late 1960s.[13]

There were multiple perspectives on the condition of Vinegar Hill. Before urban renewal, George Ferguson, a Black doctor in Charlottesville, remembers, "Those residences that people complained about, most of the properties were owned by whites renting to blacks, and a lot of them had outdoor toilets." Booker Reaves, a Black educator, observes, "Even though there were different economic levels of black people who lived in the Vinegar Hill area—some had better homes than others—they were all very closely knit, and they were people who were helpful to each other in times of stress, and they were people who would come together and work with people all over town."[14]

Like the lack of consensus about the condition, there is some dispute about the close-knit nature of Vinegar Hill. On the one hand, Alies Jones remembers, "They were nice people. I used to cross from my yard to somebody else's, and somebody'd holler across their yard to me. And we'd borrow wood and coal and stuff like that from each other. Them was good old days then. I'm talking about when I was a little girl. Friends looked out for us, and we was just neighbors, that's all, neighbors. We looked out for each other." On the other hand, Walter Jones asserts, "Do you want to know the real truth? Blacks ain't never been closely knit, not unless something comes along now, because that's why the Caucasian race has always been able to get over them, get over and do anything they want to do, whenever they want to. Because blacks never could stick together. You know, they never had the love for each other and that type of thing. A curse is on the black people, in a way of speaking."[15]

Despite the variance in opinions, there was no denying that urban renewal disrupted the African American community in Vinegar Hill. George Ferguson observes, "The renewal came about, and any time you have anything that is disrupted, there are a lot of people who don't like it. But we lived at a time of change. I would say that the majority of those homes were properties that were rented, and the few nice homes that were there, I imagine that the people were satisfied with them. But the whole area was blight." Similarly, Florence Bryant, a Black educator, contended, "The physical condition of Vinegar Hill was poor ... It doesn't matter how poor a neighborhood is, there's an affinity for the neighborhood, for the people, who live there. You're destroying family roots, which is always bad."[16]

The demolition of the historical Vinegar Hill neighborhood created immediate chaos for residents there. To be clear, not all African American students who attended BHS lived in Vinegar Hill. Some students lived in other Charlottesville neighborhoods or Albemarle County and Scottsville. At the same time, the demolition of Vinegar Hill undermined the social and economic well-being of many African American residents at a time when they just seemed to be making progress in the realm of educational equity and opportunity. Florence C. Bryant, who moved from JHS to BHS but remained there just three years, remembers, "Burley provided a rallying point for [B]lack citizens of Charlottesville and Albemarle County to demonstrate their support of the school's program."[17]

When JHS closed, most teachers moved to BHS. Besides Bryant, Alberta Hall Faulkner was another prominent educator who made the move. Mrs. Faulkner, who started her career as a librarian at JHS, served in the same role from the establishment of BHS to its end. The former teachers from JHS were not the only ones who joined the new school. New educators from the surrounding county and beyond the area joined the school during its initial and subsequent years. Having teachers and students who had been at JHS provided continuity for the students. It sped up establishing a new program and culture at the school. Bryant, Faulkner, and others helped the students and the high school program transition from JHS to BHS. "Inspired by the beautiful new facilities, the faculty put forth a special effort to design an exciting new, vital, and dynamic educational program," Bryant remembers. "The expanded facilities made possible additional course offerings, such as art, speech and drama, practical nursing, and the building trades. BHS continued the tradition of academic excellence already established at Jefferson High School." As she had done at JHS, Bryant taught English and remained involved in facilitating extracurricular activities. Although Bryant left the high school to pursue a graduate degree at the University of Virginia, other Black educators at BHS continued to build upon the foundation and legacy of JHS and other segregated Black high schools that combined to form BHS.[18]

BHS's teachers and students continued to cultivate community and consciousness. Burley's teachers were valued and respected. In the school's final yearbook, the staff dedicated the volume to the nine teachers who had been at the school from its opening: Mrs. Lillie M. Brown, Mrs. Pauline Garrett, Mrs. Emma B. Bryson, Mrs. Gladys W. McCoy, Mrs. Alberta H. Faulkner, Mrs. Thelma H. McCreary, Mrs. Zelda H. Murray, Mrs. Alma W. Pleasants, and Mrs. Commora B. Snowden. On the dedication page, the staff wrote, "We are fortunate in having nine teachers who have dedicated their services to this school for fifteen years—its entire life history. Witnessing the sad and desolate moments, as well as many proud and glorious ones, they have watched and contributed immeasurably to the growth of Burley High since its beginning in 1951." Unlike the teachers at Jefferson High School, Burley's teachers earned their degrees and were trained at institutions throughout the South and North. Of all the teachers, the staff wrote, "The value of the golden thread runs so true among the faculty members here at Jackson P. Burley High School. The wisdom, patience, and love our administrators and teachers display provide the nucleus around which revolves the aspirations of human kind [sic]. The individual preparation and contributions of our teachers are so invaluable that there can be no doubt as to their sincerity, earnestness, and dedication to our school."[19]

Drawing upon the expanded facilities, Black educators engaged students in vocational education and a college preparation curriculum. This marked a continuance of pedagogy *as* protest. Students took courses in French and Latin language, speech and drama, world and U.S. history, typing, physical science, algebra, carpentry, masonry, farm mechanics, health and physical education, chemistry, and practical nursing. During the 1965–1966 school year, the English department held its first Shakespeare festival. The department also had students read and act out scenes from Hamlet. In ninth-grade English, the students read Charles Dickens's *Great Expectations*. In the speech and drama class, students worked to "improve the art of communication by learning the technique of effective speaking." In Latin class, students translated from Caesar's *Gallic Wars*. In music classes, students were exposed to European classical music. The *Jay Pee Bee* yearbook notes, "By being a member of the band, the choir or music appreciation class the students are introduced to many renowned composers as Bach, Beethoven and Wilhousky as well as many of the great contemporaries." Based on the available source material, the English curriculum did not center on the writings of Black authors. However, Burley continued to observe and celebrate Negro History Week.[20]

Extracurricular activities provided another space for Black educators and students to interact and seek excellence. Like Jefferson High School, all students participated in Burley's extracurricular activities. In the *Jay Pee Bee*, each senior student's picture was accompanied by a list of their involvement in various activities. Burley touted several different student-run and faculty-supported organizations. These organizations included student patrol, Future Teachers of America, *Burley Bulletin* Staff (school newspaper), Choir, Marching Band, Science and Math Club, National Honor Society, Quill and Scroll Club, Dramatics, the Rainbow Art Club, and Le Cercle Francais. Students also participated in the Student Participation Association, and each homeroom class had a representative. The yearbook claims, "Voting is a responsibility. The class of '65 leads the way." Science and Math Club students participated in math and science competitions with other high schools in the state. Burley also had a host of athletic opportunities. The school offered football, track, and basketball.[21]

Math and science courses benefited from both Burley's teachers' improved facilities and expansive expertise. In math classes, students were exposed to a range of high-level math. Students took a range of math courses, including algebra, geometry, and trigonometry. Access to these courses provided students with the content knowledge and credentials to continue their education after high school. Teachers drew upon better lab facilities to expose students to more and better opportunities. In a chemistry class pictured in the school yearbook, students could be seen making calculations about how much hydrogen could be produced under various conditions. Social studies courses aimed to provide students with a broad view of history in the United States and the world, and to prepare students for future citizenship. The world history course consisted of a broad view of civilization beginning with the stone age through the present-day.[22]

The vocational education courses were separated by gender. Young women at BHS took courses in homemaking, which involved cooking and sewing. The homemaking courses aimed to provide young women with "developing skills to carry out wisely and intelligently the duties of the homemaker." The yearbook carries pictures of young women sewing and designing clothes. Young men at BHS took agriculture, carpentry, masonry, and industrial courses to study "the fundamental principles of the work and then apply their knowledge to the carrying out of a worthwhile project." Both young men and women students took courses in business education. The courses aimed to immerse students in different business occupations and help them develop proficiency. In these courses, students became more familiar with typewriters utilized by businesses in the area. Students also took a business law course. As part of the course, students visited the corporation court presided over by Judge Bridgeforth. They also observed Law Day U.S.A. and were visited by school board member Henry Mitchell.[23]

Parents and the broader Black community were welcomed to BHS. And parents reciprocated that welcoming atmosphere through their involvement in the school. Teresa Price recalls, "At Burley, I thought it was pretty interesting that we had better participation in the PTA, and that was surprising because people had to come distances to be there." Jackson P. Burley High School held open houses at the end of the school year so students and teachers could share their work. In 1962, for example, Burley held an open house and invited parents and the community. Each department shared its work with the community, including Fine Arts, Foreign Language, Health and Physical Education, Language Arts, Science and Math, Social Studies, and Vocational Studies.[24]

BHS served not just as a school. It was also a place to build and sustain Charlottesville's African American community. This had been true of JHS, too. However, the significance and importance of the high school space grew as more students attended high school from within the city and from the surrounding counties. Berdell Fleming, a student at Burley during the 1960s, recalls, "Burley was not just a school—it was the center of our culture. A lot of community events were going on at Burley." Burley provided another space for the African American community in Charlottesville and surrounding counties and cities to gather. The school also became a space where community events were held including meetings of the local NAACP.[25]

BHS's athletic program also united educators, students, and the community. "That was the thing to do. That was like the social outlet, the football games," remembers Frankie Allen, a student at Jefferson Elementary School. "People would get off work usually on Friday nights," recalls Allen, "Oh, man, that was the social event of the weekend or whatever, to go to the Burley football games, football games and basketball games." Allen never attended Burley High School. He desegregated Venable Elementary School in fifth grade and continued in desegregated schools through his graduation from LHS. However, his experience of attending football and basketball games at BHS still resonates with him and many others today.[26]

The BHS Bears football team had a long run of success. Their success on the football field drew the attention of African American and white spectators in the area. William Redd, a student and athlete at Burley, remembers, "We were the cream of the crop in Charlottesville because during those years, like in '56 when we had the big season, Lane [High School] was one and nine. [University of] Virginia was in the midst of their 28-game losing streak ... So that was the place to be. Albemarle [High School] was just being built." In other words, BHS was the place to be for football in Charlottesville. It was typical for the high schools in the area to all play on Friday nights. However, LHS had trouble garnering a sizeable crowd. As a result, William Redd remembers, "So the next time we had to play, we played on a Thursday night, and Lane played on a Friday night. So that way, they could get the crowd. The crowds were coming to our stadium."[27]

During the 1960s, relationships developed between BHS and some faculty at UVA. The university and the Charlottesville City Schools Division collaborated on a Practical Nursing program at the high school. The students received their degrees from BHS, but they received training from professors at the University of Virginia. This arrangement provided an expanded vocational training program, but it did not offer the same level of credentials that a student at the university received. The vocational route Teresa Price, a teacher at BHS, also recalls forming a partnership with Paul Gaston, a young white professor at the University of Virginia—and civil rights activist in his own right. Price helped connect Elizabeth Crenshaw, her student, with Gaston. As a result, Gaston hired Crenshaw as his secretary. The School of Engineering at UVA also started hiring students from BHS as support staff. UVA also became involved with BHS's drama department during the school desegregation era. Faculty from UVA helped stage a play at BHS, which included Patricia Edwards—a student and future educator—in a lead role. These collaborations reveal some shifts in the relationships between UVA and the city's African American community. At the same time, these collaborations existed on the margins and UVA benefitted from these engagements. The university could be trying to influence perceptions in the community or, in the case of the practical nursing program, trying to enroll more students and generate more revenue.[28]

Just as the students at JHS had done, the students at BHS created a yearbook chronicling and commemorating the previous school year. Creating a yearbook quickly became part of high school life in the United States. The yearbook changed as resources, technologies, and the world changed. In particular, the 1965 edition of the *Jay Pee Bee*—one of the last yearbooks created at the school—provides a window not only into how the world inside the school had changed since the emergence of Black high schooling in Charlottesville but also how the outside world was changing, too.[29]

The transition between JHS and BHS reflected changes and continuities in the broader political, social, economic, and educational contexts. On the one hand, the high schools were still segregated, and the curriculum and pedagogy consisted of vocational education and college prep. On the other hand, as the world was changing beyond the high school, Black educators and students became more involved in organizing and protesting for justice and equity in various areas. The social studies courses reflected those changes.

In the 1966 edition of the *Jay Pee Bee*, there is a picture of students seated in rows with their eyes focused on their desks. It is not clear what they are reading on their desks. However, the caption reads, "So that they might be prepared to take their place as future leaders of this 'Great Society,' the seniors became thoroughly grounded in the Constitution." This caption shows an awareness of national political events and the potential for political progress in the United States. Lyndon B. Johnson delivered the "Great Society" speech during a commencement address at the University of Michigan in 1964. The speech called for a massive expansion of the state in the interest of supporting marginalized people in the United States. Also, that year, the U.S. Congress passed the Civil Rights Act of 1964. The following year, Congress passed the Voting Rights Act of 1965. These national events had consequences for the African American teachers and students at Burley High School, which was clearly on their minds as they developed the text for the yearbook. The national, state, and local events of the Black freedom struggle—and the resulting white backlash—impacted Charlottesville's entire Black community, but, more specifically, the teachers and students at segregated Burley High School. It is difficult to draw direct connections between pedagogy in the classroom and protest in the community. At the same time, it is not hard to imagine students feeling empowered to seek justice when they learn about their rights as citizens through reading and learning about the U.S. Constitution.[30]

While the Charlottesville City Schools Division resisted school desegregation, tangible vestiges of Jim Crow in other public spaces were being stripped away. The city had begun to remove both the physical and metaphorical signs of segregation. The city's trains and buses were desegregated in 1956; the city also withdrew segregated signage around the same time. Meanwhile, several political organizations became prominent during the

1950s and 1960s. Simultaneously with national efforts to enfranchise African Americans, Charlottesville organizations worked to change the local circumstances. While African Americans in Charlottesville had effected change without the right to vote, as was the case in the establishment of JHS and BHS, local groups worked to remove the barriers to voting. One significant change that occurred to activists was moving voter registration from behind closed doors to out in the public. Black teachers supported this work both as volunteers and through financial means. Voting was just one aspect that drew the attention of activists at the time.[31]

The local NAACP group became more prominent during this period on various issues. Although the Black community in Charlottesville had a history of organizing during the early twentieth century, the city did not have an NAACP chapter until midcentury. Before the *Brown* decision, members of the Charlottesville NAACP "complained that facilities at Burley, only three years old, were inferior to those found at Lane and expressed alarm when the councillors tried to divert $70,000 earmarked for Burley to Jefferson." Florence Bryant was an active member during her time at JHS and BHS. Eugene Williams joined the local chapter of the NAACP when he returned to Charlottesville in 1953. When Williams first started attending NAACP meetings, the local chapter had only sixty-five registered members—and less than ten people were present. Williams soon became the chairman of the membership committee. "And the first year (1955)," he recalls, "we increased our membership from 65 members to 900 members."[32]

The local NAACP was active in developing membership and supporting school desegregation. During the following year, 1956, membership increased to fifteen hundred members. "We just developed a membership drive that motivated people to do something that they can feel proud of," remembers Williams. The increase in membership provided the means for the local chapter to be influential on issues such as school desegregation. The national NAACP commended the Charlottesville branch's "outstanding achievement" in the "successful desegregation of the public schools." Not only had the NAACP pushed for the desegregation of schools, but they also provided tutoring to Black students when CCS closed Venable Elementary and Lane High School during the 1958–1959 school year. While the local branch received an award from the national NAACP for their efforts, some of the Black students involved in school desegregation had a different view of the tutoring arrangement and experience with navigating the city's historically white schools.[33]

The NAACP was not the only organization fighting for the civil rights of African Americans in Charlottesville. In 1942, Reverend Benjamin Bunn organized and served as the chairman of the Intra-Racial Commission. Reverend Bunn was the pastor at First Baptist Church. The group comprised African American and white members. Eventually, this commission became the Charlottesville chapter of the Virginia Council on Human Relations (VCHR). Throughout the 1940s and 1950s, the group organized around Black labor and housing issues. The group's organizing strategies drew upon the work of other civil rights struggles throughout the South. The local chapters of the NAACP and VCHR collaborated on various endeavors, including protests.[34]

The VCHR made inroads in hiring practices within Charlottesville. Teresa Price taught at BHS. But she was also involved with the VCHR. The group talked to employers in Charlottesville about having more open hiring practices. Employers, including the biggest employer in the area, UVA, discriminated against Black applicants. The work of the VCHR and civil rights legislation eventually led to changes in hiring practices at UVA and other local employers led by white people. As a result of the organizing and pressure applied by the group, African Americans were hired as clerks and cashiers at Safeway. However, access to jobs was limited by the intransigence of less educated and conservative whites and educated and liberal whites. The teachers from BHS were not the only ones involved in movement activities. Their students also became involved beyond the classroom.[35]

Sit-in protests occurred throughout the South. Charlottesville was just one of many locales where sit-ins were used to desegregate public spaces. Buddy's Restaurant on Emmet Street became a prime target for desegregation. Paul Gaston's account of events has become the dominant written narrative. In 1957, Gaston arrived in Charlottesville to become a professor in the History Department at the University of Virginia. He retired in 1997. He was an active community member between his arrival and retirement, including being part of the VCHR. In May of 1963, Gaston attended a picnic at a UVA law professor's house, including people from the local branch of the NAACP. The two groups had been involved in desegregation efforts at local restaurants, motels, and theaters. They had collaborated on negotiating with these various public entities. They had not been successful in desegregating public spaces and places—with the exception of schools in Charlottesville.[36]

Near the end of the picnic, Floyd Johnson addressed the assembled people. Johnson, a young Black minister, said, "We're going to have some sit-ins . . . You're all aware of how we've negotiated patiently here for such a long time, and yet this is still a closed city. And we've got to do something about it. So, all of you would like to join the sit-in movement, come down to my church." While sit-ins had become a tactic employed by organizers and activists throughout the South at the time, Charlottesville had not yet organized one of its own. Johnson felt that it was time to escalate the fight against segregation and discrimination in the city.[37]

Johnson's call to action occurred just two months after a speech by Martin Luther King, Jr. in Charlottesville. King delivered a speech in Cabell Hall. Gaston recalled, "[King] made a speech that rocked the place. It was filled; there were a thousand folks there. Hundreds of them came up to touch him afterward. The dynamism that the man suggested was impossible to believe unless you really saw it." King's speech—and the local people's response—set the stage for individuals at the picnic to move from words to action. A few days after the picnic, Johnson hosted a workshop on how to do a sit-in. He described how everyone should protect themselves and remain non-violent, even if the situation turned violent. Many in the group believed that Charlottesville's segregationists would not become violent.[38]

After learning how to conduct a sit-in, groups of African Americans and white people conducted a series of sit-ins at local restaurants. One of the places that they targeted for desegregation was a place called Buddy's Restaurant. The tagline for Buddy's was "Just a Nice Place to Eat." Until the sit-ins, it had only been a nice place to eat for white people. The VCHR and NAACP wanted to change that.[39]

At Buddy's Restaurant, VCHR and NAACP members sat down. They were not served. The place closed without the group being served; however, they were not attacked on the first visit. The groups returned when the restaurant opened again. When the group attempted to enter the restaurant the next day, a group stood in the doorway. Gaston remembers, "It was his job [the proprietor's] to be the host of all the guests who might come to the restaurant, and to express the proprietor's sincere regrets to those who would not be welcome in the restaurant. He was a man of substantial proportions, and one had the feeling that one was not going to have a sit-in inside that restaurant that day." In response, the group formed a line led by Floyd Johnson and attempted to enter the door. But this time, they were blocked. The group blocking the entry included UVA students, white men wearing Nazi armbands, and a white supremacist group. Following this attempt to sit-in, Paul Gaston received anonymous threatening calls that evening.[40]

On Memorial Day, the white counter-protestors turned violent. When the group attempted another sit-in at the restaurant, Floyd Johnson had to leave for a while and get some food. During Johnson's absence, Gaston was placed in charge. While Gaston was inside leading the group, two individuals approached him. The individuals attacked Gaston. They hit him across the face multiple times. The two men pulled Gaston outside, and he returned to the line. The men left before the police arrived. Gaston spoke with the police. Later, after the police left, Johnson and Johnson returned to the restaurant. They met the same fate as Gaston. However, Johnson and Johnson faced greater violence and consequences. Floyd Johnson spent two nights in the hospital as a result of the violence; William Johnson avoided time in the hospital, but he was also severely beaten.[41]

Gaston, Johnson, and Johnson all filed assault charges. Lawyers from the University of Virginia represented Gaston, while Johnson and Johnson were represented by Sam Tucker, "who was a pioneer NAACP lawyer in this area." Gaston received a mixed response from students. On the one hand, students from his Southern History course applauded him when he entered the classroom for their final exam. On the other hand, a student slashed Gaston's tires in the middle of the night. Janitors and grounds crew people came to Gaston's office to offer their support. The trial occurred after finals week for the University of Virginia.[42]

All the individuals involved in the sit-in protesting for Black civil rights were acquitted. Gaston argues, "There were just too many people who were watching the trial, and even in the worst hanging court there'd have been no way that we could have been found guilty. Likewise, it would have been very difficult to find the others innocent. So, we were just acquitted, and they were found guilty and fined by the judge ten dollars and given thirty-day suspended sentences." Buddy's Restaurant did not become desegregated because of the sit-in demonstrations. No more protests occurred at the restaurant. Buddy's Restaurant never desegregated; instead, it closed. The owner closed the restaurant when the Civil Rights Act of 1964 passed.[43]

While Gaston's account has become the dominant narrative about these sit-ins, he was not the only one there. Black students at BHS, like the students at Moton High School, fought for justice. Berdell McCoy Fleming, a student at BHS, was also involved. Fleming was born in Charlottesville at the University of Virginia Hospital. Most of her experiences being educated and serving as an educator occurred in Charlottesville. When Fleming was growing up, the Charlottesville City Schools Division did not yet offer kindergarten. So, she attended the Janie Porter Barrett Daycare Center—the oldest preschool in central Virginia. Fleming attended the Jefferson Elementary School for grades one through seven. Fleming recalls, "[T]hey were solid teachers [at Jefferson Elementary School] and community members, so you saw them in other places. You saw them in church. And girl scout activities."[44]

After seventh grade at Jefferson, Fleming transferred to BHS. "Burley was not just a school—it was the center of our culture," recalls Fleming. "A lot of community events were going on at Burley." BHS had "absolutely wonderful teachers." Fleming's mother, Gladys McCoy, taught at BHS. Her mother had attended Ohio State University. She taught French at Burley and was fluent. Upon graduating from BHS, Fleming left the city to participate in college at Norfolk State University.[45]

Despite never being mentioned in Gaston's "official" account, Fleming participated in the sit-ins at Buddy's Restaurant. Fleming felt obligated to join the sit-in since she had not desegregated LHS. Donald Martin, one of the twelve Black students involved in desegregation, was one of her friends growing up. After he finished each day at LHS, Fleming recalled Martin walking over to BHS to hang out with his friends. Fleming's best friend—whose mother was a teacher—also participated in the sit-in. Mrs. Palmer, a woman from Fleming's church, and some Student Nonviolent Coordinating Committee (SNCC) members trained Fleming and her friend Alicia Lugo. "We were just teenagers and told to get the training," recalls Fleming, "We were told to take a book and read." She remembers being taunted, things being thrown, and people spitting on her. Nevertheless, she continued to stand. Fleming cites Mrs. Palmer as the reason for staying there during the sit-in.[46]

There's no doubt that historian Paul Gaston played an integral role in the local sit-in movement. However, by centering himself as the story's hero, other individuals have been left out of the story until recently. Fleming and her friend wanted to be involved in the local Black freedom struggle. From

Fleming's perspective, it was the least she could do as her peers desegregated Lane High School. Fleming's perspective is essential for another reason, too. Often, when historians focus on high school students, there is a tendency to view students as conflicting. Of course, there are examples of generational tensions between Black youth and Black adults. However, in Fleming's case, Mrs. Palmer was integral to her participation in the sit-in.

By the spring of 1967, BHS had employed Black educators and enrolled Black youth for over fifteen years. While students like Patricia Edwards and Berdell Fleming have fond memories of their teachers, not all students and parents were satisfied with their experience at BHS. Based on Edwards's conversations with her peers at LHS and her experiences at BHS, she believes her parents were right. Edwards speaks glowingly about how her teachers cared for students' academic and personal well-being. She credits her teachers as the reason for pursuing a career as a teacher. The local NAACP approached other students about becoming students in the city's desegregated schools. Randolph White served as editor of the *Charlottesville-Albemarle Tribune*, a local Black newspaper; his son attended Burley. White claimed he had to hire a professor at the University of Virginia "to teach him something he should have had at Burley." And while White's son went on to graduate from Howard University, Burley lost its accreditation in December 1966. The Southern Association of Colleges and Schools dropped Burley from the association's list of approved secondary schools. One reason for the loss of accreditation stemmed from the qualifications of the school's teachers. Some teachers did not have a bachelor's degree recognized by the Southern Association of Colleges and Schools, while five others were teaching classes they were not certified to teach.[47]

As school desegregation at LHS accelerated during the mid-to-late 1960s, BHS lost students. Rather than splitting all the city's high school students between Burley and Lane, Superintendent George C. Tramontin and the Charlottesville City Schools Division placed the burden of desegregation on Black students. The enrollment at BHS went from 410 students in 1964 to just 151 in 1966. The number of Black educators also dropped from forty-two to thirty-one over the same period. Black educators continued to leave as it became apparent that the Charlottesville City Schools Division would be forced to desegregate LHS. The *Burley Bulletin*, the student newspaper, tracked where teachers ended up after leaving Burley High School. Based on their reporting, one teacher went to Lane; six teachers went to the junior high schools, one to the sixth-grade center at Jefferson, one to Albemarle High School, four to schools outside the area, and two to graduate school. The Charlottesville City Schools Division did not assign teachers based on their qualifications and experience. CCS placed teachers based on the division's needs. Burley's vice principal, for instance, "was assigned to teach mathematics and science in the Jefferson Sixth Grade Center." He had only taught high school students throughout his thirty-three-year career in the city schools.[48]

When the Charlottesville City Schools Division—alongside other school divisions in Virginia and school districts across the South—were pushed by the courts to implement full-scale school desegregation, they made hundreds of decisions about which schools would be desegregated. This meant choosing to keep some schools open while closing other schools. As with school desegregation, historically Black schools bore the brunt of the school closures. In Charlottesville, rather than split all the city's public school students between BHS and LHS, the Charlottesville City Schools Division decided to close BHS and crowd all public high school students into LHS. This would have long-term consequences for Black teachers and students, but it also affected the experiences of all students at the school during the late 1960s and early 1970s.

Besides the decisions to close schools, school divisions across Virginia also made hiring decisions for the era of school desegregation. Gladys McCoy's experience was common. McCoy, the mother of Berdell McCoy Fleming, taught at BHS and then transferred over to LHS. In 1968, the Charlottesville City School Board decided not to renew McCoy's contract for the upcoming school year. McCoy responded to the board's decision by filing a lawsuit against the board and Superintendent Edward W. Rushton. Filing in the federal court, McCoy sought a restraining order and financial damages resulting from her unemployment. Before the board had decided to fire McCoy, they had reassigned her to serve as an assistant librarian across several elementary and junior high school divisions. She countered that this assignment violated the stipulations of her contract: It not only undermined her earning potential during the upcoming school year, but it would also impact her future retirement earnings, too. McCoy's lawsuit also asserted that the School Board "avoided employing Negroes as principals and have followed a course of action which will steadily diminish the percentage of Negros among professional personnel" in the Charlottesville City Schools Division. McCoy faced the fate of thousands of Black educators who were either demoted or dismissed by their school divisions and districts in the South.[49]

Like Black high schools throughout the South, BHS was converted into a middle school. Since BHS was a joint venture by the Charlottesville City Schools Division and the Albemarle County Schools Division, closing the school required more logistics involving both divisions. One of the biggest challenges with closing the school, from the perspective of the divisions, was how to handle the ownership of the building. "In April 1968, the county finally bought Charlottesville's interest in Burley at a price of $700,000." Not everyone in Charlottesville agreed to sell the BHS building to the county schools. Anne Holden asserts, "The Burley plant was in good condition, and during the debate, Burley was described by the Charlottesville city manager as the best-constructed school in the city. Burley is located on a seventeen-acre campus that some considered too valuable a piece of property for the city to let go, regardless of the building. There was a feeling in the black community that the school board did not want to take on another formerly black school that whites would have to attend on a desegregated basis." Whether or not the School Board intended to avoid questions about desegregating BHS, the school building became the property of the Albemarle County Schools Division. And it remains so today.[50]

PART TWO

The Origins and Limits of the Desegregated High School

CHAPTER FOUR

"A Little More Defiant, a Little More Militant"

Lane High School, 1959–1974

Well, that entailed that we were a little more defiant, a little more militant, just less in terms of the same old, same old. We wanted to say, well 'you don't have black history, you don't have this, you don't have that . . . why is the principal, why is the staff doing this?' We definitely came in asking questions. Of course during those days, the Black Panthers and the militancy and the fist raising happening.
—Charles Alexander, a student at Lane High School

She never looked at me. She stood with her back to me. 'College? You need to get that notion out of your head and pick up a trade.' I was devastated. I was crushed.
—James Bryant, a student at Lane High School

Donald Martin and John Martin grew up on Charlottesville's Lankford Avenue in the late 1940s and 1950s. They attended Jefferson Elementary School and, like their peers at the time, would have attended BHS. However, instead of attending and graduating from BHS, the Martin brothers, alongside their fellow student, French Jackson, became the first Black students at Lane High School and bore the burden of desegregating LHS. Donald Martin was just twelve years old at the time. When Governor J. Lindsey Almond ordered the closure of schools in Charlottesville, Donald Martin, John Martin, and French Jackson attended a "basement school" during the fall of 1958. Unlike the schools in Prince Edward County, which remained closed for five years, the Charlottesville City Schools Division reopened before the end of the school year. Lane High School reopened in February 1959; however, only white students returned to the school. Jackson and the Martin brothers remained in limbo. The Charlottesville City Schools Division did not allow them to enroll at Lane High School, but their lawyers advised them against returning to Burley High School to maintain standing. So, they remained in the basement

Table 4. Black students at Lane High School, 1959–1963

Year	1959	1960	1961	1962	1963
Students	3	7	16	26	42

Source: Charlottesville Public Schools, "Outline of Charlottesville School Integration Case," December 2, 1963, 2–3.

school until the end of the school year 1959. John Martin recalls that the makeshift schooling arrangement was a "waste of time."[1]

Finally, on September 8, 1959, Jackson and the Martin brothers desegregated LHS. Built on the land of a formerly Black neighborhood and using the support of federal funds from the Works Progress Administration, Lane High School sat down the hill from Jefferson High School. White columns framed the three-story red-bricked building's front entrance. On their first day, Jackson and the Martin brothers did not initially enter the school through the front door. "They told us to go to the rear door," recalls Donald Martin, "It was locked." They returned to the front of the school, where a group of white people lined the path leading to the front door. They screamed racist epithets at the young Black men and other comments, including "Go back to your kind" and "Stay away from my daughter." Not only did Jackson and the Martin brothers face a white racist entrance to the school, but they did so without any other Black people in Lane High School's classrooms.[2]

During the initial period of school desegregation, African American educators remained at the city's segregated schools. In comparing his experience at desegregated Lane High School and at segregated Jefferson Elementary School, John Martin asserted, "The teachers were excellent—better than some at Lane." At Lane High School, he dealt with a "somewhat hostile" physical education teacher and an algebra teacher who seldom called on him in class. Martin did have some better experiences at Lane with his English teacher, June Webster, and his Spanish teacher, Hebe Redden. A few white students at Lane also showed him moments of kindness; however, the school ultimately pushed him out. Martin did not graduate from Lane. The school's administration accused him of being a "gang member" and of "throwing rocks." Martin denied both accusations but eventually left LHS. He attended and graduated from Virginia Randolph High School in Richmond, Virginia.[3]

Donald Martin had a slightly different outcome. He credited his time at Jefferson Elementary and his upbringing for preparing him well for what he would face at LHS. "In spite of what people may have said, Jefferson [Elementary] had prepared me well," remembers Martin. "I had no academic problems, felt no deficiency in training, and was able to pick up where I was and move forward. I never felt academically intimated. In fact, I remember helping some of my white classmates with their homework." But he still faced many of the same challenges that his brother faced. Martin managed to survive and graduated from Lane. Due to the location of his childhood home, he had regular interactions with white folks. "I lived race relations every day," Martin remembers, relying on various strategies to navigate the white space at Lane High School. For example, in the hallways, Martin "would look at the person's eyes," and he received a range of reactions. "Some of them looked straight past me and through me as though I were invisible.... Others looked straight at me, acknowledged me and smiled. Still others looked at me with hostility. In any case, those reactions were a gauge of how my day would go, positive or negative."[4]

In the classroom, Donald Martin had mixed experiences with white teachers. "My Spanish teacher was very pleasant. I mastered Spanish to the level that I tutored some of the other students," recalls Martin, "I remember that my English teacher was very demanding, but she treated me just like she did the other students in her class and didn't do me any favors. My government teacher was my favorite teacher. He inspired me to major in political science in college." Besides the experiences with individual teachers, Martin noticed the difference between teachers' expectations of him at Lane High School, particularly in comparison with how he was treated at Jefferson Elementary. Martin claims, "The teachers didn't expect me to achieve, and clearly not to excel. Going to high school was just a matter of getting through the day. I did just enough to get by, enough not to be exceptional, not to stand out, just enough to blend in and not call attention to myself. I felt that any attention I might get would be negative. My whole notion was to make the experience just as painless as possible."[5]

Beyond the classroom, Martin had limited engagement with extracurricular activities. He participated in the school's Spanish club. However, his participation in that club resulted from a class requirement and not necessarily a genuine desire to participate in the club's activities. He did not participate in athletics for most of his time at LHS. In his senior year, he played varsity basketball. This experience of playing basketball did not change his overall assessment of attending Lane High School as one of the first Black students to do so. "It was something I had to do, not something for full actualization," remembers Martin. "High school should fulfill the cultural, social, and academic needs of the students. I was interested in only academics. I walked to school with my buddies in the morning and entered the building at 9, and I left school at 3:20 in the afternoon, rejoined my buddies and returned home. That was my school day." Being one of the first Black students and one of just a few Black people in the school building, Martin's high school experience, for the most part, became narrowed on academics. He graduated from high school and attended college at Virginia State University.[6]

Throughout the 1960s, a small group of African American students opted to follow in the footsteps of Jackson and the Martin brothers to enroll at Lane High School. This small group of students continued to face white resistance and racism—all with few African American teachers, counselors, and administrators in the building. When the Charlottesville City Schools Division was forced by federal courts to desegregate all the schools fully, they decided to close Jackson P. Burley High School. After closing Burley, the Charlottesville City Schools Division crowded all the city's high school students into a single building at Lane. Neither the building nor the people within were prepared for full-scale desegregation. By the late 1960s, not only were all the city's Black high school students attending Lane, but they were also growing increasingly frustrated by the hostile environment and racist behaviors of their white peers, teachers, and the school's administrators.[7]

The Massive Resistance campaign in the Commonwealth of Virginia, generally, specifically in Charlottesville, gave way to other forms of white resistance. The Commonwealth of Virginia enacted new legislation which allowed for school desegregation. But it was on the terms of white politicians, white superintendents, white educators, and white community members. The "Freedom of Choice" program required African American students to apply to desegregate historically white schools. Black students and their families had to complete an application to the school division and undergo a lengthy process to gain admission. On the one hand, the process was less cumbersome than suing the school division to desegregate; on the other hand, white

Photograph of Lane High School, circa 1963, from the front of the building reproduced from *The Chain*, 1962–1963. Courtesy of Charlottesville High School Media Center.

students did not have to undergo any process. This "Freedom of Choice" period lasted in Charlottesville from the fall of 1959 to the fall of 1966.[8]

Initially, Lane High School's building did not create problems for school desegregation. However, during the Freedom of Choice era, the number of Black students increased steadily from 3 to 122. The Charlottesville City Schools Division required African American students to apply for admission at the city's historically segregated white schools, including Lane High School. Some scholars have called the white students, teachers, and administrators part of the "moderate" faction; however, those who remained at these desegregated schools should more aptly be referred to as "passive resistors." By contrast, the massive resistors tried a new tactic sweeping Virginia and the South. Using tuition credits from the Commonwealth of Virginia, they founded Rock Hill Academy. Rock Hill served as the city's high school segregation academy.[9]

The absence of several hundred white students during this period did, however, alleviate enrollment pressures as more Black students sought admission and enrolled at Lane High School. By 1966, Black students constituted ten percent of the Lane High School's population. But at Rock Hill Academy, fewer than a hundred white students enrolled, and the number dwindled by the year. In most cases, the students who left Rock Hill Academy returned to Lane High School. When full-scale school desegregation took hold, Black students constituted twenty percent of the student population. Since the Charlottesville City Schools Division had long been in denial that school desegregation would occur, they did not have adequate facilities to handle all the city's high school students in a single building.[10]

While the student population at Lane High School was shifting, the faculty and staff at Lane High School were also changing. Due in part to the closure of Burley High School, Black educators began desegregating Lane High School. As school desegregation took hold in Charlottesville, African American educators eventually joined African American students at Lane High School. Like their students, African American educators were outnumbered. To varying degrees, the teachers new to the school became involved with Black student organizing and activism. Teresa Price and Lorraine Williams were among the first. Price and Williams started their career at BHS before desegregating LHS. They were involved in organizing and activism beyond the BHS classroom, which continued during their time at LHS.[11]

Price worked on various fronts to agitate for justice and equity. She counted on working with the VCHR local branch. She taught courses such as bookkeeping and shorthand that prepared students for future employment as secretaries. She connected her civil rights work outside the classroom with the business education courses by working behind the scenes to secure jobs for her Black students. As mentioned in chapter three, one of her former students, Elizabeth Crenshaw, went to work for Paul Gaston at the University of Virginia. She also invited the local State Farm Insurance company to test students' proficiency in her classroom. Price reasoned that her students would perform better in that environment. Some of her students secured employment with State Farm, which suggests Price's reasoning was well founded.[12]

Business education courses did not provide an easy entry point for discussing the civil rights movement. However, Price employed a creative approach to engaging her students on the topic. When she moved to Lane High School, she started teaching a course called "Notehand." The course aimed to prepare college-bound students to take notes. Price did more than teach students to take notes. She made a pact with students that half the class would focus on taking notes while the other half of the forty minutes would be spent discussing race relations. One young Black woman was enrolled in the course; the remaining students were young white women. Price fielded questions from students and asked them questions. The pact between Price and the students was important because the mayor's daughter was enrolled in the course. The dialogue between Price and the students on race and racism had significant potential for backlash. While this approach did not root out the racism present at LHS, no less Charlottesville, Price's attempt, placed in the social and political context of the time, was subversive.[13]

Several young and new teachers in the school division significantly impacted school desegregation and Black students. Most white teachers at Lane High School were resistant to change. However, one white teacher aimed to become an ally of Black educators and students at Lane High School. Susan Cone Scott, a white woman from Richmond, had become an English teacher around the same time Price and Williams desegregated Lane. Scott arrived in Charlottesville to earn a graduate degree in English at the University of Virginia. Teaching at Lane High School only occurred after earning her degree. During her time, Scott allied herself with Black teachers and students.[14]

Scott taught different levels of English. As a white woman with access to money, privilege, and power, she had little idea of what her students—both Black and white—faced beyond the classroom. She spent time getting to know her students and using that information to create a curriculum and pedagogy that would engage students. Susan Cone Scott was one teacher who advocated for African American students. Miss Scott was a young English teacher when Charles Alexander attended high school. "We were sort of supportive of her . . . we sort of like created a little bond with her. I don't know—because she was young and attractive, or what—but she was sort of a little more open." With only three black teachers on the faculty at the time, advocacy from teachers such as Scott made a difference for Alexander and his fellow students. Scott started teaching at Lane High School in the fall of 1966 and taught at Lane until January 1969. She grew up in the West End of Richmond and remembers, "[T]he only Black people I knew were servants, and I knew something was wrong." Scott attended Sweet Briar for three years. At Sweet Briar, she was "involved in some Civil Rights work." Before her senior year, she transferred to Barnard in New York City. She had left Virginia for New York City when she was twenty-one. She swore that she "would never come back to the South." However, she returned to Virginia and pursued a master's degree in English literature at the University of Virginia. And when a teaching job became available at Lane, "it was like a realization that it was where my roots were, and I needed to stay here."[15]

Scott had close relationships with Lane's African American teachers, including Lorraine Williams and Teresa Price. She remembers, "They were wonderful.... They kept their sense of humor, they kind of held their own dignity, and they did not tell me much about what was going on. I was probably going to them and babbling about what was going on ... their humor was wonderful, and no, they did not complain once." While Scott became friends with Williams and Jackson, Scott believes they "were very isolated." Scott remembers, "I suspect that's why Lorraine was in her classroom rather than up in the teacher's lounge. Because most of the long-term, senior teachers who had made sure they taught in the basement schools, were now facing Black teachers in their schools." In other words, the teachers who were willing to support massive resistance through continuing education when Lane was closed were teaching African American students. If those teachers had been unwilling to teach in those schools, it would have created additional pressure for Superintendent Ellis and Governor Lindsay to open the schools.[16]

At Lane, Scott taught English and French. She recalls, "At that point they had a tracking system, or level system, and I taught mostly fourth level students, which means that they were reading on a fifth to seventh grade level, they were given books with Sir Gowan [sic] and the Green Knight in it for tenth grade. And they were mostly Black." The school was not well equipped to meet these students' needs. "I'm not even sure that year I had any college bound [sic] students. And basically, most of my students I had to fabricate a curriculum for and get materials from outside the school that they could use." Most of her students were in their first year at Lane because they had transferred from Burley. "Lane was already overcrowded, and I forget the figures, whether it was 300 students or 500 students. They needed to build a new school, but under those circumstances, there was a lot of close physical contact because you were so crowded."[17]

Scott taught English to many students who were behind in reading. Rather than use the textbook provided by the school, she drew upon a text called *Hooked on Books*. "It was a little paperback book, and here I am with these, all these low-level students and I mean low-level students, on their reading abilities, and they weren't all Black. There were White kids in there, too." *Hooked on Books*, according to Scott, was a book by "two psychologists who worked with juvenile delinquents." She used her own money to purchase materials for the class and utilized the pedagogical techniques described by Daniel Fader and Elton McNeil. Each student was provided a thick spiral notebook. Students were required to write at least one page a day. If they reached the one-page threshold, then they were given an "A." "The idea is that writing for most students is painful," contended Scott. "They get papers back with red marks all over them, and it's just a way to expose yourself to criticism." For Scott, using this approach to writing provided students with a safe space to develop their writing abilities.[18]

Scott admits that this approach allowed some students to copy from a book. She contended that they were still working on their handwriting even if they were copying from another book. For many students, the journal became a place where they could put down ideas and issues that they were grappling with. Scott also used prompts to spur students' writing and thinking. One day, she asked students about reincarnation. After explaining the term, she asked students what they would like to return to life as. "And my Black male students, there was a preponderance in every class that they wanted to come back as [a] poodle. And I don't think it's just because I had a standard poodle. And they would say, 'Because the poodle is loved, brushed, and washed,'" Scott remembers. "I mean, it was mind-blowing. Often, it was the toughest, meanest boys in the class that would say this." Overall, Scott viewed her pedagogical approach as a success. "They loved it," she remembers. "You gave them their own book. It didn't cost any . . . I mean it was such a minimal technique. You know I got the newspapers, the [Daily] *Progress* would give you free newspapers, so I told them to read classified ads.[19]

During the 1968 school year, the Black students started an Afro-American Club. Scott served as the sponsor at first. The group focused on learning about Black writers. Scott possessed no previous training, nor had she been exposed to African American writers in graduate school at the University of Virginia. She tried to learn about and read books by African American authors, but "it was such a busy time." Scott's time as sponsor of the Afro-American Club was short-lived for two reasons. First, serving as the faculty sponsor for the Afro-American Club made Scott a target of the LHS administration. "What happened to all of us White, rebellious teachers," asserts Scott, "is that as more radical people began to advise the young people, they began to push us out too. Because they didn't want some good-hearted White person being the sponsor of the Afro-American club." Second, Black students in the club wanted a change. Scott remembers, "They wanted an African American. They were beginning to think that if you weren't Black, you could not comprehend the Black experience." Scott was hurt when the African American students sought a different advisor. "It's like, huh, now I'm nowhere," Scott remembers, "The White staff and faculty don't like me, and now you're doing this." However, her ego and feelings became an impediment to truly meeting the needs of the high school's Black students.[20]

Despite being pushed out of the role, Scott supported Black student protests at LHS—behind the scenes. She recalls, "The first time they all walked out, they came and got me" and "it happened to be my free period and I went up there and they kind of welcomed me to the meeting." When the students walked out during this period, they ended their walkout at a church on the corner of Gordon Avenue and 14th Street. Teachers were not allowed to leave the school during their free period for any reason—let alone protest. "I was a rebel," Scott contends. "I was furious about what was going on, and I did it. Within the next couple of months, they gathered in the main front hall of Lane, and by then, it was mostly Black [students], but there'd be a few White students in a group like this. People who believed what was going on was wrong." In response to the protest in the front hall, Principal Nichols addressed the crowd standing on a box. Scott remembers that Nichols "really had a gift for saying the wrong thing." Nichols pleaded with students and said, "I'm a fair person, I'm fair to everybody." As he was pleading with the students, he would seek support from Scott. She did not support Nichols. Nichols never sought retribution against her, though. "I don't think he dared. I don't think they dared." During this same period, Scott started connecting with the Black community through organizing with the local Democratic Party. She met Eugene Williams through the local party.[21]

The late 1960s and early 1970s marked a shift in Black student and educator organizing and activism at Lane High School. Some students also approached the school, teachers, and students with different methods to instigate change. Black students such as Charles Alexander, James Bryant, Corlis Turner, and others fought the racism they faced at LHS. These individuals did not have a single means or vision for seeking equitable educational opportunities. Corlis Turner was a Black student involved in the Lane cheerleading squad in school and the NAACP chapter outside of school. In a profile, the *Lanetime* reported, "Corlis is quite proud of the racial balance on the squad this year. She feels that this aspect has eliminated a great deal of tension in certain areas at Lane." According to Corlis Turner, "The girls on the squad get along very well together and all are receptive of suggestions and new ideas." At the time of the profile, she wanted to attend Morgan State University. She also served as treasurer for the local NAACP chapter. "Being in the NAACP," asserted Turner, "has helped me a great deal as far as leadership is concerned. Last year, we worked with such activities as Voter Registration." She attended both the statewide and national conventions of the NAACP during her time at LHS.[22]

Charles Alexander was the youngest member of "The Charlottesville Twelve." Born in Charlottesville, Alexander attended a private kindergarten in the city. The local NAACP approached his mother, Elizabeth Taylor, about becoming one of the students desegregating Venable Elementary School for his first-grade year. Alexander, like his desegregating counterparts in high school, spent his first-grade year in the offices of the Charlottesville City Schools Division and received private tutoring there. He desegregated Venable alongside Raymond Dixon, Regina Dixon, Maurice Henry, Marvin Townsend, William Townsend, Sandra Wicks, Roland T. Woodfolk, and Ronald E. Woodfolk. During the entirety of his experience at the Charlottesville City Schools Division, Alexander only attended desegregated schools.[23]

Alexander entered Lane High School in the mid-1960s. His experience attending desegregated schools and awareness of organizing and activism led to a more radical approach to instigating change. He joined forces with other Black youth, who collectively called themselves "The Wrecking Crew." "The Wrecking Crew" included Alexander and another prominent student named Cherry Pie. On their approach to making changes at Lane High School, Alexander recalls, "Well, that entailed that we were a little more defiant, a little more militant, just less in terms of the same old, same old. We wanted to say, well 'you don't have black history, you don't have this, you don't have that . . . why is the principal, why is the staff doing this?' We definitely came in asking questions. Of course, during those days, the Black Panthers and the militancy and the fist raising happening."[24]

James Bryant did not identify as a militant in the same way as Charles Alexander. However, he also experienced racism and resistance at Lane High School. Bryant was born and raised in Charlottesville. In 1960, he started first grade at Jefferson Elementary. He stayed at Jefferson until fifth grade. During his sixth-grade year, Bryant had his first white teacher and first experience attending school with white students. As a result of living in public housing, he thinks the white teachers believed he had lower aspirations, "When we integrated into the white schools, it was very, very different," he recalls. "Teachers thought we couldn't read." As he continued to attend desegregated schools, Bryant made other observations about the schools, including Black students being tracked into the lower math and English classes.[25]

In 1969, Bryant entered LHS as a sophomore. "It was really bad at Lane because there were a lot of racial issues and problems," Bryant recalls. One instance at Lane reveals how Bryant experienced racism. He remembers going to see the guidance counselor, Miss Garrett. "She never looked at me. She stood with her back to me. 'College? You need to get that notion out of your head and pick up a trade.' I was devastated. I was crushed," Bryant recalls. He left the room crying. Miss Woodset, the only Black guidance counselor at LHS, agreed to work with Bryant. At that moment, Bryant vowed he would never do the same thing if he ever became a teacher. And he did become a teacher. Despite the trauma caused by Miss Garrett, Bryant would eventually attend Virginia Union University and become a music teacher in Madison County. He observes, "With all the trauma and drama [at Lane], I figured it was a good fit for me."[26]

Several Black students worked to effect change at LHS and in the city. The Raiders Club was composed of black youth and aimed to "help and improve their community." The club had sixteen members, with students aged twelve to seventeen. The only requirement for joining the club was "an ability to get along with people and to work wholeheartedly for the improvement of the community." Van Johnson, the group's president, was a sophomore at Lane. According to Johnson, the club was formed "when a group of friends and neighbors decided to organize in order to do volunteer work in the community." Bobby Walker served as the vice president, Glenda Walker as the secretary, Sabrina Walker as the assistant secretary, and Melvin Walker as the treasurer. The club raised funds through "dances, bake sales, cook-outs, and the sale of a variety of products." The money was donated to St. Paul's Episcopal Housing Task Force. In addition to engaging in community work, the club also had a basketball and a wrestling team. They also took field trips to Washington, D.C., and Richmond. The club also hiked in various locations around Albemarle County on the weekends. Reverend C. H. Brown, the club's sponsor, chaperoned the group on these outings. The club also had a monthly newspaper called *The Raider Progress*.[27]

Black organizing and activism manifested in several ways. Radical Black and white students participated in a limited run of an alternative newspaper called *Blast*. The newspaper wrote about the Black Panthers and Che Guevara while also highlighting local happenings at Lane High School in the community. Away from the school-sanctioned newspaper, the *Lanetime*, students chronicled the rise of social movements throughout the United States, including Charlottesville. The existence of *Blast*, although brief, reveals how students at the high school were aware of protest and organizing beyond their community. In one of the few issues of the alternative newspaper, the editors wrote, "The purpose of our existence is simple. We want to provide Lane High School with a paper it can believe in. We don't want to submit our articles to 'Higher authority' for approval. . . . Any contributions are welcome. Space and money permitting, we'll print all you send us, no matter whether it's by Tiny Cheetham or Cherry Pie. We want to say something to the student ear; we want to speak from the student's mind."[28]

The height of Black student protest at LHS occurred in 1968. Bryant was an active participant in the fight against racism during his time at LHS. He recalls, "We fought throughout that period for racial equality. We didn't have any black administrators. We didn't have any black teachers. So, we marched and we protested. Whenever we would march and leave the school, we would go to my church—my godfather's church, Trinity Episcopal Church. It was formerly located on 10th and Page. We knew that Reverend Mitchell would meet us there. The late Mr. George Ferguson, leader of the NAACP, would meet us there to console us and try to give us guidance." Since the school lacked a critical mass of African Americans, the students left the school space and sought out a more welcoming space. Eventually, the students' activism yielded actions by the school's administrators and division. Lane hired a single Black administrator and some Black teachers who had recently graduated from the University of Virginia during the late 1960s and early 1970s.[29]

In May 1968, LHS hosted a senior class carnival on a Friday evening. In the middle of the night, after the carnival, six white students riding in a car threw a glass bottle and struck a Black student walking home. The student's injuries required treatment at the University of Virginia Hospital. Rumors about the assault circulated throughout the city over the weekend. For the Black students at Lane High School, the assault marked a tipping point. Since the beginning of token school desegregation, some white students, teachers, and administrators at Lane High School verbally and, at times, physically assaulted Black students. On the Monday after the carnival—in response to the recent assault but also the general atmosphere at LHS—Black students organized a walkout and composed a set of demands. Their demands included hiring more Black teachers and counselors and creating a "Negro History course." While their demands responded to the local context, they echoed other Black high school students throughout the United States. Also, Black high school students were not the only ones in Charlottesville who sought to reform the curriculum in the 1960s and 1970s.[30]

A similar push for curriculum reform was ongoing at the University of Virginia, just a few miles away from Lane High School. As a result of protests and organizing by a "biracial coalition of progressive students and faculty," UVA established the Afro-American Studies program in 1970. UVA joined colleges and universities across the United States that developed Black Studies courses, majors, institutes, and departments during the 1960s and 1970s.[31]

Responding to the demands of African American students, the Charlottesville City Schools Division purchased new materials centered on Black history and the Black experience in the United States. With few exceptions, educators at Lane High School lacked the expertise to teach Black history or Black Studies courses. So, they outsourced the work, at first, to Dr. Edgar A. Toppin. Dr. Toppin, a professor at Virginia State College and a prominent member of the Association for the Study of African American Life and History, created a televised Black history course for college students at Virginia State College and Virginia Commonwealth University called "Americans from Africa: A History."[32]

Dr. Toppin was born in Harlem, New York City. Before arriving at Virginia State College in 1964, he earned a bachelor's and master's degree in history from Howard University and a doctoral degree from Northwestern University. He taught at Alabama State University, the University of

Akron, North Carolina College, San Francisco State University, and Western Reserve University. He authored several academic articles and three books: *Pioneers and Patriots*, *A Mark Well Made*, and *The Unfinished March*. His wife was a native Virginian, and they settled in Chesterfield County, Virginia. When creating the curriculum, Dr. Toppin's three kids attended second, seventh, and tenth grades.[33]

Dr. Toppin developed "Americans from Africa" during the mid-1960s with a grant from the Old Dominion Foundation. Overall, the course aimed "to tell the neglected story of persons who constitute one-ninth of the population of the United States today" and to develop "better understanding and harmony among students by increasing the awareness of the part that all Americans have played in the making of this nation." The past and present were inextricably linked based on Dr. Toppin's framing for the course. "By emphasizing the historical role of the American Negro, generally omitted from schoolbooks, the series hopes to contribute to easing the tensions and crises of the present." Although he never references specific events or tensions, there were several at the time. Protests against racial inequities had occurred throughout the 1960s in Los Angeles, Detroit, and Newark. Soon, the country would be dealing with the assassination of Dr. Martin Luther King Jr. By including the Black experience in U.S. history courses, Dr. Toppin believed students would be better equipped to understand contemporary issues and potentially mitigate future racial violence.[34]

Dr. Toppin's "Americans from Africa: A History" offered a comprehensive and contemporary account. The course covered topics from the arrival of enslaved Africans to Virginia in 1619 to the rise of Black Power. Despite covering many issues, the range of African and African American experiences covered by "Americans from Africa" was limited. Dr. Toppin crafted a narrative focusing on great African American men. The curriculum spotlighted the lives and work of Frederick Douglass, Booker T. Washington, and W. E. B. Du Bois, Marcus Garvey, and Martin Luther King Jr. The curriculum examines the debate between Washington and Du Bois. Referencing *The Souls of Black Folk*, Dr. Toppin writes that Du Bois "urged Washington to permit the free airing of diverse views rather than give white America the impression that all blacks agreed with Atlanta Compromise and the Tuskegee plan of education." The debate between Washington and Du Bois does not include Black women such as Nannie Helen Burroughs, Mary McCleod Bethune, and Anna Julia Cooper—who were all Washington and Du Bois contemporaries.[35]

In 1969, "Americans from Africa" became a part of the junior U.S. history course at Lane High School. The same course was also used at the nearby junior high school. Once a week, usually on Friday, students would watch a lecture from Dr. Toppin. Dr. Toppin prerecorded the lectures at a television studio in Richmond, Virginia. Then, teachers played lectures on a television in the classroom. In addition to the lecture, each lesson included background information and a bibliography for the teachers. Teachers were expected to read the background information and facilitate discussion after the lecture. Based on the responses of Black students in the classes, the history teachers did not read the background information and prepare for the lesson. Since the teachers had received an education that did not adequately center on the experience of Black people in the United States, they were ill-prepared to support the curriculum. The lack of white teacher preparation and motivation meant the curriculum could only be so effective.[36]

Despite being provided a revisionist perspective on the history of the United States, Black students and community members were unsatisfied with the new arrangement. On the one hand, the course added the Black experience to U.S. history. It drew upon expert knowledge for the curriculum, and the lessons did cover ostensibly controversial topics at the time, including slavery, the civil rights movement, and the Black Power Movement. On the other hand, the Black experience was just an additive component of the course. And Black heterosexual men were centered in the curriculum. No matter how comprehensive the content was, it was delivered through an impersonal medium. Lane High School's white history teachers were not equipped to support the lecture, either, and students "complained that the teachers did not know enough about black history."[37]

As a result of the shortcomings of the televised courses, Lane's African American students continued to engage in protest *for* pedagogy. In November 1968, they organized another walkout and "demanded more black teachers, an expanded black history course, and fairer treatment from white teachers." They also sought alternative means of learning Black history, including a teach-in on Africa hosted by the local chapter of the Virginia Council on Human Relations. They also found support from beyond the school and their communities. College students and professors at the University of Virginia supported Black high school students in a few ways. The newly formed Afro-American Studies program at UVA would help provide the people and pedagogy to underpin the development of a Black Studies elective course at Lane High School.[38]

Black Studies elective courses in American high schools expanded during the 1960s and 1970s. Mr. James Wright taught one such course at Eau Claire High School in Columbia, South Carolina. "By prominently including African American leaders and other minority icons from history in his curriculum, he embraced his role as a teacher activist, promoting hidden histories and engaging with issues of race and social justice." Wright's curricular decisions made a difference for his students as did his pedagogical decisions. According to Derrick Alridge, he drew upon "videos, filmstrips, and music to bring African American history to life for his students." Alridge argues, "Wright's passion for teaching and his dedication to liberating his students with the knowledge of black history impacted generations of students in Columbia and throughout South Carolina. Although not an activist in the traditional sense, Wright used black history as an activist tool to educate his students."[39]

Like Eau Claire High School, Lane High School established a Black Studies elective course in 1971. When Lane's student newspaper announced the course's addition to the curriculum, the article offered a range of student opinions. One student (who asked to remain anonymous) observed, "It's the one course that students have been pushing for." Another student, Nancy Allen, contended, "I think it will improve race relationships because it will develop more understanding between the races." Yet another student, Michael Lewis, noted, "I don't think too many people are taking it and that more people of different races need to take it." Bernadette Whitsett was hopeful about the course's influence on the school, "I feel it's a step in the right direction in improving race relations." Susan Chiles asserted, "It's a good idea, and every school should have one." And Clarence Wells claimed, "The course within itself is a really good course and to make it, you've got to work really hard."[40]

Lane High School hired Anthony Sherman to teach the Black Studies elective course. Sherman was among the first Black undergraduates at the University of Virginia. The Lane High School yearbook described the course as "enveloping the black man's history, culture, and literature." Sherman hoped the course would "develop an appreciation of blackness." He used two primary texts for the course: John Hope Franklin's *From Slavery to Freedom* and William Loren Katz's *Eyewitness: The Negro in American*

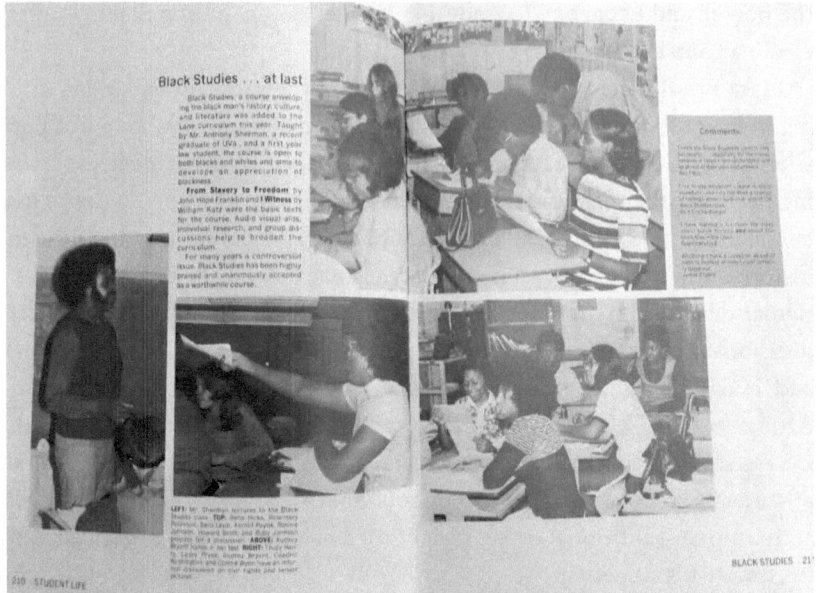

The Chain yearbook page is dedicated to the first year of teaching Black Studies at Lane High School. On the left is Anthony Sherman, a Black man with a beard and an afro, who was the first instructor for the course. Courtesy of Charlottesville High School Media Center.

History. Franklin's text served as a textbook, while Katz's book, a collection of primary source documents, was a supplementary text. Sherman used various pedagogical approaches to teach the course, including visual aids, research projects, and group discussions.[41]

The course used John Hope Franklin's third edition, *From Slavery to Freedom*. The revised edition marked the twentieth anniversary of the book's publication. Franklin laid out the most notable changes to the newest version in the preface. He wrote, "I feel constrained to add that even the revolutionary developments of the last decade should not obscure the fact that this is essentially a history and not a contemporary tract. Therefore, these developments have been valuable for historians not only in themselves but also in the new perspectives they provide us as one looks at the past, even in remote events. These new perspectives are reflected in some of the revisions of the earlier parts of the book." *From Slavery to Freedom* offered a broad account of the Black experience, beginning with Africa and ending with the civil rights movement. The book spends three chapters tracing life in Africa before moving to the slave trade. In Virginia, Franklin spotlights topics such as Black schools, slave revolts, Black delegates to the Constitutional Convention, and Black colleges.[42]

Sherman supplemented the course readings with William Loren Katz's *Eyewitness: The Negro in American History*. The book offered an array of contextualized primary source materials spread over nineteen chapters. Each chapter started with a brief overview of the topic, followed by several eyewitness accounts (primary sources). The book commences with "The Opening of New Worlds"—the first contact between Europeans, Native Americans, and Africans. Katz writes of the first contact between whites and indigenous peoples, "For all who came to these shores, America was a land of freedom, hope, and opportunity. For all—except the Negro. He came in chains and, for hundreds of years, had to fight just to be free. With few friends, and against almost hopeless odds, black men and women struggled to stay alive, and to share in the American drama of human dignity and justice for all."[43]

Franklin's *From Slavery to Freedom* and Katz's *Eyewitness* combined to provide a different perspective on American history. Indeed, students in the Black Studies elective course were exposed to an account of history that had been previously hidden. And, given the presence of these texts in the school yearbook, the school's administration and, more than likely, the division's administration were aware of the inclusion of these texts in the course. For much of the course, the Black Studies course focused on the African American experience from a historical perspective. However, it also reactively tackled a recent event: the civil rights movement.

Both Franklin and Katz spend a chapter on the civil rights movement. Franklin refers to it as the "Negro Revolution," while Katz refers to it as "America's Civil Rights Revolution." The final chapter of Katz's book covers the civil rights movement. In particular, he spotlights the *Brown v. Board of Education* decision, the Montgomery Bus Boycott, and the March on Washington. The chapter introduction cites W. E. B. Du Bois, and Katz notes that on the day Du Bois died, "hundreds of thousands of Americans were moving toward Washington, D.C. to voice their protest against all color-lines in the United States." These protestors, Katz asserts, "were taking part in a long historic process, deeply embedded in their nation's history. And they were contributing to the fulfillment of America's commitment to equal justice for all."[44]

The eyewitness accounts for the Civil Rights Revolution include the NAACP's response to the *Brown* decisions and recollections from Central High School students in Little Rock, Ark. The student recollections are derived from a broadcast segment by Mrs. Jorunn Ricketts, a Norwegian news correspondent. Mrs. Ricketts interviewed six students: three white young women, one white young man, one young African American man, and one young African American woman. In response to a question from Mrs. Ricketts about how the National Guard troops ended up at Central High School, Ernest Green, the African American young man, responded, "It is because our government—our state government—was against the federal law.... Our country is set up so that we have forty-eight states, and no one state has the ability to overrule our nation's government. I thought that was what our country was built around. I mean, that is why we fight. We fought in World War II together—the fellows that I know died in World War II; they died in the Korean War. I mean, why should my friends get out there and die for a cause called 'democracy' when I can't exercise my rights—tell me that."[45]

Katz includes a short passage from this interview. The Central High School students conducted several interviews with news organizations throughout the school year. This selection, titled "Voices from Central High School," is significant for several reasons. First, a Norwegian correspondent conducted the interview. Katz could have included any number of interviews with American journalists. However, he chose a foreign journalist's interview. By doing so, he situated the civil rights struggles, such as school desegregation, within a global context. Second, this interview focuses on the views of high school students who were just a decade removed from high school students exposed to this text. Indeed, this interview centers on the perspective of high school students from different racial groups at Central High. Although no students from LHS's elective course cited this specific example, it is not hard to imagine how this source would resonate with high school students attending a desegregated high school such as LHS.[46]

Franklin also addresses the crisis at Central High School. In the wake of the *Brown* decisions, Franklin writes, "Taking their cue from the call for massive resistance by the Virginia Senator, Harry F. Byrd, all of the eleven states of the old Confederacy enacted interposition, nullification, or protest resolution against the Supreme Court decision in the school desegregation cases." After spotlighting the role played by one of Virginia's senators and most prominent politicians, Franklin turns to Little Rock. "Not until

President Eisenhower sent federal troops in response to the governor's defiance of the court order did the Negro children gain admission to the school. The weeks and months of intimidation and harassment of the children on the part of the white students and their parents suggested how bitter and harsh the resistance would be." Such a passage would hit very close to home for the teachers and students sitting in a classroom, and the building closed just a decade earlier in response to the *Brown* decision.[47]

The Black Studies elective course continued to use similar pedagogical approaches and curricular resources. However, a different teacher taught the course during each year of the course's existence. Anthony Sherman lasted just over half of the year. Sherman taught two course sections—one during the fifth and the other during the sixth period. In total, there were thirty-seven students enrolled in the two class periods. After Sherman left Lane, Stanley Ryan taught the Black Studies course. Originally from Brooklyn, New York, Ryan graduated from South Carolina State and was pursuing a master's degree at the University of Virginia. In an interview with the school newspaper, Ryan contended that Black Studies would be "effective" under his watch because he aimed "to cover various aspects of Black culture such as religion, music, the arts, folktales and myths." Ryan stayed at Lane for a year, teaching the Black Studies elective and English courses, before departing Charlottesville. He left the city to teach freshman composition at the State University of New York at Albany. Lena Banks and Celia Parrot followed Sherman and Ryan's footsteps by briefly teaching the course before moving on.[48]

Teacher turnover took a toll on the course's reputation. Some Black students expressed their frustration in the pages of *Lanetime*. Rather than focus on teacher turnover, some students blame their peers. In April 1973, Clarice Jones penned a letter to the editor. She wrote,

> I think most of the students at Lane High School are letting a great opportunity of learning about Black history and culture slip through their fingers by not signing up for the magnificent Black History course here at Lane. This year we have a good instructor and more books and materials than we've had in previous years. After fighting so long for Black Studies at Lane, less than 25 people are enrolled in the class. Black students need this course more than the average white person because it teaches us so much about ourselves that will better enable us to really achieve a broader sense of Black awareness.

Jones specifically called out Black students without fully contextualizing the lack of enrollment. She did offer some context based on anecdotal data.[49]

Jones cited several reasons for the enrollment decline. "I've heard various reasons from Black students as to why they haven't enrolled in the class. Some include no room on the schedule and 'it's too hard.' To them I'd like to say there is no subject more relevant to your success in life as Black Studies should be. Most Black people go about life not really knowing anything about their past. How can you have any kind of self-identity if you don't know about or understand your history and culture?" Jones expressed disappointment with students who deemed the course too hard "because Black Studies is no harder than English, government or any other courses we have to take. We as a race are in no position to pass by a course like this with a lazy and apathetic attitude." Jones concluded by reminding students of the stakes. "Last year there were two classes of Black Studies, this year there is only one. After fighting for this worthwhile class let's not let it be cancelled due to a lack of interest. This is a great opportunity to gain knowledge of ourselves and our glorious heritage. Let's extend our sense of Black pride and Black awareness by taking a truly relevant course next year."[50]

The Black Studies elective course faced several challenges. On the one hand, since the course was an elective, it meant that students chose to enroll in the course. Enrolled students possessed some level of interest in the course, which could not be said of all courses at the high school. On the other hand, it meant that most students could opt out of the course. Based on the enrollment numbers and experiences relayed by students in the class during its brief existence, most students did not take the course. Due to the course's designation as an elective, it also meant that students taking remedial courses did not have the space to enroll. Black students at Lane were overrepresented in remedial courses. At any rate, issues regarding Black enrollment in this Lane elective would soon become moot: In the spring of 1974, Lane High School closed, replaced by Charlottesville High School, located approximately a mile and a half north.[51]

For most of the school's existence, LHS did not participate in Negro History Week and, later, Black History Week. Even as Black students and educators desegregated the school, the high school did not initially offer special programming during February. This shifted as more and more Black students arrived on campus, establishing and developing Black History programming during February. The experiences of Esther Vasser and Diane Price and their students, like James Bryant, reveal the opportunities and challenges of organizing and facilitating a Black History program in a desegregated school setting.[52]

Esther Vasser taught English at LHS. Vasser only stayed for a single but consequential year at the school. She grew up in Newport, Tennessee, attending all-Black schools in the 1950s and 1960s. For college, she applied to the University of Tennessee. Tennessee admitted her. However, while administrators were open to desegregating the university, the housing on campus and surrounding it in Knoxville was not open to her. Vasser decided to leave the state of Tennessee altogether and attend Howard University in Washington, D.C. At Howard University, she studied English.[53]

Vasser arrived in Charlottesville, alongside her husband, to attend graduate school at the University of Virginia during the late 1960s. Vasser earned her master's degree in English, while her husband earned a law degree. By then, there were more Black students at the University of Virginia than in the era of Nathaniel Ridley, Booker Reaves, and Florence Bryant when they earned their graduate degrees just a decade earlier. However, the number of Black students and women still paled in comparison to the number of white male students. When she attended graduate school at the University of Virginia, she recalls white students calling her "Zulu" as she walked around. Vasser finished her degree before her husband finished law school. So, while he finished law school, she took a job at Lane High School teaching three different sections of English.[54]

Vasser was one of the only Black educators teaching the school's academic courses. She looked "young enough to be a student at the time." She had an afro and wore Afro-centric clothing, including a turban. Her appearance at Howard University and in Washington, D.C., at the time did not look out of the norm; however, in Charlottesville and at Lane High School, her look was vastly different from her colleagues.[55]

The English courses at Lane were tracked by ability. Ability tracking existed before Black students arrived at Lane; however, it existed along socioeconomic lines. The enrollment of Black students only exacerbated tracking along a mixture of racial and socioeconomic lines. Vasser insisted upon teaching a level three course—the lowest tracked course. The level three course had the highest concentration of Black students across Vasser's course load. In all her classes, relationships with students centered on ensuring that all students felt "comfortable in the classroom." And that included white students, too.[56]

Vasser characterized her approach toward the majority of her course's reading list as "protest literature." Vasser's approach represented a continuation of pedagogy *as* protest. She taught students through the art and noted that "artists are our revolutionaries." She had been exposed to that art at Howard. It was not a conscious decision to teach those books; it just felt normal to her. In order to have a "well-rounded education," Vasser asserted, "you had to deal with more than English literature and American literature because those classes did not include writers who looked like me." Vasser's reading list included Richard Wright, Ralph Ellison, Nikki Giovanni, and Langston Hughes. Students in level three were exposed to Black literature for the first time—she remembers getting special approval from the school's administration for the curriculum. "I think I received approval because nobody had read that." Vasser did not have to hide the books away as Benjamin Tonsler and other fugitive pedagogues had done during the Jim Crow era. Vasser and her students either benefited from a change in the consciousness of white administrators or, more likely, benefited from their ignorance of African American literature. But not everyone was so naive.[57]

Vasser did receive one complaint—from a white student's parent. The white parent was enraged that her student had read Ralph Ellison's *Invisible Man*. Vasser, however, did not end up in any trouble with the school's administration as a result of the situation. The parent seemed cowed by the shame that she had not read the book and protested having her student read the book out of sheer bigotry.[58]

In addition to her duties in the classroom, Vasser served as the coordinator of the Negro History Week assembly in February 1972. Because the auditorium could not hold the entire student body, the same programming was staged on February 15 and 16. The first assembly occurred without incident and concluded with the singing of the Black National Anthem, otherwise known as "Lift Every Voice and Sing." However, with the singing of the Black National Anthem at the second assembly's conclusion, an incident erupted.[59]

The program consisted of a dance, songs, a play, and poetry readings by Black students. Students on stage encouraged everyone in the auditorium to stand up and sing along to the Negro National Anthem. As the students on stage and in the crowd stood up and sang along, a group of approximately fifty white students walked out of the back of the auditorium. There was a dispute about whether the students were seated together in three rows, as interviewed Black and white students believed, or that the white students were scattered throughout the auditorium, as Principal John E. Huegal believed. Either way, there was no disputing that a significant number of white students walked out of the assembly.[60]

There was yet another dispute about the white student walkout. On the one hand, some white students claimed that they were leaving the assembly because they thought it was over. On the other hand, some Black students claimed the walkout was organized "as an insult to blacks" and against the Negro National Anthem. Their claims were bolstered by the fact that the program had occurred the day before, so the white students in attendance during the second assembly knew how the program would end. What's more, Harry A. Tinney, one of the white Charlottesville City School Board members, defended the white students by saying, "They felt that there is only one national anthem and to stand for another was just not right. I think they associated 'black national anthem' with 'black fists,' 'Black Panthers,' and 'black violence.'" So while Black students were only "hurt, disappointed, and angered" by the white students who walked out, they were also frustrated by the nonresponses of faculty, staff, and administrators who were present at the assembly. No one did anything to stop the white students from leaving the assembly. Nor were any of the white students held responsible for their actions.[61]

LHS had a policy for students who left the assembly without permission. Leaving an assembly resulted in students being suspended by the school administration. In a previous incident, Black and white teachers, with the support of the school administration, had suspended Black students for five days after they left an assembly or class before they were allowed to leave. However, in the aftermath of the white student walkout, the school's administration did not suspend any students.[62]

African American students responded to the school administration's lack of action. A day after the second Negro History Week assembly, Black students walked out of class. They sang "We Shall Overcome" to the school's auditorium. One hundred Black students stayed in the auditorium and refused to leave. One day of protest was not enough to get the school administration's attention, so the following day, another two hundred students joined the students from the previous day in the auditorium. This protest represented the students attempt to use protest as pedagogy. They wanted to teach their white peers, teachers, and administrators, that Black students at LHS would not tolerate racism and discrimination. In discussing the consequences of the white student walkout, one Black student asserted, "[a]ll the progress we've made over the past three years was killed in 15 minutes. I walked out of that assembly and saw white faces, not friends."[63]

Although the administrators at Lane High School did not suspend any of the white students who walked out, they did close school on the Friday following two days of Black student protests in the auditorium. Superintendent Edward Rushton ordered the closure of Lane High School and the other schools in the division. Rushton claimed he wanted to calm things down among students and faculty and meet with students and faculty without school being in session. "It's a problem of human relations that has to be resolved, and we are not doing it because of any fear of violence." While the school and division administrators characterized the incident as a single interpersonal conflict, Black teachers and students had a very different perspective.[64]

Black teachers and students viewed the incident within a more extended history of racism and discrimination in Charlottesville, Virginia, and the United States. Esther Vasser asserted, "Everybody knows the protest didn't begin with Black Culture Week. People are going to have to learn to become sensitive to other human beings. We tried to expose white people to what we value (during the cultural assembly), but when we did, whites felt persecuted. Whites don't want to accept the things that were and the things that are a part of our culture." The white students who walked out were not an aberration; they carried on the legacy of their ancestors in the city and state who would rather close schools than desegregate them. The white students were supported in both overt and tacit ways, too. The school board gave them cover, and the administration did nothing to punish the students.[65]

Not everyone on the division's school board agreed with the decision not to punish the white students. Reverend Henry B. Mitchell highlighted the connection between the city's only public high school and its relationship to the community, asserting, "[W]hat happened at Lane is but a reflection of what can happen to the community at large. This means community in its broadest sense—state, national, and local." Mitchell, one of two Black board members on the Charlottesville City School Board, continued saying, "I don't believe we're any closer now than we were 20 years ago to a solution to the race problem whether at Lane or any other place." As it turned out, that was the last time Vasser would coordinate Negro History Week at Lane. She left Lane High School at the end of the school year—and never taught high school again.[66]

The year after Vasser left LHS, Diane Price arrived there. Price lived all over the world during her childhood. Her father served in the United States military, which led to the family making stops in Japan and Germany. She also spent significant time in Virginia, including a brief time in Charlottesville, where she attended the Jefferson Elementary School. The local NAACP approached Price and her family about potentially becoming one of the students to desegregate the Charlottesville City Schools Division. However, Price's family moved away from Charlottesville before school desegregation.[67]

Like Vasser, Price attended Howard University. She earned a bachelor's and master's degree in German from 1965 to 1971. "I left Howard with a big Afro and being quite militant," Price recalls, "but knowing when to tone it down and when to be militant." Price received an offer from Lane High School to teach German and government. She accepted and moved to Charlottesville.[68]

Price, alongside other teachers, assumed the role of coordinating the Negro History Week program until Lane closed in 1974. She knew what had occurred during the previous year. Like Vasser and other Black educators at the time, she had a strong awareness of how few Black educators there were at the school and even fewer who taught academic subjects. Upon her arrival at Lane, Price learned about the white student walkout and its consequences during the previous year. People within the Black community told Price that some white teachers had encouraged the white students to walk out during the singing of the Negro National Anthem. So, in preparing and observing the program, Price understood what could happen.[69]

Price did not face the backlash and white resistance Vasser had faced the previous year. She remembers receiving flowers and notes about the program she facilitated at Lane. For the program, the students interviewed one of the stars of the basketball team, did a reenactment of Rosa Parks, and a live "Soul Train." It was an assembly at the end of the week. They had guest speakers throughout the week and posters in the hallways. While Price would continue coordinating the Black History Week and, later, Month program as LHS closed and Charlottesville High School opened, she would become increasingly disillusioned by the lack of integration of the Black experience in all classes throughout the school year.[70]

These recommendations and opinions informed subsequent themed weeks and celebrations. Price, along with Mrs. Lena Banks and students, went on to organize Black Culture Week in 1974. The week took place during February 11–15. The theme was "We Came, We Saw, We Conquer." They planned to have speakers with open attendance on Monday, panel discussions for all students on Tuesday and Wednesday, and a show in two parts on Thursday and Friday. Students heard from various speakers and participated in panels about topics near and far. On Tuesday, students discussed whether school integration was a success or failure and whether Black Culture Week was a helpful event or a hindrance. Jane Frier, Mamie Estes, Cindy Williams, Regina Brown, Kathy Smith, Leslie Crickenberger, Margaret Vaughn, and Selma Waffle participated as panelists. On Wednesday, students discussed "communication problems between the races at Lane." The students who participated in that discussion included Mark Scott, Pam Scott, Julia Turner, Rennie Johnson, Dot Shelton, Bernard Whitsett, Thomas Dickerson, and Rene Johnson, who served as the moderator. An assembly capped the week off. It included skits, a fashion show, and a dance program modeled on "Soul Train." And it ended with students singing the Black National Anthem—"Lift Every Voice and Sing"—without incident.[71]

After Black Culture Week concluded, an editorial offered an assessment of the week. Overall, the editorial felt the week was successful. "Everything seemed to go smoothly, with the exception of a Rap Session or two. During these sessions the students spoke freely, and many points of view were heard, but sometimes things got a little out of hand and off subject. There was too much bickering about things like who was sitting next to who and who ate with who, etc., creating friction when there was no point to it." After noting some of the challenges, the editorial highlighted the positions and larger significance of the week's events. In particular, the editorial discussed why there's a need for the week. "The speakers, panels and productions gave students a unique opportunity to learn about what was left out of their history courses. As enjoyable as it is, Black Culture Week should not be necessary. It should be part of all American and Virginia history courses. Black culture is a part of every American's culture. The general attitude seems to be Black students telling about their private history, and white students looking at it as something removed from their own history. But the whole mess is *American* history, and it all happened at the same time. If people could take some of their stubborn racial pride and stick it to their national pride, things might straighten out."[72]

African American students, from Donald Martin in the early days to Michael Lewis near the end of the school's existence, faced racism and discrimination. Yet despite those challenges, they did find ways to survive and thrive at Lane High School. Before he graduated, *Lanetime* profiled Michael Lewis. "Michael Lewis, a six-foot-tall senior, has set his goal to become the 'baddest' [sic] disc jockey in the U.S." Lewis attended Wilberforce University, where he intended to study radio and television. He chose Wilberforce partly because of "the college's co-op program, which allows a student to obtain a job in his major field of studies." The profile included a retrospective of Lewis's time at the school: "As a sophomore, Michael was a member of the track team, but due to his having trouble with his knees and because he felt there was racial prejudice on the team, he was forced to quit in his junior year. In spite of this, he was quite successful as he finished sixth in the regions in the 40-yard dash and finished fifth in the district." In reflecting on his time at Lane, Lewis called the school "disgusting and troublesome." Lewis was a member of the Student Council Association at Lane. He served as a senior class representative in the Student Council Association. In response to a question about what he hopes to see at Lane after he graduates, Lewis asserted that "the educational program at Lane will change in that it will prepare students better in the fields of their interest." This was a hope that many had as Lane High School closed and Charlottesville High School opened.[73]

During the era of school desegregation, African American youth became more visible and overt in their approach to instigating change at Lane High School. The mere presence of French Jackson and the Martin brothers at the historically white Lane High School challenged the status quo of segregation in education. The overt protest of Black youth led to a shift in the school's pedagogical approaches and initiated reform efforts aimed at greater justice and equity at the high school. A small group of Black students, including Charles Alexander and "The Wrecking Crew," led direct action to enact change, including walkouts and petitions. Not all African

American students participated in protests, but they were all impacted by the reforms and attempts at reform. While students were the most visible participants in the struggle for equity and justice at Lane High School, Black educators provided support in less visible ways within and beyond the school setting.

Like the African American students who initially desegregated Lane High School, African American educators faced a lack of critical mass and support from the school's administration. Esther Vasser strongly influenced the students she taught, such as James Bryant. She brought her experience and protest pedagogy into the classroom. While many students appreciated her approach, she only spent a year at Lane High School. The white students and white administrators at the school pushed her out during the fallout over the walkout during Negro History Week. The school lost as Vasser went on to a long career in higher education, business, and government. Vasser left Charlottesville with her husband and taught college courses. Eventually, she became involved in government and business relations in Virginia. Her work in government and business culminated in taking a position in President Obama's administration.[74]

CHAPTER FIVE

"Because Racism Was So Deeply Ingrained"
Charlottesville High School, 1974–2001

I was equally sure that, because racism was so deeply ingrained in the fabric of the American society, Charlottesville High School could not possibly have been immune.
—Florence C. Bryant, educator at Charlottesville High School, 1989

The problems the report addresses are rooted in the issues surrounding educational achievement for blacks and in the complex social and historical conditions which underlie race relations in Charlottesville.
—Robert Templin, Introduction to "Race Relations and Education in Charlottesville," 1985

Something had to be done about the overcrowding at LHS. In the years before LHS closed, overcrowding became a point of conversation within the school division and city politics. As early as 1970, local politicians like Charles Barbour criticized Edward Rushton, the Charlottesville City Schools Division Superintendent, about the division's lack of attention to overcrowding and its consequences at the high school. The relatively brief period of school desegregation made clear the need for changes at Lane High School. The physical space at Lane High School did not, in and of itself, create problems between students, teachers, and administrators. But it did exacerbate issues at the city's first desegregated high school.[1]

At the beginning of the desegregation era, only a few Black students enrolled at LHS; at the same time, some white students attended the city's segregationist academy, Rock Hill Academy. As more and more African American students enrolled at Lane and fewer white students enrolled at Rock Hill Academy, the Lane building could not accommodate all the city's potential high school students. The problems with the building and the student body's size should not have surprised the city's politicians and school administrators. However, it does seem that some within the city and school division did not believe desegregation would ever happen. Once the full-scale desegregation occurred, the Charlottesville City Schools Division, School Board, and City Council moved slowly to rectify the situation.[2]

The Charlottesville City Schools Division did reorganize the schools' configuration to ease high school overcrowding. When the high schools were segregated, Jackson P. Burley High School and Lane High School included eighth graders. This continued as school desegregation continued. Eighth-grade students were moved to Walker Junior High School, and LHS consisted of ninth through twelfth-grade students until it closed. Some of the Lane High School classes were held at the Jefferson School. Students walked from Lane High School to the former Jefferson Elementary School building during the day. Reorganizing the school system and having some students attend classes elsewhere did help with overcrowding. However, these two solutions did not rectify the situation. So, administrators began exploring options to find a long-term solution for overcrowding at the high school.[3]

Three proposals to rectify the situation emerged. First, administrators proposed adding to and remodeling the Lane High School building. This option would have retained the school's central location but also created another major problem. During the renovation of the LHS building, students would still need a place to attend classes and participate in extracurricular activities. The city's schools were already strapped for space. Finding excess space at other schools would have proved difficult, and the school division had already been dealing with the issue for several years.[4]

Second, they proposed building two high schools at either end of the city. This option would have provided high school campuses near different population centers. It would have also solved the space problems without figuring out another solution for where students would attend school and participate in extracurricular activities during construction. A bond measure of $7,000,000 to finance two high schools failed. Even if the bond had passed, there would have been several negative consequences for proponents of school desegregation. Since housing in Charlottesville had become more and more segregated due to Jim Crow policies during the early twentieth century and the "urban renewal" of the Vinegar Hill neighborhood, the two high schools would have likely led to resegregation of the city's high schools.[5]

Third, they proposed building a single yet much larger high school in another part of the city. This would allow the city's school division to build the new high school without interrupting classes and activities at Lane High School. The new high school would replace Lane High School but would continue with a desegregated environment. The additional space at the new high school would relieve the overcrowding problems that had plagued LHS. However, the new high school would be located beyond a ten-mile radius of the city's center. This new location would create inequitable access to the school building.[6]

Despite the concerns about the different locations, the third proposal became a reality. Throughout the era of segregated schools, the Black and white high schools had all been in the middle of the city, near downtown. JHS, BHS, and LHS formed a triangle, with each school within walking distance. The new high school's location in the northern part of the city meant that many students could no longer walk to the high school. This was particularly true for students of lower socioeconomic status, both African American and white, but the burden of travel fell disproportionately on the city's African American residents. Longtime educator Florence C. Bryant recalls, "The students, faculty, and community had developed a sense of devotion and loyalty toward the school by working together in informal settings outside the classroom. Those opportunities were denied to the students at CHS, and an important avenue for developing positive race relations was lost. Several factors—the location of the school and the lack of opportunities for students to interact in mutually interesting settings outside the structured classroom—all affected the degree and quality of integration at CHS."[7]

Beyond the location, the new high school stirred other small yet consequential questions. Residents debated what the new high school would be named, what the new high school's mascot would be, and what the curriculum and pedagogy of the new high school would be. On the one hand, many white residents wanted to retain and continue the history of LHS. They believed the new high school should remain "Lane High School"—named for James W. Lane, a white educator and early superintendent of the Charlottesville City Schools Division—and the Black Knight mascot. On the other hand, many African American residents wanted the new high school to provide a fresh start with a new name and mascot. The School Board settled on Charlottesville High School yet continued with

A side view of Charlottesville High School (1974–present). Courtesy of the author.

the Black Knight as their mascot. The school's yearbook continued to be called *The Link*, yet the school's newspaper became the *Knight Time Review*. This new student newspaper became central to a brewing conflict at the high school in the 1980s.[8]

Florence C. Bryant was on the cusp of retirement. After a long career in education at several different schools in the Charlottesville City Schools Division, Bryant was ready for retirement. The Charlottesville City Schools Division, though, had other plans. Charlottesville High School hired Bryant as an assistant principal. Her main task was to continue developing and implementing a new curriculum. The high school's new curriculum was known as the "innovative high school model" and was supported by a program called "Project Change." Before CHS opened, John E. Huegal, principal of LHS since 1968, left Lane a year early to oversee the building of the new high school and to start the development of the latest programming at Charlottesville High School. In an article about the new curriculum, Holly Smith wrote,

"Students entering the school in September will have four schools to choose from. The largest sub-school will have a traditional curriculum and be called the School of General Learning. Ninth and tenth grade students will be assigned to this school and eleventh and twelfth grade students not selecting another sub-school will continue to attend the General Learning School." Two other sub-schools included a Career School focused on vocational training and a Fine Arts School focused on jewelry making, weaving, and radio and television production. Finally, the last sub-school was known as the Community School. Students wrote their learning objectives in the Community School and plotted their curricular foci.[9]

On the one hand, the model offered students more choices within the curriculum. There were various elective options and unique opportunities, including participating in the school's radio station. On the other hand, the innovative high school seemed a lot like the old high school: tracked and unequal. Bryant recalls,

> In the beginning, Charlottesville High School was operated as a three-in-one school. The design of the building enhanced the implementation of that concept, and the instructional personnel were assigned accordingly. One school centered on the curriculum of basically semester courses. Course credits were recorded at the end of each semester, and the students selected a whole new set of courses. The units earned were determined at the end of the term. Another school centered on basically an accelerated curriculum. The students were allowed to pursue a wide variety of independent study projects. The recording of credits was similar to that of the school above. The third school followed a traditional program of general studies. All of the courses were full-year, with credits determined only at the end of the school year. Gradually, most students moved away from the first two options and elected to take the traditional general studies program. Eventually, the three-schools-in-one concept was phased out in consideration of students' preferences.[10]

The new building and curriculum could have led to different outcomes for the students at Charlottesville High School. However, the tracking and treatment of students remained similar to the practices found at Lane High School. It might look positive to have the "curriculum designed to fit individual." However, implementing such a system can lead to individuals fitting into prescribed roles based on race, gender, and class.[11]

Conflicts between white teachers and Black students remained the norm. Bryant observed from her vantage point as assistant principal: "A lack of understanding between the students and some of their teachers was revealed in some of the students' perceptions. They continually complained about prejudicial and discriminatory treatment in some of their classes." Black students felt that many CHS teachers did not believe they could achieve academically. African American students also complained to Bryant about the inequalities related to class and school discipline. The perceptions of African American students stemmed from interactions with their teachers, like the experience of students at Lane High School. However, Bryant also noted the power of nonverbal communication from white teachers toward African American students. "Prejudice and discrimination can be manifested in a variety of ways: tone of voice, eye movement, body language, brash rebuffs, to name a few," asserted Bryant. "Students are perceptive enough to recognize such behaviors, no matter how subtle they may appear."[12]

The lack of opportunities to engage in extracurricular activities also shaped how students felt in the school. Since the days of JHS, extracurricular activities created community among participants and the wider community. The lack of proximity between students' homes and the school had consequences for travel to and from school. However, the issue was particularly acute for students who wanted to participate in athletics and extracurricular activities. Since the students could not quickly or safely walk home after school, many chose to skip these activities because they did not have transportation available after extracurricular activities concluded. There are a range of factors involved in whether students participate in athletics and extracurricular activities; however, the new location of the high school only exacerbated inequality at the new high school.[13]

Compared with the final years at Lane High School, the first decade of CHS included few notable incidents of Black student protest. This does not suggest that CHS, or the surrounding community, existed in a post-racial utopia. In 1975, conflicts erupted between Black youth and security guards at a Safeway grocery store on West Main Street—the street linking the University of Virginia community with the downtown areas of Starr Hill, Vinegar Hill, and Preston Avenue. The conflicts originated with the arrest of a young man allegedly shoplifting from the store. The incidents led to the city organizing events like concerts and dances to give youth "something to do." Following the "Safeway Riots," the city and other researchers published reports pointing to the continued challenges in the school system and the city's only public high school.[14]

Sociologists from the nearby University of Virginia conducted and wrote both studies with the cooperation of the Central Piedmont Urban Observatory and the City of Charlottesville. The first report focused broadly on various facets of the city's life, including education. Released during the second year of CHS's existence, the report noted the mild approval of the city's public high schools. Since CHS had not been around for long, the report's findings about high school education in the city pointed more toward the general feeling rather than a specific evaluation of the new high school. However, the report pointed to concerns about racism and discrimination in the city as a whole. Another UVA report was published in 1979. It detailed the results of a survey study with various stakeholders at Charlottesville High School, including students, parents, administrators, the school board, and community members.[15]

Overall, the reports pointed to several ways systemic racism existed in the Charlottesville City Schools Division and, more specifically, at the high school. Black students and parents cited the curriculum reform, which exacerbated tracking at the high school during the transition from LHS to CHS, as a significant problem. The report also included a range of test scores at various levels of schooling, with a familiar conclusion: there was an achievement gap between Black and white students. Another follow-up study was conducted in 1981 by University of Illinois professor Frederick Rodgers. His report warned that the current state of the school system would lead to future problems, stating, "More pressure is likely to come from black parents regarding the achievement performance and active participation of their children in programs that lead to higher status and better paying job [sic] in our society."[16]

The return of African American student protests in the city's high school originated with a newspaper article in the *Knight Time Review*. Just as Jefferson High School had *The Jeffersonian*, Jackson P. Burley High School had the *Burley Bulletin*, and Lane High School had the *Lanetime*, Charlottesville High School had the *Knight Time Review*. Like those other newspapers, yet unlike *Blast*, the newspaper was school-sanctioned and overseen by the school's faculty advisor. So, ostensibly, the faculty advisor read and signed off on each edition of the *Knight Time Review*. This arrangement between students and faculty had become the norm in high schools throughout the United States during the second half of the twentieth century.[17]

From CHS's inception, Principal Huegal had been at the helm. He left LHS early to oversee the building and create a fresh start at CHS. However, he retired before the 1983–1984 school year. Florence C. Bryant recalls that the new principal, Principal David H. Garrett, struggled in his new role, and there was an overall lack of communication between various people at the school. Garrett, a white man, was an ex-Marine and had served as principal at the Burnley-Moran Elementary School. When he took on the new role at Charlottesville High School, he cited a need for "a new challenge." His background in the military shaped his approach to administration. Garrett asserted, "I believe in an orderly atmosphere in school. I believe kids should be told the rules and the reasons for them. And they should be followed." Garrett's approach to building community and disciplining students came to a head with the release of a newspaper article following Black History Month.[18]

On Friday, March 2, 1984, the *Knight Time Review* ran a story called "Grading Black-White Relations: 17 Years After Integration." At the time, about 470 students out of 1,369 identified as African American. The article consisted of anonymous quotes from students at the high school. The article's author noted the limitations of their approach, including the lack of perspectives from around the high school. The article's approach was not the only problem. The article's anonymous racist comments had immediate consequences. White students in the article commented on their views of Black students at the high school. One white student was quoted as saying that the only reason Black students came to school "was to get heat." They continued saying, "They just mess around... come to school 'cause they don't have nothing else to do... they just come to smoke herb and all that stuff." Black students reacted to the contents of the newspaper article in several ways, including violence. Principal Garrett and the school's administration decided to close the school early on Friday.[19]

The fallout from the newspaper article escalated due to another separate yet related incident. On the morning of Monday, March 6, when students arrived at the high school the day after the article, there were racist epithets painted on a concrete wall near the school's parking lot. The signs included one that said, "N****** must die," and another said, "Seniors for White Supremacy." Principal Garrett and other faculty members arrived at the school in time to see the signs. However, Garrett claimed they did not have enough time to paint over or remove the signs before students arrived. The signs led to fights breaking out between Black and white students. Some Black students went to the school's library and overturned bookcases. Other students refused to get off the bus. Principal Garrett called the police to the scene at the high school. Rather than hold school on that Monday, Principal Garrett closed school beginning at 11 A.M. The school's administration held an emergency faculty meeting.[20]

All students returned to school the next week. Garrett, the school administration, and teachers wore buttons that said, "I Care." Garrett read a statement over the loudspeaker apologizing for the article and its contents, particularly the "insensitivity of some of the statements." Then, most students attended an extended first-period class to discuss the article and the aftermath. Approximately 150 African American students refused to participate in their first period, and they were sent to the school's gymnasium to meet with Florence C. Bryant, Diane Price, and other African American community leaders from around the city. Garrett characterized the meeting as African American students learning how to handle "racial problems without violence." African American students had not written the article; they had not signed off on the publication of the article; they had not painted racist inscriptions on the parking lot wall. Responding to the situation with violence was not the core of the problem; the problem was the racist comments in the newspaper and on the parking lot wall.[21]

Beyond the school, there were various perspectives on the newspaper article and its aftermath. Cindy Stratton, the president of the local NAACP, drew parallels to the tensions at LHS during desegregation and the current CHS situation. Stratton had attended LHS as a student and recalled how "That was a really difficult time." Stratton states, "Charlottesville has not changed much over the last 15 years socially." George Ferguson provided a slightly different perspective. Ferguson claimed, "Things have changed tremendously. Charlottesville is a unique place. I think the communication between the races is better here than in some Virginia towns. The university has something to do with it because it brings together different kinds of people." William Smith also offered his perspective. Smith, a minister at Westminster Presbyterian Church, asserted, "Racism is always here, so why should we be surprised (when racial tensions flare)? We get too comfortable, because tensions go underground for a while."[22]

Stratton offered five recommendations to the Charlottesville City Schools Division in a prepared statement she shared at Zion Union Baptist Church. She asserted, "I think the incident has opened a lot of people's eyes who thought the situation was peachy-keen." The recommendations did not focus just on the high school but viewed the problem more broadly. She identified how one of the problems with the tracking system originates with teachers' attitudes toward Black students, which "relegates them to second class [sic] activities and poor preparation for life in today's world." She called to fire the faculty advisor for the *Knight Time Review*. She called for involving students to a greater degree in school policymaking, including professional development programs on human relations in schools, and placing the division's best teachers "to the schools and students which have the most serious problems."[23]

This situation placed Florence C. Bryant in a challenging situation. Bryant felt caught between her identity as a Black woman, a prominent person in the local Black community, and an administrator at CHS. In reflecting on the situation, Bryant wrote,

> I felt caught between my position as an administrator, who needed to defend the integrity of the school's program, and my position as a [B]lack person, who needed to defend the legitimacy of the [B]lack students' perceptions of racism and inequality at Charlottesville High. I felt totally ineffectual on both counts. I knew that the school board and school administration had continuously sought ways to raise the motivational levels of the students and to encourage all students to develop their potentials to the fullest. Many special programs had been implemented, especially to raise the achievement levels of the underachievers, but obviously success in that regard had not been fully attained. On the other hand, I was equally sure that, because racism was so deeply ingrained in the fabric of the American society, Charlottesville High School could not possibly have been immune.[24]

A few months after the Black student protests at CHS, Bryant decided to retire from the school division. Her decision was not surprising. Bryant had worked in the Charlottesville City Schools Division since World War II. She cited the challenges of dealing with the white teachers' negligence in dealing with the racist article and her struggle to meet the needs of Black students at the time. She also cited another factor: the *A Nation at Risk* report. The report had been published the previous year. Having seen the contours of educational reform in the United States, she strongly sensed that the report would lead to widespread changes in the American educational system, influencing all schools, including CHS.[25]

After Bryant departed from the high school, a local report addressing the situation in Charlottesville was released. In October 1985, about a year and a half after the publication of the newspaper article, the Social Development Commission/School Board and Task Force on Race Relations released "Race Relations and Education in Charlottesville." The report had been commissioned a year earlier. In the opening pages, the authors provided a rationale for the report, asserting, "In response to growing awareness in the community that a study of race relations was needed, the Social Development Commission elected to make race relations their major priority for 1985." The report then cited "the incident at Charlottesville High School" as another sign that the city needed to address racism and discrimination in the city and the schools. The creation and dissemination of the report revealed a desire, at least by some in the community, that something needed to be done in response to Black student protests.[26]

The report noted the complex factors involved in explaining the roots of and solutions for racism in education and other areas of Charlottesville. "The problems the report addresses are rooted in the issues surrounding educational achievement for blacks and in the complex social and historical conditions which underlie race relations in Charlottesville," the authors wrote in the preface. "They are based on community issues such as housing, unemployment, and inequities in the standards of life of various neighborhoods; conditions which have been shaped both by history and by circumstance." This analysis of the situation represents a more sophisticated understanding of the relationship between schooling and society. It revealed an understanding that schools do not exist in a vacuum and are entangled with the broader community.[27]

The report then pivoted to discussing school desegregation and its consequences. "The desegregation of the public schools was only the beginning of the move toward racial understanding and socio-economic equality," wrote the authors. "This report will focus on problems which relate to public education and community relations; the two are inseparable: problems found in the schools originate in the community, yet we look to schools to solve those problems."[28]

During and after the report's release, the Task Force met with various groups to discuss race and education in the city. The groups included school administrators, school board members, teachers, representatives from the Black community, community interest groups, and Charlottesville High School students. Including the Charlottesville High School students seems to have been a direct response to the Black student protest in the spring of 1984. The Task Force focused on describing the problems *and* finding solutions to those problems. Racism and inequality continued to plague CHS; however, Black educators and students also continued to fight for justice at the nexus between pedagogy and protest. As had been the case at LHS, Black educators and students often bore the burden of creating greater educational opportunities.

Diane Price was among the few Black teachers who moved from LHS to CHS. She continued to teach German and U.S. government, leading the planning and facilitation of Black History Week at Charlottesville High School and later, in 1976, Black History Month—at Charlottesville High School. She remained one of the few African American educators at the high school throughout her long tenure.[29]

When Price moved from Lane High School to Charlottesville High School, she continued facilitating the Black History program. In 1976, two years after the new high school opened, Black History Week became Black History Month, which coincided with the American Bicentennial celebration. Dr. Edgar Toppin, creator of "Americans from Africa" and the President of the Association for the Study of African American Life and History, was instrumental in the change. The transition to Black History Month shaped school events and curricula throughout the United States, including Charlottesville. During this era, Price grew frustrated by the lack of integration of Black history and the Black experience across the curriculum at Charlottesville High School. She threatened to stop facilitating the Black History Month programming unless other teachers stepped up to desegregate their curriculum. Price sought one hundred percent participation from other faculty members in the pursuit of incorporating Black history across the curriculum. She received their assurances and continued her work on the Black History program in February.[30]

Price did not leave teachers on their own. She helped them revise their curriculum so Black history was integrated throughout the curriculum and coursework. While subjects like English and government provided more opportunities to explore Black history, other subjects like math and science proved more challenging. This challenge did not dissuade Price from affecting change at the high school. Price ensured the physical education classes had a lesson plan alongside the science and math classes. They had guest speakers. Students signed up to research famous African Americans. Price recalls, "It wasn't just Martin Luther King or Rosa Parks. We had other people. We had bulletin boards." On the bulletin boards one year, there was information about Black teachers who had attended Historically Black Colleges and Universities. This activity helped center the Black teachers at the school and helped all students learn more about their teachers before they became teachers.[31]

Price had the opportunity in her German classes to take students outside Charlottesville to visit Germany and use their language. In her government classes, she used the "Eyes on the Prize: America's Civil Rights Movement" documentary on the civil rights movement. The documentary was initially aired on public television from 1987 to 1990. Price habitually recorded programs on video tapes and then used them in her classroom. Teaching "Eyes on the Prize" marked a shift in the pedagogical approach to understanding government in the United States. Also, the documentary dealt with many issues close to home, including Venable Elementary School and Lane High School closures. Rather than just understanding the structure of the United States and how the system of government should work, Price encouraged students to appreciate how change has been and could be enacted.[32]

Price's pedagogical approach within her classroom manifested the "warm demander" archetype. In a newspaper profile of her teaching, Price asserted with a smile, "Students think they will coast through their senior year—and then they get me." Price encouraged her students to become active in civic life through her courses. "My goal is to help them become contributing members of society. I tell them they're going to be voters—not non-voters—and people who read and know how to make up their minds about issues." Price provided extra credit to her students for "attending city council and school board meetings, or for helping tally votes at party headquarters after a local election." She had students focus on politics and government not just at the local level but also to follow national politics.[33]

Price had students connect their learning in the classroom with issues beyond the school in other ways, too. She encouraged students to write essays for the local American Civil Liberties Union (ACLU) competition on the Bill of Rights. Two of Price's students won the competition in 1983. Price did not just tell students about the competition, but she also provided the support and scaffolding to help them be successful. In the government classes, Price had students "thoroughly" study the Bill of Rights and Constitution before they composed their essays. Beth Schrank, the essay competition winner, said Price "[is] hard sometimes, but she is a good teacher. She wasn't going to let anyone slide by."[34]

Diane Price was not the only African American teacher who moved from LHS to CHS. Garwin DeBerry also spent a brief period at LHS. As chronicled earlier, DeBerry desegregated LHS but later transferred back to BHS after Lane's administration would not allow him to participate in extracurricular activities. DeBerry graduated from Jackson P. Burley High School and attended Virginia State College. He played fullback and linebacker on the football team at Virginia State and earned a bachelor's degree in health, physical education, and driver's education. DeBerry did not return to Charlottesville immediately after college graduation. He moved to Passaic, New Jersey, with his wife, Marilyn. He coached football and taught at an elementary school. He played semiprofessional football for the Jersey Jays.[35]

Eventually, DeBerry returned to Charlottesville to coach football at LHS. Henry Mitchell, a pastor at Trinity Episcopal Church, recruited DeBerry to return to Charlottesville and helped him secure a coaching position at LHS. In 1972, DeBerry became an assistant coach under Tom Theodose—the coach who would not allow him to play when he attended LHS. "It was just a great experience with him and he was just like man I just wish you had been able to play, and I said yeah well that's water under the bridge now, let's get this coaching thing going," remembers DeBerry. In 1979, DeBerry succeeded Theodose as the head coach at Charlottesville High School. In succeeding Theodose, he became the area's first Black head football coach.[36]

African American principals and administrators faced staggering job losses in the wake of the *Brown* decisions. Like Florence C. Bryant, other Black educators bore significant responsibility in leading the school and teaching their classes amid the continued racism within the school division and, more specifically, the high school. Wilbert T. Lewis assumed the role of vice principal at Charlottesville High School upon Bryant's decision to retire. Lewis did not start his career in Charlottesville. He grew up in Lynchburg, Virginia, and attended the city's segregated schools: Dunbar Elementary and Dunbar High School. He attended and graduated from Virginia Union College with a degree in chemistry and mathematics. Lewis had initially planned to work as a chemist at the National Institute of Health in Washington, D.C. However, he received a call from the superintendent of the Lynchburg City Schools—out of nowhere, at least from Lewis's perspective at the time—offering him a job as a sixth-grade teacher.[37]

Lewis worked as a sixth-grade teacher for a year. Then, he moved to Lynchburg's Dunbar High School, where he taught math. During the summers, while he was still teaching, Lewis pursued graduate study at Western Kentucky University. He earned a master's degree in school administration and counseling. He held administrative positions in the Lynchburg City Schools before graduating the last all-Black class at Dunbar High School in 1970. He served as principal at desegregated Dunbar High School for the next two years. Those two years would be Lewis's last in Lynchburg.[38]

Dr. Bass recruited Lewis to the University of Virginia, where he pursued his doctorate and worked at the Consultative Center for School Desegregation. The Consultative Center for School Desegregation was related to the university; however, it did not have a formal office and received federal funding for operations and research support. The Center worked with school divisions around the state to support teachers and administrators during the initial decades of school desegregation, including Lane High School. Lewis's work with the Center prepared him for the opportunities and challenges of leading within a desegregated school like Charlottesville High School.[39]

After graduating from the University of Virginia with his doctorate, Lewis worked as a math coordinator and assistant personnel director at the Albemarle County Schools Division offices. He spent a brief time there before becoming an assistant principal at Charlottesville High School in the fall of 1984 and, later, principal in 1989. In 1984, Lewis joined a new team of administrators at the high school, including a new principal, Richard D. Greig. Shortly after becoming principal, Lewis sat for an interview with a local newspaper.[40]

Lewis spoke about several issues specific to Charlottesville High School. However, he commented on issues facing other high schools in the United States at the time. Asked about the environment he wanted to see at the high school, Lewis wanted it to be "an inviting place and warm place. We want teachers to feel good about teaching here, we want kids to feel good about coming." Lewis was, of course, referring to all students at the high school. He also commented on the two major issues facing the high school at the time: tracking and "dropouts." Lewis spoke about the consequences of tracking and the concomitant expectations placed on students. "Because I'm disadvantaged does not mean that I've got to be dumb." He then noted that teachers' expectations and standards for students mattered in how students viewed themselves within the high school. "I have never equated intelligence with being rich or poor," asserted Lewis. He spoke at length about the concept of tracking and called for meeting the needs of students in equitable ways.[41]

Patricia Edwards, a former student at Jefferson Elementary School and BHS, returned to Charlottesville during the 1970s. Edwards attended the Hampton Institute before transferring to Virginia State College. She taught at the McGuffey Special Education Center in her first teaching job out of college, with brief stints at schools in Charlottesville and then Charlotte, North Carolina, and Pinellas, Florida. After moving around, Edwards returned to Charlottesville and took a position at Charlottesville High School as a special education teacher, having earned a master's degree in education at the University of Virginia. Edwards and Price were among the few Black educators at Charlottesville High School during the late twentieth century and into the early twenty-first century.[42]

Collectively, Black teachers and administrators at CHS made a significant impact on the lives and educational experiences of youth. They drew upon the tradition of Black excellence cultivated in the segregated schooling spaces at JHS and BHS and historically Black institutions of higher education to create equitable educational opportunities for Black students in desegregated spaces. At the same time, Black educators—whether in the classroom or school system—were often fighting against the ingrained racism of the Charlottesville City Schools Division system.

Charlottesville High School remains the only public high school in the city. It opened in response to overcrowding at Lane High School and, for some, was an opportunity for a fresh start. While the new high school did ease overcrowding, it created new problems due to its new location outside of the city's downtown area. In the early years and subsequent decades, Black teachers and students faced a series of local and national changes and continuities at the high school. The mid-1980s included two events that represented those changes and continuities: the release of the *A Nation at Risk* report in 1983 and the Black student protests at the high school in 1984. The report marked a shift from a focus on "equity" in education to a focus on "excellence." While education reform was shifting at the national level, the Black student protests revealed how "racism was so deeply ingrained" in Charlottesville and its high schools.[43]

The relationship between protest and pedagogy represented another continuity. On the one hand, Diane Price brought her pedagogical approaches to Charlottesville High School. Her teaching approach represented both pedagogy *as* protest and pedagogy *for* protest. Price employed pedagogical methods in her U.S. government course that departed from the typical approach as she focused on the significance of the civil rights movement. She did not just want her students to learn about the politics of the past; she also provided opportunities for students to apply their learnings in class through visits to the Charlottesville City School Board meetings and entering writing contests for the local chapter of the ACLU. Price's approach was not the norm at the high school; however, it shows what one teacher could and did accomplish amid a period of standardization and accountability. On the other hand, Black teachers were not the only ones who faced challenging situations and aimed to provide a more relevant pedagogical approach.[44]

In 1994, Wilbert T. Lewis ended his tenure as principal of Charlottesville High School. He moved from Charlottesville High School to the Charlottesville City Schools Division offices, where he served as the Assistant Superintendent of Personnel. Lewis retired in 2003 and passed away in 2015. Lewis and Florence C. Bryant, who is still alive, are part of a unique generation of African American educators. They grew up attending segregated schools in Virginia, from elementary school through college. Then, they started their careers teaching in segregated schools before becoming part of the desegregation process. Not only did they desegregate schools as educators, but they were part of the first wave of Black graduate students at historically white higher education institutions.[45]

Lewis and Bryant became school administrators with unique stories. Unlike many of their peers across Virginia, including Gladys McCoy, who lost her job, and Booker Reaves, who was demoted to an administrative role at the division, Lewis and Bryant remained in important and socially prestigious positions of leadership in schools. (Positions of administration at the high school level are often viewed as more prestigious than ones at the elementary level.) At the same time, Lewis and Bryant faced a particularly challenging political, social, and economic context at Charlottesville High School. The Charlottesville City Schools Division leaned on them to lead the school through difficult times as racism continued to be an issue for Black teachers and students. Moreover, the demands of school reform efforts at the national level meant that Lewis, Bryant, and their colleagues faced greater scrutiny over test scores and student attendance.[46]

Conclusion

"The Statues Coming Down Is the Tip of the Iceberg"

The statues coming down is the tip of the iceberg. There are larger systems that need to be dismantled. Educational equity is a good place to start.
—Zyahna Bryant, a former student at Charlottesville High School and the University of Virginia

Charlottesville has "big dinosaur bones in the closet," and one day, they're going to step out and have flesh on them.
—Berdell Fleming, a former student at Jackson P. Burley High School

The dynamic relationship between protest and pedagogy continues today in Charlottesville. Some of the people involved in this relationship are familiar, while others are less so. Collectively, they have continued the legacy of African American high school educators and students who propelled and sustained the Black freedom struggle during the twentieth century.

Florence Coleman Bryant and Charles Alexander are no longer involved in the Charlottesville City Schools Division as students or educators. However, since leaving the school division, they have been involved in various endeavors related to public pedagogy and remembering their lived history. Following Bryant's retirement as an administrator at CHS, she has worked on several books and manuscripts related to her life, Charlottesville, and the local history of African American education. She has also been interviewed a few times in the past few decades, including an interview for the TIM Project. The collective archive she developed during several decades of work constitutes yet another chapter of her pedagogy, which began in the classrooms of JHS and BHS. Few others have such a firsthand account of how Charlottesville, the Black freedom struggle, and the American high school had changed *and* remained the same during the twentieth century.[1]

Since graduating from LHS, Charles Alexander left Charlottesville to attend college at South Carolina State in Orangeburg, South Carolina. He did not finish his degree and spent some time away from the city, living and working in Richmond and Atlanta. Across those cities, he became involved as a speaker, educator, and organizer. In 2011, when the historical marker, "The Triumph of the Charlottesville Twelve," was unveiled, Alexander returned to Charlottesville and participated in a roundtable discussing school desegregation and its consequences. More recently, Alexander worked to establish the Black History Pathway. Alexander described the initiative's purpose at the unveiling of the Black History Pathway historical marker on April 8, 2023. At the ceremony, Alexander asserted, "The sign means to maintain and observe the rich history and contributions of the African-American community in Charlottesville and Albemarle [County]."[2]

Other African American educators and students have worked to remember the history of Black high schools. In particular, the alums and former educators at BHS have been involved in organizing the establishment of other markers and memorials to observe and celebrate what the school meant to them and the African American community. The Burley Varsity Club has spearheaded several efforts to remember the contributions of athletes and coaches at the high school. Two historical markers are situated outside of the Burley Middle School gym, spotlighting the life and work of Black coaches and educators. BHS alums have also helped build a monument wall and bench to highlight all the people involved at Burley, such as students, staff, educators, and administrators. The center of the wall reads, "With reverence and steadfast hearts, we honor the memory of our beloved Burley High School and Mr. Jackson P. Burley. Minds were molded and shaped by the dedicated administrators, teachers, and staff who guided us. The legacy of this grand institution will live forever."[3]

These efforts to remember the past have helped advance a more robust and nuanced understanding of the history of African Americans in Charlottesville. While many African American educators and students have led these efforts in the past, there have been more recent efforts by current students in the Charlottesville City Schools Division.

During the past decade, Zyahna Bryant has played an integral role in fighting for justice, liberation, and educational opportunities. In 2016, Bryant, an African American student at Charlottesville High School, crafted and circulated an online petition arguing for removing the Robert E. Lee statue in one of the city's downtown parks. Nearly a hundred years earlier, during the Jim Crow era, the Lee statue had been commissioned and placed by the city to perpetuate the Lost Cause narrative and uphold white supremacy. "As a teenager in Charlottesville that identifies as black, I am offended every time I pass [the Lee statue]," wrote Bryant in the petition. "I am reminded over and over again of the pain of my ancestors and all of the fighting that they had to go through for us to be where we are now. Quite frankly I am disgusted with the selective display of history in this city. There is more to Charlottesville than just the memories of Confederate fighters. There is more to this city that makes it great." Bryant's petition represented more recent instances of African American high school students involved in protest *as* pedagogy and protest *for* pedagogy.[4]

On the one hand, Bryant's petition manifested protest *for* pedagogy as she aimed to deconstruct white supremacist ideology infused in the city's public pedagogy. Removing the statue would topple a monument to white supremacy and racial oppression in the physical landscape of the city. Statues do not themselves enact white supremacy and racial oppression; however, they signal what and who a city values. On the other hand, the petition manifested protest *as* pedagogy because it educated the broader community about the statue, which had been part of the city's landscape for nearly one hundred years. Many people had walked past the statue and perhaps known the history and purpose of the monument, yet no one had put into writing a proposal to remove it—even if they disapproved of its existence. Bryant's petition also led to questioning other monuments to white supremacy and racial oppression in the city and at the nearby University of Virginia.[5]

The petition garnered the attention of the Charlottesville City Council. The Council, including Wes Bellamy, an African American man and Vice-Mayor, voted to remove the Lee statue. This vote set off a series of events that thrust the city into the national spotlight and drew the attention of white supremacist groups. In August 2017, white supremacists rallied around the Thomas Jefferson statue on the grounds of the University of Virginia and attacked the city and its residents. The white nationalist protest led to a multitude of other harms, seen and unseen, to people and places in the city; however, the white supremacist violence did not change

Table 5. Demographics of Charlottesville High School, 2020

Racial/ethnic group	Black or African American	White	Hispanic	Asian
Percentage of student population	29%	41.8%	14.2%	4.6%

Source: "Charlottesville High School" *Segregation Explorer,* Accessed on May 14, 2024. https://edopportunity.org/segregation/explorer/.

the minds of the City Council, who continued to work toward removing the statue.[6]

Meanwhile, amid the effort to remove the Lee statue, Zyahna Bryant also became involved in protests against racial violence and for justice and educational equity at Charlottesville High School. CHS remains open today. While CHS has remained unchanged physically since it opened in 1974, the school's demographics have changed slightly in the past few decades. Nearly forty-two percent of the students identify as white, and twenty-nine percent identify as Black or African American. However, the number of students identifying as Hispanic or Latina/o/x has increased to over fourteen percent—a significant jump since the turn of the twentieth century. More than two-thirds of all students who attend CHS are eligible for free lunch.[7]

In March 2019, a white male student at Charlottesville High School sent a threatening message through an online platform detailing how he would harm African American and Latino/a/x students. Charlottesville High School's Black Student Union, organized by Zyahna Bryant, did not wait for CHS or the Charlottesville City Schools Division's administrators to respond to the incident. Instead, Bryant and the other African American and Latino/a/x students organized their responses. They composed a petition with several demands. Rather than writing the petition down on a piece of paper and circulating it to the school and division's administration, the students posted their demands on a YouTube channel with a parade of students describing them individually. The students walked out of their classes the following week at CHS alongside the online petition video.[8]

The Statues Coming Down | 131

Zyahna Bryant, second from left, first row, and other Black students protest outside of Charlottesville High School in response to online racist posts and racial inequalities at the school. Courtesy of Zach Roberts, Charlottesville, Va., ZUMA Wire/Alamy Stock Photo.

On the one hand, African American and Latino/a/x students were responding to an immediate threat, much like African American students had done at Lane High School in 1968. They wanted the administration at the high school and the division level to respond urgently and unequivocally to denounce the violent speech. On the other hand, the African American and Latino/a/x students situated their demands in a broader framework, which meant highlighting the institutional racism and inequality at Charlottesville High School and within the Charlottesville City Schools Division. Although the online threats were the catalyst for the walkout, the students at CHS understood these problems as larger than one precipitating event. Indeed, as this book reveals, their demands consisted of issues with deep roots in the history of high schools in Charlottesville but also, in some cases, a slight shift or nuance concerning previous demands by African American students in the city.[9]

Students demanded changes in hiring practices, curriculum, and pedagogy at CHS. They requested more teachers of color in all classes, particularly in honors and Advanced Placement (AP) classes. The students demanded greater participation—across the school—in courses centering on the African American experience. CHS did have an African American history course. However, similar to the situation at LHS, the course was a regular-track elective history course. So, not only was the course not part of the higher tracks of courses, but it was also not part of the core curriculum. As related to African American history, their demands also included more specific requirements regarding the course's quality. They sought "A high standard of programming associated with Black history."[10]

Students' demands also reflected the unique inequalities they faced at CHS. Students demanded that every student be tested for "QUEST" or, as it is known in other school divisions and districts, gifted and talented. They demanded greater access to college resources beyond the high school's Advancement Via Individual Determination (AVID) program. At a high school with a significant population of students with parents, guardians, and family members employed by or associated with the University of Virginia, the disparities between the privileged students and others were more significant.[11]

Finally, the students' demands reflected changes in the implementation of school community policies and consciousness regarding different approaches to mental health and safety. In terms of school discipline, students demanded an end to "the excessive suspending and policing of [B]lack middle and high school students by creating a diverse board of staff, students, parents, to oversee equitable and effective discipline." Students did not call for the end of school resource officers as many other students have done in different cities. However, they did call for "racial bias and culturally sensitive training for all resource officers." Finally, the students demanded an improved security system and the use of "mental health practices that are culturally relevant and racially aware."[12]

Almost fifty years earlier, African American students at Lane High School made similar demands during the height of school desegregation. Their demands revealed both the changes *and* continuities in Black education, curriculum, pedagogy, and the American high school in Charlottesville. This book has illuminated those changes and continuities, beginning with the fight for a Black high school in the city and concluding with the consequences of the organizing and activism of Bryant and their peers. How this story is remembered—or forgotten—in Charlottesville is essential for understanding the past and cultivating a new and more progressive vision for the *city*— *and* cities and communities across the United States.[13]

Although Bryant and the other students involved in the initial formation of the Black Student Union have since graduated high school, other students at CHS have continued to organize in support of different issues and causes. They have organized and protested in solidarity with other high school students throughout the nation around the problems of climate change, transgender rights, and gun violence in the United States. Linking local, state, national, and international issues together is a characteristic of historical social movements, as well as more contemporary social movements. However, the extent certainly varies depending on the political, social, economic, and educational contexts.[14]

On July 9, 2021, the City of Charlottesville removed the Robert E. Lee statue in a downtown park from its perch. Zyahna Bryant was among the many people present as the cranes lifted the statue off its pedestal. At the event, Bryant asserted the need to not only rid the city of statues dedicated to perpetuating white supremacy but also to fight for justice and equity more broadly. "The statues coming down is the tip of the iceberg. There are larger systems that need to be dismantled. Educational equity is a good place to start."[15]

Bryant's organizing for the removal of the statue yielded a significant change in the city's physical landscape. In her interview with the media at the event, Bryant noted the importance of the moment while also drawing attention to the structural issues impacting the African American community in Charlottesville, particularly around education. Bryant's organizing efforts within and beyond Charlottesville High School have continued the work of many African American high school students and educators in the past. And the work continues.

NOTES

Introduction

1. Hyres, "Dedication to the Highest of Callings," 148, 150–54. Depending on the era, I use Jefferson Colored Graded/Elementary School or Jefferson Elementary School. Also, I use African American and Black interchangeably throughout the book, while not capitalizing "white" unless it is capitalized within a quote. For more on this approach, see Nicole Meir, "Why We Will Lowercase White," Associated Press, July 20, 2020, https://www.ap.org/the-definitive-source/announcements/why-we-will-lowercase-white/.

2. Hyres, "Dedication to the Highest of Callings," 155–57, 160–62.

3. Don Devore, "Integration at Lane, Venable Carried Out Without Incident," *Daily Progress*, September 8, 1959: 1, 3; Charles Alexander, interview with Phyllis Leffler, Lorenzo Dickerson, and George Gilliam, "No Playbook," July 28, 2022; and Charles Alexander, interview with Liz Sargent and Alexandria Searls, "Jefferson School Interviews, Vol. 1," June 17, 2004.

4. Charles Alexander, interview with Liz Sargent and Alexandria Searls, "Jefferson School Interviews, Vol. 1," June 17, 2004; and Holden, *The Bus Stops Here*, 92–99.

5. The use of "educators" instead of just "teachers" is intentional. "Educators" encompasses both teachers and administrators. Throughout the book, I use "teachers," "administrators," and "educators" to specify the position of the adults involved in schools. On Black student activism, see Danns, "Chicago High School Students' Movement for Quality Public Education, 1966–1971"; Willis, *Audacious Agitation*; Franklin, *The Young Crusaders*; and Hale, *A New Kind of Youth*. On Black teacher activism, see Baker, "Pedagogies of Protest"; Loder-Jackson, *Schoolhouse Activists*; Walker, *The Lost Education of Horace Tate*; Alridge, "Teachers in the Movement"; and Alridge, Hale, and Loder-Jackson, *Schooling the Movement*. On the relationship between Black teachers *and* students in the Black freedom struggle, see Givens, *Fugitive Pedagogy*; and Hale, *A New Kind of Youth*.

6. Historians of the African American experience have debated different frameworks for understanding social movements in the twentieth century. This book employs the framework of "the Black freedom struggle" as opposed to "the long civil rights movement." The book begins before and ends after the "long civil rights movement" and the story evinces the changes and continuities in the

African American experience, which transcends the narrow moment of the Civil Rights era. On these frameworks and the debate between scholars, see Hall, "The Long Civil Rights Movement" and Cha-Jua and Lang, "The 'Long Movement' as Vampire."

7. On the history of Black youth and educator activism, see previous footnote. On youth and educator protest, more broadly, in the United States, see Graham, *Young Activists*; Schumaker, *Troublemakers*; and Shelton, *Teacher Strike!* On changes and continuities in pedagogy in American schools, see Cuban, *How Teachers Taught*; Zimmerman, *Whose America?*; Burkholder, *Color in the Classroom*; Givens, *Fugitive Pedagogy*; Hines, *A Worthy Piece of Work*; and Yacovone, *Teaching White Supremacy*.

8. On the institutional story of the American high school, see Anderson, *The Education of Blacks in the South*; Labaree, *The Making of an American High School*; Reese, *The Origins of the American High School*; Steele, *Making a Mass Institution*; and Kitzmiller, *The Roots of Educational Inequality*. On the rise and fall of Black high schools, see Anderson, *The Education of Blacks in the South*; Cecelski, *Along Freedom Road*; Walker, *Their Highest Potential*; Driskell, *Schooling Jim Crow*; Hale, *A New Kind of Youth*; and Nocera, Steele, and Hensley, "Standardization, White Supremacy, and Racial Self-Definition."

9. On school closures and their impacts in Black communities, see Ewing, *Ghosts in the Schoolyard* and Morris, Parker, and Negrón, "Black School Closings Aren't New."

10. Zyahna Bryant, "Change the Name of Lee Park and Remove the Statue," Change.Org Petition, 2016, accessed August 18, 2024, https://www.change.org/p/charlottesville-city-council-change-the-name-of-lee-park-and-remove-the-statue-in-charlottesville-va.

11. "Our Schools: Charlottesville City Schools," https://charlottesvilleschools.org/contactus.

12. Moore, *Albemarle: Jefferson's County*, 7, 9–10, 16–20, 23–25, 463; Taylor, *Thomas Jefferson's Education*, 15–17, 101–9, 159; and Zehmer, Sewell, and Johnston, *Educated in Tyranny*, 1–4.

13. Taylor, *Thomas Jefferson's Education*, 7, 101–9. On the lives of African Americans at Monticello and UVA, see Gordon-Reed, *The Hemingses of Monticello*; and Zehmer, Sewell, and Johnston, *Educated in Tyranny*, 27–41.

14. Saunders and Shackelford, *An Oral History of Vinegar Hill*, 43.

15. Erickson, "How/Should We Generalize?" 96.

16. "Teachers in the Movement Oral History Project," https://teachersinthemovement.com/.

17. On student-generated documents, see Hyres and Steele, "Reimagining the High School Experience."

18. Author's picture, May 27, 2018; Don Devore, "Integration at Lane, Venable Carried Out Without Incident," *Daily Progress*, September 8, 1959; and Graham Moomaw, "Charlottesville 12 Recall Experiences," *Daily Progress*, November 20, 2011: 6.

19. Author's picture, May 27, 2018. On *Brown v. Board of Education*, see Kluger, *Simple Justice*; Patterson, *Brown v. Board of Education*; and Daugherity, *Keep On Keeping On*.

Chapter One. "A Long, Hard Struggle and a Lot of Agitation"

Epigraphs are from Bryant, *Rebecca Fuller McGinness*, 36 and "Papers Pertaining to Jefferson High School," n.d., Accession #13523, Albert and Shirley Small Special Collections, University of Virginia Library, Charlottesville, Va.

1. "A Colored Educator Dead," *Daily Progress*, March 7, 1917; and Williams, *Self-Taught*, 208.

2. Williams, *Self-Taught*, 208; and Taylor, *Thomas Jefferson's Education*, 159–60.

3. "A Colored Educator Dead," *Daily Progress*, March 7, 1917; Williams, *Self-Taught*, 17–35, 185; and Anderson, *The Education of Blacks in the South*, 4–32.

4. "A Colored Educator Dead," *Daily Progress*, March 7, 1917; Anderson, *The Education of Blacks in the South*, 4–32; and Butchart, *Schooling the Freed People*, 17–51, 78–119.

5. "A Colored Educator Dead," *Daily Progress*, March 7, 1917; Williams, *Self-Taught*, 17–35, 36–47, 185; Anderson, *The Education of Blacks in the South*, 4–32; Span, *From the Cottonfield to the Schoolhouse*, 23–48; and Butchart, *Schooling the Freed People*, 117–19. On the development of public schools in the North and South during the antebellum era, see Kaestle, *Pillars of the Republic*; Moss, *Schooling Citizens*; Webber, *Deep Like the Rivers*; and Baumgartner, *In Pursuit of Knowledge*.

6. Vance, "Freedmen's Schools," 430–38; Butchart, *Schooling the Freed People*, 24; and Lee, "Crucible in the Classroom," 35–37.

7. Carkin, *The Reminisces of Philena Carkin*, 104–6; Lee, "Crucible in the Classroom," 35–37; and "Death," *The Southern Workman*, 1917: 252.

8. Anderson, *The Education of Blacks in the South*, 33–78; Watkins, *The White Architects of Black Education*, 47–61; Carkin, *The Reminisces of Philena Carkin*, 104–6; and "A Colored Educator Dead," *Daily Progress*, March 7, 1917.

9. Hume, "The Membership of the Constitutional Convention of 1867–1868," 468–69; and Moore, *Albemarle: Jefferson's County*, 228–29.

10. Hume, "The Membership of the Constitutional Convention of 1867–1868," 468–69; and Moore, *Albemarle: Jefferson's County*, 228–29. On the move away

from white teachers to African American teachers, see Fairclough, *A Class of Their Own*, 5, 89.

11. "The Lynching of John Henry James," *Virginia Encyclopedia*, accessed November 15, 2024, https://encyclopediavirginia.org/entries/lynching-of-john-henry-james-1898-the/ and Moore, *Albemarle: Jefferson's County*, 368–69.

12. Tarter, *The Grandees of Government*, 265–66.

13. Tarter, *The Grandees of Government*, 257, 261; and Coleman, *That the Blood Stay Pure*, 4.

14. Watkins, *The White Architects of Black Education*, 161–74; and "Robert Edward Lee Sculpture," Application to the National Register of Historic Places, June 19, 1996, accessed April 6, 2025, https://www.dhr.virginia.gov/historic-registers/104-0264/.

15. Saunders and Shackelford, *An Oral History of Vinegar Hill*, 1.

16. Saunders and Shackelford, *An Oral History of Vinegar Hill*, 9, 12.

17. Saunders and Shackelford, *An Oral History of Vinegar Hill*, 9, 12.

18. Saunders and Shackelford, *An Oral History of Vinegar Hill*, 11.

19. Bryant, *Rebecca Fuller McGinness*, 7–8.

20. Bryant, *Rebecca Fuller McGinness*, 7–8; and Moore, *Albemarle: Jefferson's County*, 111–27.

21. Bryant, *Rebecca Fuller McGinness*, 34–36.

22. Bryant, *Rebecca Fuller McGinness*, 34–36.

23. Bryant, *Rebecca Fuller McGinness*, 34–36.

24. Bryant, *Rebecca Fuller McGinness*, 37.

25. Bryant, *Rebecca Fuller McGinness*, 34–35, 36.

26. Bryant, *Rebecca Fuller McGinness*, 39.

27. On the development of high schools in the South, see Anderson, *The Education of Blacks in the South*, 186–237. On the origins and development of the high school in the North, see Reese, *The Origins of the American High School*; Labaree, *The Making of an American High School*; and Steele, *Making a Mass Institution*.

28. Anderson, *The Education of Blacks in the South*, 189–90, 236–37.

29. Moore, *Albemarle: Jefferson's County*, 320–21; French, "African American Civic Activism and the Making of Jefferson High School"; and Salmonowicz, "Race and Education in a Southern School System," 53.

30. Moore, *Albemarle: Jefferson's County*, 320–21.

31. Anderson, *The Education of Blacks in the South*, 192–93; and Jones, *Negro Education*, 15–16.

32. French, "African American Civic Activism and the Making of Jefferson High School," 52.

33. Saunders and Shackelford, *An Oral History of Vinegar Hill*, 10–11.

34. Saunders and Shackelford, *An Oral History of Vinegar Hill*, 13–14.

35. Saunders and Shackelford, *An Oral History of Vinegar Hill*, 13–14.

36. French, "African American Civic Activism and the Making of Jefferson High School," 52.

37. French, "African American Civic Activism and the Making of Jefferson High School," 48, 52.

38. French, "African American Civic Activism and the Making of Jefferson High School," 31, 48; and Bryant, *Rebecca Fuller McGinness*, 36–37.

39. Bryant, *Rebecca Fuller McGinness*, 37; and Records of the Charlottesville School Board, 1869–2006, #14210, Albert and Shirley Small Special Collections, University of Virginia Library, Charlottesville, Va., Box 66, Folder 17.

40. French, "African American Civic Activism and the Making of Jefferson High School," 55; and "Papers Pertaining to Jefferson High School," n.d., Accession #13523, Albert and Shirley Small Special Collections, University of Virginia Library, Charlottesville, Va.

41. "Papers Pertaining to Jefferson High School," n.d., Accession #13523, Albert and Shirley Small Special Collections, University of Virginia Library, Charlottesville, Va.

42. Moore, *Albemarle: Jefferson's County*, 320–21; French, "African American Civic Activism and the Making of Jefferson High School"; and Salmonowicz, "Race and Education in a Southern School System," 53.

43. Records of the Charlottesville School Board, 1869–2006, #14210, Albert and Shirley Small Special Collections, University of Virginia Library, Charlottesville, Va., Box 66, Folder 1.

44. French, "African American Civic Activism and the Making of Jefferson High School," 60, 63.

45. Moore, *Albemarle: Jefferson's County*, 324–25; and Records of the Charlottesville School Board, 1869–2006, #14210, Albert and Shirley Small Special Collections, University of Virginia Library, Charlottesville, Va., Box 66, Folder 1.

46. French, "African American Civic Activism and the Making of Jefferson High School," 60, 63.

47. French, "African American Civic Activism and the Making of Jefferson High School," 63.

Chapter Two. "Pillars of This Town"

Epigraphs are from William Gilmore, interview with Lynn Carter, "Jefferson School Interviews, Vol. 1," August 31, 2004; and "Principal's Message to the Students," *The Jeffersonian*, October 26, 1945.

Notes to Chapter Two

1. Booker Reaves and Donna Reaves, interview with Ashlin Smith and Jean Hiatt, "Ridge Street Oral History Project," September 8, 1994.

2. Booker Reaves and Donna Reaves, interview with Ashlin Smith and Jean Hiatt, "Ridge Street Oral History Project," September 8, 1994.

3. Patrice Grimes, "Jefferson School"; Pocahontas Sellers, Mary Sellers Carter, and Virginia Carter, interview with Jean Hiatt and Roulhac Toledano, "Ridge Street Oral History Project," August 13, 1994; and "Facts to Remember About Charlottesville," *The Reflector* (Charlottesville, Va.), April 7, 1934, accessed October 26, 2016.

4. U.S. Census Bureau, Literacy, 1930, prepared by Social Explorer, accessed December 11, 2017; and "Night School for Adults," *The Reflector* (Charlottesville, Va.), June 23, 1934, accessed October 26, 2016, http://www2.vcdh.virginia.edu/saxon/servlet/SaxonServlet?source=/xml_docs/rp_news/raceplace_news.xml&style=/xml_docs/rp_news/raceplace_news.xsl&level=single&order=none&item=va.np.reflector.06.23.34.

5. Records of the Charlottesville School Board, 1869–2006, #14210, Albert and Shirley Small Special Collections, University of Virginia Library, Charlottesville, Va., Box 81, Folders 2–4. The archivists have labeled these folders as "Jefferson High School drop-outs." However, the use of that term at this time is ahistorical. "Drop-out" as a social category did not exist until after World War II.

6. "Race and Place Newspapers." There are approximately a year and a half of newspapers that still exist. For more on this collection, see "Race and Place Newspapers: *The Reflector*," http://www2.vcdh.virginia.edu/saxon/servlet/SaxonServlet?source=/xml_docs/rp_news/raceplace_news.xml&style=/xml_docs/rp_news/raceplace_news.xsl&level=single&order=none&item=va.np.reflector.08.19.33.

7. "Scottsboro or Charlottesville," *The Reflector* (Charlottesville, Va.), August 26, 1933, accessed October 26, 2016, http://www2.vcdh.virginia.edu/saxon/servlet/SaxonServlet?source=/xml_docs/rp_news/raceplace_news.xml&style=/xml_docs/rp_news/raceplace_news.xsl&level=single&order=none&item=va.np.reflector.08.26.33.

8. "Hope on the Horizon," *The Reflector* (Charlottesville, Va.), February 17, 1934, accessed October 26, 2016, http://www2.vcdh.virginia.edu/saxon/servlet/SaxonServlet?source=/xml_docs/rp_news/raceplace_news.xml&style=/xml_docs/rp_news/raceplace_news.xsl&level=single&order=none&item=va.np.reflector.02.17.34.

9. De Corse, "Charlottesville," 7.

10. De Corse, "Charlottesville," 7–10.

11. "Negro Relief in Charlottesville," *The Reflector* (Charlottesville, Va.), November 18, 1933, accessed October 26, 2016, http://www2.vcdh.virginia.edu

/saxon/servlet/SaxonServlet?source=/xml_docs/rp_news/raceplace_news
.xml&style=/xml_docs/rp_news/raceplace_news.xsl&level=single&order
=none&item=va.np.reflector.11.18.33.

12. Bernadine Gines, Ruth Harris, and Frances Wood, interview with Lois McKenzie, "Jefferson School Interviews, Vol. 1," August 31, 2003; and Kenneth Martin, interview with Alexandria Searls, "Jefferson School Interviews, Vol. 2," March 17, 2003. Martin's account of students walking to Jefferson High School is mentioned by several individuals interviewed as part of the Jefferson School Oral History Project; Rudolph Goffney, interview with Chana Ewing, "Jefferson School Interviews, Vol. 1," August 31, 2002.

13. Dr. Braxton Coles, interview with Jacky Taylor, "Jefferson School Interviews, Vol. 1," August 31, 2002.

14. Dr. Braxton Coles, interview with Jacky Taylor, "Jefferson School Interviews, Vol. 1," August 31, 2002.

15. Records of the Charlottesville School Board, 1869–2006, #14210, Albert and Shirley Small Special Collections, University of Virginia Library, Charlottesville, Va., Box 81, Folders 2–4.

16. Bernadine Gines, Ruth Harris, and Frances Wood, interview with Lois McKenzie, "Jefferson School Interviews, Vol. 1," August 31, 2003; and Kenneth Martin, interview with Alexandria Searls, "Jefferson School Interviews, Vol. 2," March 17, 2003.

17. Booker Reaves and Donna Reaves, interview with Ashlin Smith and Jean Hiatt, "Ridge Street Oral History Project," September 8, 1994.

18. Hyres, "Dedication to the Highest of Callings," 148–65.

19. Wingfield, *A History of Caroline County*, 167; and Bryant, *Memoirs of a Country Girl*, 97.

20. Bryant, *Memoirs of a Country Girl*, 107–108; and Anderson, *The Education of Blacks in the South*, 235–37.

21. Wingfield, *A History of Caroline County*, 172–74; Simmons, *An Oasis in Caroline County, Virginia, 1903–1969*; and Bryant, *Memoir of a Country Girl*, 111–12.

22. Bryant, *Memoirs of a Country Girl*, 112–13, 114; and Givens, *Fugitive Pedagogy*, 199.

23. Bryant, *Memoirs of a Country Girl*, 141; and Florence Bryant, interview with Alexandria Searls, "Jefferson School Interviews, Vol. 1," March 12, 2003.

24. Rudolph Goffney, interview with Chana Ewing, "Jefferson School Interviews, Vol. 1," August 31, 2002; and Teresa Price, Jane Foster, and Gene Foster, interview with Jacky Taylor and Liz Sargent, "Jefferson School Interviews, Vol. 2," June 29, 2003.

25. Rudolph Goffney, interview with Chana Ewing, "Jefferson School Interviews, Vol. 1," August 31, 2002; Priscilla Whiting, interview with Jacky Taylor and

Liz Sargent, "Jefferson School Interviews, Vol. 2," June 9, 2003; and William Gilmore, interview with Lynn Carter "Jefferson School Interviews, Vol. 1," August 31, 2002.

26. Rudolph Goffney, interview with Chana Ewing, "Jefferson School Interviews, Vol. 1," August 31, 2002.

27. "Deluxe Glee Club to Make Formal Bow," *The Reflector* (Charlottesville, Va.), April 21, 1934, accessed October 26, 2016, http://www2.vcdh.virginia.edu/saxon/servlet/SaxonServlet?source=/xml_docs/rp_news/raceplace_news.xml&style=/xml_docs/rp_news/raceplace_news.xsl&level=single&order=none&item=va.np.reflector.04.21.34.

28. Teresa Price, Jane and Gene Foster, interview with Jacky Taylor and Liz Sargent, "Jefferson School Interviews, Vol. 2," June 29, 2003; and *The Crimson*, 1940, 1941, 1942, 1944, 1945, 1946, 1947, 1950, 1951. All students at the Jefferson School and Jefferson High School were represented in a class picture for their respective grade. However, the seniors received individual pictures, which included a list detailing their extracurricular involvement.

29. Rudolph Goffney, interview with Chana Ewing, "Jefferson School Interviews, Vol. 1," August 31, 2002.

30. "Jefferson School Notes," *The Reflector* (Charlottesville, Va.), April 21, 1934, accessed October 26, 2016, http://www2.vcdh.virginia.edu/saxon/servlet/SaxonServlet?source=/xml_docs/rp_news/raceplace_news.xml&style=/xml_docs/rp_news/raceplace_news.xsl&level=single&order=none&item=va.np.reflector.04.21.34.

31. Laura Robinson, interview with Ashlin Smith, "Jefferson School Interviews, Vol. 2," August 31, 2002.

32. Rudolph Goffney, interview with Chana Ewing, "Jefferson School Interviews, Vol. 1," August 31, 2002; and Bernadine Gines, Ruth Harris, and Frances Wood, interview with Lois McKenzie, "Jefferson School Interviews, Vol. 1," August 31, 2003.

33. Florence Bryant, interview with Alexandria Searls, "Jefferson School Interviews, Vol. 1," March 12, 2004.

34. Givens, *Fugitive Pedagogy*, 160.

35. "Jefferson School Notes," *The Reflector* (Charlottesville, Va.), November 11, 1933, accessed October, 26, 2016, http://www2.vcdh.virginia.edu/saxon/servlet/SaxonServlet?source=/xml_docs/rp_news/raceplace_news.xml&style=/xml_docs/rp_news/raceplace_news.xsl&level=single&order=none&item=va.np.reflector.11.11.33; "Jefferson School Notes," *The Reflector* (Charlottesville, Va.), February 24, 1934, accessed October 26, 2016, http://www2.vcdh.virginia.edu/saxon/servlet/SaxonServlet?source=/xml_docs/rp_news/raceplace_news

.xml&style=/xml_docs/rp_news/raceplace_news.xsl&level=single&order=none&item=va.np.reflector.02.24.34; and "Church Notes," *The Reflector* (Charlottesville, Va.), February 24, 1934, accessed October 26, 2016, http://www2.vcdh.virginia.edu/saxon/servlet/SaxonServlet?source=/xml_docs/rp_news/raceplace_news.xml&style=/xml_docs/rp_news/raceplace_news.xsl&level=single&order=none&item=va.np.reflector.02.24.34.

36. Wilkerson, "The Negro School Movement in Virginia"; and Nocera and Hyres, "Rebel With a Cause."

37. Wilkerson, "The Negro School Movement in Virginia"; and Anderson, *The Education of Blacks in the South*.

38. Barksdale, "A Comparative Study," 56.

39. William Gilmore, interview with Lynn Carter "Jefferson School Interviews, Vol. 1," August 31, 2002.

40. William Gilmore, interview with Lynn Carter "Jefferson School Interviews, Vol. 1," August 31, 2002.

Chapter Three. "To Take Their Place as Future Leaders"

Epigraphs are from the *Jay Pee Bee*, the Jackson P. Burley High School Yearbook, 1965; and Berdell Fleming, interview with Derrick Alridge and Chenyu Wang.

1. Wilkerson, "The Negro School Movement in Virginia" 20; "Oglesby Says Ruling Will Kill State's Public School System," *Daily Progress*, May 17, 1954; and Gaston and Hammond, "Public School Desegregation," 2. On equalization policy in North Carolina, see Thuesen, *Greater Than Equal*.

2. Barksdale, "A Comparative Study," 56; Virginia Foundation for the Humanities, "Jackson P. Burley School," *African American Historic Sites Database*, accessed December 5, 2016, http://www.aahistoricsitesva.org/show/220; "Burley High Opens With Fall Session," *New Journal and Guide* (Norfolk, Va.), September 15, 1951: A4; "The Way We Were," *Negro History Bulletin* 44 (1), January–February–March, 1981: 14; and Smith, *Unforgettable*.

3. Sellers, "New $1,400,000 High School Dedicated."

4. Virginia Foundation for the Humanities, "Jackson P. Burley School," *African American Historic Sites Database*, accessed December 5, 2016, http://www.aahistoricsitesva.org/show/220; "Burley High Opens With Fall Session," *New Journal and Guide* (Norfolk, Va.), September 15, 1951: A4; Barksdale, "A Comparative Study," 44; and "The Way We Were," *Negro History Bulletin* 44 (1), January–February–March, 1981: 14.

5. Virginia Foundation for the Humanities, "Jackson P. Burley School," *African American Historic Sites Database*, accessed December 5, 2016, http://www.aahistoricsitesva.org/show/220; and "Burley High Opens With Fall Session," *New Journal and Guide* (Norfolk, Va.), September 15, 1951: A4.

6. Sellers, "New $1,400,000 High School Dedicated."

7. Sellers, "New $1,400,000 High School Dedicated." For more on educational plants or parks and their role in desegregation, see Erickson, "Desegregation's Architects."

8. Sellers, "New $1,400,000 High School Dedicated."

9. Kluger, *Simple Justice*; Titus, *Brown's Battleground*; Bonastia, *Southern Stalemate*; and Hale, *A New Kind of Youth*, 96–102, 203.

10. Daugherity, *Keep On Keeping On*; and Gaston and Hammond, "Public School Desegregation."

11. Records of the Charlottesville School Board, 1869–2006, #14210, Albert and Shirley Small Special Collections, University of Virginia Library, Charlottesville, Va., Box 1, Folder 93; Box 2, Folders 4, 11, 17, 18. On students deemed eligible for school desegregation, see Box 2, Folders 31, 32–36; Stephon Dingle, "Former Football Coach Reflects on Segregated 1960s at Lane High School," *CBS 19 News*, http://www.newsplex.com/home/headlines/Former-Football-Coach-Reflects-On-Segregated-1960s-294441101.html; and Records of the Charlottesville School Board, 1869–2006, #14210, Albert and Shirley Small Special Collections, University of Virginia Library, Charlottesville, Va., Box 1, Folder 93.

12. Daugherity, *Keep On Keeping On*, 69, 70, 75; Holden, *The Bus Stops Here*, 87–93; "Letters from Mrs. Hattie L. DeBerry to Fendall Ellis," September 23, 1960, June 16, 19, 1962, Albert and Shirley Small Special Collections, University of Virginia Library, Charlottesville, Va., Box 1, Folder 93; and Patricia Edwards, interview with Kelly Martin and Alexander Hyres.

13. Saunders and Shackelford, *An Oral History of Vinegar Hill*, 2–4.

14. Saunders and Shackelford, *An Oral History of Vinegar Hill*, 27, 30.

15. Saunders and Shackelford, *An Oral History of Vinegar Hill*, 29, 27.

16. Saunders and Shackelford, *An Oral History of Vinegar Hill*, 28; Florence Bryant, interview with Alexandria Searls, "Jefferson School Interviews, Vol. 1," March 12, 2003; Florence Bryant, interview with Lindsey Jones, Derrick Alridge, and Alexander Hyres.

17. Bryant, *Memoirs of a Country Girl*, 141–42.

18. Bryant, *Memoirs of a Country Girl*, 141–42; and Smith, *Unforgettable*, 258–59.

19. *Jay Pee Bee*, Jackson P. Burley High School Yearbook, 1966; Patricia Edwards, interview with Kelly Martin and Alexander Hyres; and Berdell Fleming, interview with Chenyu Wang and Derrick Alridge.

20. *Jay Pee Bee,* Jackson P. Burley High School Yearbook, 1966; Smith, *Unforgettable,* 60–83, 88–102; Patricia Edwards, interview with Kelly Martin and Alexander Hyres; Berdell Fleming, interview with Chenyu Wang and Derrick Alridge; and Teresa Price, interview with Derrick Alridge and Nora Ferguson.

21. *Jay Pee Bee,* Jackson P. Burley High School Yearbook, 1966; and Smith, *Unforgettable,* 88–102.

22. *Jay Pee Bee,* Jackson P. Burley High School Yearbook, 1966.

23. *Jay Pee Bee,* Jackson P. Burley High School Yearbook, 1966; and Teresa Price, Jane and Gene Foster, interview with Jacky Taylor and Liz Sargent, "Jefferson School Interviews, Vol. 2," June 29, 2003.

24. Albert and Shirley Small Special Collections, University of Virginia Library, Charlottesville, Va., Broadside 1962. C4 J2; and Teresa Price, Jane and Gene Foster, interview with Jacky Taylor and Liz Sargent, "Jefferson School Interviews, Vol. 2," June 29, 2003.

25. Berdell Fleming, interview with Derrick Alridge and Chenyu Wang.

26. Frankie Allen, interview with Phyllis Leffler.

27. William Redd, interview with George Gilliam and Annie Valentine, October 11, 2021.

28. Teresa Price, Jane and Gene Foster, interview with Jacky Taylor and Liz Sargent, "Jefferson School Interviews, Vol. 2," June 29, 2003; and Kenneth Martin, interview with Alexandria Searls, "Jefferson School Interviews, Vol. 2," March 17, 2003.

29. *Jay Pee Bee,* Jackson P. Burley High School Yearbook, 1965.

30. *Jay Pee Bee,* Jackson P. Burley High School Yearbook, 1965.

31. Teresa Price, Jane and Gene Foster, interview with Jacky Taylor and Liz Sargent, "Jefferson School Interviews, Vol. 2," June 29, 2003; and Moore, *Albemarle: Jefferson's County,* 435.

32. Ablemarle-Charlottesville NAACP, http://www.albemarle-cvillenaacp.org/about-us/; Moore, *Albemarle: Jefferson's County,* 434; Eugene Williams, interview with Jacky Taylor and Liz Sargent, "Jefferson School Interviews, Vol. 2," February 17, 2004; and Teresa Price, Jane and Gene Foster, interview with Jacky Taylor and Liz Sargent, "Jefferson School Interviews, Vol. 2," June 29, 2003.

33. NAACP Papers, "Thalheimer Awards: 1960 Winning Branches," reproduced from the Collections of the Manuscript Division, Library of Congress.

34. Moore, *Albemarle: Jefferson's County,* 433; Teresa Price, Jane and Gene Foster, interview with Jacky Taylor and Liz Sargent, "Jefferson School Interviews, Vol. 2," June 29, 2003; and Teresa Price, interview by Derrick Alridge and Nora Ferguson.

35. Teresa Price, Jane and Gene Foster, interview with Jacky Taylor and Liz Sargent, "Jefferson School Interviews, Vol. 2," June 29, 2003; and Teresa Price, interview with Derrick Alridge and Nora Ferguson.

36. Zinn, *SNCC: The New Abolitionists*, 16–39; Carson, *In Struggle*; Brown-Nagin, *Courage to Dissent*; Morgan and Davies, *From Sit-Ins to SNCC*; and Gaston, "Sitting In" in the 'Sixties, 1–2, 6.

37. Gaston, "Sitting In" in the 'Sixties, 1–2, 6.

38. Gaston, "Sitting In" in the 'Sixties, 9; and "White Moderates Must Speak Out, Says King," *New Journal and Guide*, April 6, 1963.

39. Gaston, "Sitting In" in the 'Sixties, 9; and "Negroes Continue Demonstrations; Mass Arrests Are Made in Tallahassee," *The Free Lance Star*, May 31, 1963: 1.

40. Gaston, "Sitting In" in the 'Sixties, 9, 10–11; and "Negroes Continue Demonstrations; Mass Arrests Are Made in Tallahassee," *The Free Lance Star*, May 31, 1963: 1.

41. Gaston, "Sitting In" in the 'Sixties, 14; "Negroes Continue Demonstrations; Mass Arrests Are Made in Tallahassee," *The Free Lance Star*, May 31, 1963: 1; and "Negroes Halt Restaurant Protests," *Richmond Times-Dispatch*, June 1, 1963: 2.

42. Gaston, "Sitting In" in the 'Sixties, 14–16; and "Negroes Halt Restaurant Protests," *Richmond Times-Dispatch*, June 1, 1963: 2.

43. Gaston, "Sitting In" in the 'Sixties, 18–19; and "Negroes Halt Restaurant Protests," *Richmond Times-Dispatch*, June 1, 1963: 2.

44. Berdell Fleming, interview with Derrick Alridge and Chenyu Wang.

45. Berdell Fleming, interview with Derrick Alridge and Chenyu Wang.

46. Berdell Fleming, interview with Derrick Alridge and Chenyu Wang.

47. Holden, *The Bus Stops Here*, 80.

48. Holden, *The Bus Stops Here*, 79–81; and "Where the Faculty Went," *Burley Bulletin*, November 1966.

49. "Teacher Sues School Board, Charlottesville Denies Discrimination," *Richmond Times-Dispatch*, September 27, 1968; On Black educators' demotions and dismissals, see Fenwick, *Jim Crow's Pink Slip*.

50. Holden, *The Bus Stops Here*, 81.

Chapter Four. "A Little More Defiant, a Little More Militant"

Epigraphs are from Charles Alexander, interview with Liz Sargent and Alexandria Searls, "Jefferson School Interviews, Vol. 1," June 17, 2004; and James Bryant, interview with Danielle Wingfield-Smith.

1. Lisa Provence, "On Brown's 50th: Why Charlottesville Schools Were Closed," *The Hook*, April 8, 2004, http://www.readthehook.com/94922/cover-long-and-winding-road-city-residents-recall-integration-battles; Mearns, *Civil Rights U.S.A.*, 161–67, 168–74; and Daugherity, *Keep On Keeping On*, 69, 70, 75.

2. Devore and McKown, "Integration at Lane, Venable Carried Out Without Incident," *Daily Progress*, September 8, 1959; and Lisa Provence, "On Brown's 50th: Why Charlottesville Schools Were Closed," *The Hook*, April 8, 2004, http://www.readthehook.com/94922/cover-long-and-winding-road-city-residents-recall-integration-battles.

3. Devore and McKown, "Integration at Lane, Venable Carried Out Without Incident," *Daily Progress*, September 8, 1959; and Lisa Provence, "On Brown's 50th: Why Charlottesville Schools Were Closed," *The Hook*, April 8, 2004, http://www.readthehook.com/94922/cover-long-and-winding-road-city-residents-recall-integration-battles.

4. Devore and McKown, "Integration at Lane, Venable Carried Out Without Incident," *Daily Progress*, September 8, 1959; Lisa Provence, "On Brown's 50th: Why Charlottesville Schools Were Closed," *The Hook*, April 8, 2004, http://www.readthehook.com/94922/cover-long-and-winding-road-city-residents-recall-integration-battles; and Bryant, "One Story about School Desegregation," 67–70.

5. Bryant, "One Story about School Desegregation," 67–70.

6. Bryant, "One Story about School Desegregation," 67–70.

7. Mearns, *Civil Rights U.S.A.*, 161–67, 168–74; Holden, *The Bus Stops Here*; George King, interview by Derrick Alridge; and Patricia Edwards, interview with Alexander Hyres.

8. Daugherity, *Keep On Keeping On*, 59–78.

9. Daugherity, *Keep On Keeping On*, 79–123; Gaston and Hammond, "Public School Desegregation," 10–11; and Moore, *Albemarle: Jefferson's County*, 436. The city's segregation academy elementary school was called Robert E. Lee Elementary.

10. Holden, *The Bus Stops Here*, 54, 75.

11. Teresa Price, interview with Derrick Alridge and Nora Ferguson; and Teresa Price, Jane and Gene Foster, interview with Jacky Taylor and Liz Sargent, "Jefferson School Interviews, Vol. 2," June 29, 2003.

12. Teresa Price, interview with Derrick Alridge and Nora Ferguson; and Teresa Price, Jane and Gene Foster, interview with Jacky Taylor and Liz Sargent, "Jefferson School Interviews, Vol. 2," June 29, 2003.

13. Teresa Price, interview with Derrick Alridge and Nora Ferguson; and Teresa Price, Jane and Gene Foster, interview with Jacky Taylor and Liz Sargent, "Jefferson School Interviews, Vol. 2," June 29, 2003.

14. Susan Cone Scott, interview with Jacky Taylor and Liz Sargent, "Jefferson School Interviews, Vol. 2," May 18, 2004.

15. Susan Cone Scott, interview with Jacky Taylor and Liz Sargent, "Jefferson School Interviews, Vol. 2," May 18, 2004; and Charles Alexander, interview with

Liz Sargent and Alexandria Searls, "Jefferson School Interviews, Vol. 1," June 17, 2004.

16. Susan Cone Scott, interview with Jacky Taylor and Liz Sargent, "Jefferson School Interviews, Vol. 2," May 18, 2004.

17. Susan Cone Scott, interview with Jacky Taylor and Liz Sargent, "Jefferson School Interviews, Vol. 2," May 18, 2004.

18. Susan Cone Scott, interview with Jacky Taylor and Liz Sargent, "Jefferson School Interviews, Vol. 2," May 18, 2004.

19. Susan Cone Scott, interview with Jacky Taylor and Liz Sargent, "Jefferson School Interviews, Vol. 2," May 18, 2004.

20. Susan Cone Scott, interview with Jacky Taylor and Liz Sargent, "Jefferson School Interviews, Vol. 2," May 18, 2004.

21. Susan Cone Scott, interview with Jacky Taylor and Liz Sargent, "Jefferson School Interviews, Vol. 2," May 18, 2004.

22. Records of the Charlottesville School Board, 1869–2006, #14210, Albert and Shirley Small Special Collections, University of Virginia Library, Charlottesville, Va., Box 66, Folder 44; and "Turner Devotes Time to Cheering; Clarke Reflects on Japanese Culture," *Lanetime*, October 20, 1970, Albert and Shirley Small Special Collections, University of Virginia Library, Charlottesville, Va.

23. Charles Alexander, interview with Liz Sargent and Alexandria Searls, "Jefferson School Interviews, Vol. 1," June 17, 2004.

24. Charles Alexander, interview with Liz Sargent and Alexandria Searls, "Jefferson School Interviews, Vol. 1," June 17, 2004.

25. James Bryant, interview with Danielle Wingfield-Smith.

26. James Bryant, interview with Danielle Wingfield-Smith.

27. Ramona Paige, "Black Raiders League Works for Community," *Lanetime*, March 25, 1970.

28. *Blast*, 1969, Albert and Shirley Small Special Collections, University of Virginia Library, Charlottesville, Va.

29. James Bryant, interview with Danielle Wingfield-Smith.

30. Charles Alexander, interview with Liz Sargent and Alexandria Searls, "Jefferson School Interviews, Vol. 1," June 17, 2004; Holden, *The Bus Stops Here*, 82–87; James Bryant, interview with Danielle Wingfield-Smith; and author phone call with James Bryant, October 15, 2018.

31. Harold, "'Of the Wings of Atalanta,'" 41–69.

32. Holden, *The Bus Stops Here*; Toppin, *Americans from Africa*; and Franklin, "In Memoriam," 187.

33. Toppin, *Americans from Africa*; and Franklin, "In Memoriam," 187.

34. Toppin, *Americans from Africa*, i.
35. Toppin, *Americans from Africa*, 28.
36. Toppin, *Americans from Africa*; and Holden, *The Bus Stops Here*, 89.
37. Holden, *The Bus Stops Here*, 89–90.
38. Holden, *The Bus Stops Here*, 93; and "Teach-In: Africa," Papers of the Virginia Council on Human Relations, Charlottesville-Albemarle Chapter, #9606, Albert and Shirley Small Special Collections, University of Virginia Library, Charlottesville, Va., Box 6.
39. Alridge, "Teachers in the Movement," 21–23.
40. "Sherman Teaches First Black Studies Course," *Lanetime*, September 23, 1971, Albert and Shirley Small Special Collections, University of Virginia Library, Charlottesville, Va.
41. "Sherman Teaches First Black Studies Course," *Lanetime*, September 23, 1971, Albert and Shirley Small Special Collections, University of Virginia Library, Charlottesville, Va.; *The Chain*, Lane High School Yearbook, 1972, 210–11; Wingfield-Smith, interview with James Bryant; and author phone call with James Bryant.
42. Franklin, *From Slavery to Freedom*.
43. Katz, *Eyewitness*, 3.
44. Katz, *Eyewitness*, xix, 474.
45. Katz, *Eyewitness*, 496.
46. Katz, *Eyewitness*, 496.
47. Franklin, *From Slavery to Freedom*, 619–20.
48. "Lane . . . A Better Place to Be Says One of Lane's New Teachers" *Lanetime*, September 28, 1972; and Judy Nye, "Hello Mrs. Banks," *Lanetime*, January 17, 1974, Albert and Shirley Small Special Collections, University of Virginia Library, Charlottesville, Va.
49. Clarice Jones, "Letter to the Editor," *Lanetime*, April 19, 1973, Albert and Shirley Small Special Collections, University of Virginia Library, Charlottesville, Va.
50. Clarice Jones, "Letter to the Editor," *Lanetime*, April 19, 1973, Albert and Shirley Small Special Collections, University of Virginia Library, Charlottesville, Va.
51. Bryant, *Memoirs of a Country Girl*, 159–61.
52. Esther Vasser, interview with James Bryant and Derrick Alridge; and Diane Price, interview with Danielle Wingfield and Gabriel Benn.
53. Esther Vasser, interview with James Bryant and Derrick Alridge.
54. Esther Vasser, interview with James Bryant and Derrick Alridge.
55. Esther Vasser, interview with James Bryant and Derrick Alridge.
56. Esther Vasser, interview with James Bryant and Derrick Alridge.

57. Esther Vasser, interview with James Bryant and Derrick Alridge.

58. Ralph Ellison, *The Invisible Man*; and Esther Vasser, interview with James Bryant and Derrick Alridge.

59. Esther Vasser, interview with James Bryant and Derrick Alridge; and Tom Luce, "Anthem Sparks Charlottesville 'Reappraisal,'" *Richmond Times-Dispatch*, February 27, 1972.

60. Esther Vasser, interview with James Bryant and Derrick Alridge; and Tom Luce, "Anthem Sparks Charlottesville 'Reappraisal,'" *Richmond Times-Dispatch*, February 27, 1972.

61. Esther Vasser, interview with James Bryant and Derrick Alridge; and Tom Luce, "Anthem Sparks Charlottesville 'Reappraisal,'" *Richmond Times-Dispatch*, February 27, 1972.

62. Esther Vasser, interview with James Bryant and Derrick Alridge; and Tom Luce, "Anthem Sparks Charlottesville 'Reappraisal,'" *Richmond Times-Dispatch*, February 27, 1972.

63. Esther Vasser, interview with James Bryant and Derrick Alridge; Tom Luce, "Anthem Sparks Charlottesville 'Reappraisal,'" *Richmond Times-Dispatch*, February 27, 1972; and Bryant, *Memoirs of a Country Girl*.

64. Esther Vasser, interview with James Bryant and Derrick Alridge; and Tom Luce, "Anthem Sparks Charlottesville 'Reappraisal,'" *Richmond Times-Dispatch*, February 27, 1972.

65. Esther Vasser, interview with James Bryant and Derrick Alridge; and Tom Luce, "Anthem Sparks Charlottesville 'Reappraisal,'" *Richmond Times-Dispatch*, February 27, 1972.

66. Esther Vasser, interview with James Bryant and Derrick Alridge; and Tom Luce, "Anthem Sparks Charlottesville 'Reappraisal,'" *Richmond Times-Dispatch*, February 27, 1972.

67. Diane Price, interview with Danielle Wingfield and Gabriel Benn.

68. Diane Price, interview with Danielle Wingfield and Gabriel Benn.

69. Diane Price, interview with Danielle Wingfield and Gabriel Benn.

70. Diane Price, interview with Danielle Wingfield and Gabriel Benn.

71. David Holiday, "Black Culture Week a Success: Final Assembly," *Lanetime*, February 21, 1974, Albert and Shirley Small Special Collections, University of Virginia Library, Charlottesville, Va.

72. "Editorial," *Lanetime*, February 21, 1974, Albert and Shirley Small Special Collections, University of Virginia Library, Charlottesville, Va.

73. "Seniors Express Views of Lane," *Lanetime*, May 30, 1973, Albert and Shirley Small Special Collections, University of Virginia Library, Charlottesville, Va.

74. Esther Vasser, interview with James Bryant and Derrick Alridge.

Chapter Five. "Because Racism Was So Deeply Ingrained"

Epigraphs are from Bryant, *Memoirs of a Country Girl*, 179; and Templin, "Race Relations and Education in Charlottesville," 8.

1. "Ruston Says Plan for Lane is Temporary," *Daily Progress*, May 28, 1970: 9.
2. Holden, *The Bus Stops Here*, 40–43; and Gaston and Hammond, "Public School: Desegregation," 10–13.
3. Holden, *The Bus Stops Here*, 79.
4. Bryant, *Memoirs of a Country Girl*, 158; and Cathy Perkins, "The Bumpy Road to Progress," *Daily Progress*, July 15, 1973: 1.
5. Bryant, *Memoirs of a Country Girl*, 158; Saunders and Shackelford, *An Oral History of Vinegar Hill*, 37–101; and Cathy Perkins, "The Bumpy Road to Progress," *Daily Progress*, July 15, 1973: 1.
6. Bryant, *Memoirs of a Country Girl*, 163; and Cathy Perkins, "The Bumpy Road to Progress," *Daily Progress*, July 15, 1973: 1.
7. Bryant, *Memoirs of a Country Girl*, 163; and Cathy Perkins, "The Bumpy Road to Progress," *Daily Progress*, July 15, 1973: 1.
8. Bryant, *Memoirs of a Country Girl*, 163 and; "Your Right to Say It: Favors Change," *Daily Progress*, June 2, 1973: 4.
9. Bryant, *Memoirs of a Country Girl*, 160–61; and Holly Smith, "Curriculum Designed to Fit Individual," *Richmond Times-Dispatch*, April 22, 1974: 1.
10. Bryant, *Memoirs of a Country Girl*, 160–61; and Holly Smith, "Curriculum Designed to Fit Individual," *Richmond Times-Dispatch*, April 22, 1974: 1.
11. Holly Smith, "Curriculum Designed to Fit Individual," *Richmond Times-Dispatch*, April 22, 1974: 1.
12. Bryant, *Memoirs of a Country Girl*, 163–64.
13. Bryant, *Memoirs of a Country Girl*, 163–64.
14. "Integration: How Far Are We," *Charlottesville Observer*, March 15–21, 1984: 3.
15. Hadden and Erickson, "Charlottesville"; and Kirshstein and Wilken, *High School Education in Charlottesville*.
16. Kirshstein and Wilken, "High School Education in Charlottesville"; and Rodgers, "Report on Race, Class, and Socioeconomic Status of Students."
17. Hyres and Steele, "Reimagining the High School Experience," 1–5.
18. Bryant, *Memoirs of a Country Girl*, 163–64; and Julie Young, "'Challenge' Awaits Garrett at High School," *Daily Progress*, May 16, 1983.
19. "Charlottesville High School Reopened Today After Defiant Students Were Sent Home," *United Press International*, March 6, 1984; "Charlottesville High

Reopens as Racial Tension Eases," *Washington Post*, March 7, 1984; and Dan Genest and Kathy Hoke, "School's Problems Probed," *Daily Progress*, March 7, 1984.

20. "Charlottesville High School Reopened Today After Defiant Students Were Sent Home," *United Press International*, March 6, 1984; "Charlottesville High Reopens as Racial Tension Eases," *Washington Post*, March 7, 1984; and Dan Genest and Kathy Hoke, "School's Problems Probed," *Daily Progress*, March 7, 1984.

21. "Charlottesville High Reopens as Racial Tension Eases," *Washington Post*, March 7, 1984; Diane Price, interview with Danielle Wingfield and Gabriel Benn; Dan Genest and Kathy Hoke, "School's Problems Probed," *Daily Progress*, March 7, 1984; and Julie Young, "CHS Settles Into Normal Routine," *Daily Progress*, March 8, 1984.

22. "Integration: How Far Are We," *Charlottesville Observer*, March 15–21, 1984: 3.

23. Cynthia Stratton, "CHS Student Newspaper Inflames Racial Tension; NAACP Calls for Journalistic Integrity," *Charlottesville Observer*, March 8, 1984: 2.

24. Bryant, *Memoirs of a Country Girl*, 178–79.

25. Bryant, *Memoirs of a Country Girl*, 179; and "People Around Town," *Charlottesville Observer*, June 7, 1984.

26. Templin, "Race Relations and Education in Charlottesville," 8.

27. Templin, "Race Relations and Education in Charlottesville," 8.

28. Templin, "Race Relations and Education in Charlottesville," 8.

29. Diane Price, interview with Danielle Wingfield and Gabriel Benn.

30. Diane Price, interview with Danielle Wingfield and Gabriel Benn.

31. Diane Price, interview with Danielle Wingfield and Gabriel Benn.

32. Diane Price, interview with Danielle Wingfield and Gabriel Benn; and Hampton, "Eyes on the Prize: America's Civil Rights Movement."

33. Emily Smith Gray, "Teacher," *Charlottesville Observer*, August 16, 1984: 7; and Diane Price, interview with Danielle Wingfield and Gabriel Benn.

34. Emily Smith Gray, "Teacher," *Charlottesville Observer*, August 16, 1984: 7–8; and Diane Price, interview with Danielle Wingfield and Gabriel Benn.

35. Meredith Grabois, "CHS Coach Celebrates Miles Stone with Black Knights," *Charlottesville Observer*, October 19, 1999.

36. Meredith Grabois, "CHS Coach Celebrates Miles Stone with Black Knights," *Charlottesville Observer*, October 19, 1999.

37. Wilbert T. Lewis, interview with Derrick Alridge and Alexander Hyres.

38. Wilbert T. Lewis, interview with Derrick Alridge and Alexander Hyres.

39. Wilbert T. Lewis, interview with Derrick Alridge and Alexander Hyres.

40. "People Around Town," *Charlottesville Observer*, August 30, 1984.

41. Chris Edwards McNett, "CHS's New Principal Preaching a Message of Student Potential," *Charlottesville Observer*, August 17–23, 1989.

42. Patricia Edwards, interview by Kelly Martin and Alexander Hyres.

43. On this period of school reform, see Vinovskis, *From A Nation at Risk to No Child Left Behind*; and Schneider, *Excellence for All*.

44. Gray, "Teacher," *Charlottesville Observer*, August 16, 1984: 7; Diane Price, interview with Danielle Wingfield and Gabriel Benn; and Ladson-Billings, *The Dreamkeepers*.

45. Wilbert T. Lewis, interview with Derrick Alridge and Alexander Hyres; and "Wilbert Thomas Lewis, Jr.," *Daily Progress*, April 15, 2016.

46. Wilbert T. Lewis, interview with Derrick Alridge and Alexander Hyres; and "Wilbert Thomas Lewis, Jr.," *Daily Progress*, April 15, 2016.

Conclusion

First epigraph is from Hawes Spencer and Michael Levenson, "Charlottesville Removes Robert E. Lee Statue at Center of White Nationalist Rally," *New York Times*, July 9, 2021, https://www.nytimes.com/2021/07/09/us/charlottesville-confederate-monuments-lee.html; and Ben Paviour, "Charlottesville Removes Robert E. Lee Statue that Sparked a Deadly Rally," National Public Radio, July 10, 2021, https://www.npr.org/2021/07/10/1014926659/charlottesville-removes-robert-e-lee-statue-that-sparked-a-deadly-rally. Second epigraph is from Berdell Fleming, interview with Chenyu Wang and Derrick Alridge.

1. Hyres, "Dedication to the Highest of Callings," 148–65.

2. Hyres, "Barbara Johns and Beyond," 461–63; Graham Moomaw, "Charlottesville 12 Recall Experiences," *Daily Progress*, November 20, 2011: 6; and "Black History Pathway Finally Unveiled," https://www.cbs19news.com/story/48686710/black-history-pathway-finally-unveiled.

3. "Burley Alumni Celebrate School's Legacy with New Plaque," *Daily Progress*, April 16, 2022, https://dailyprogress.com/news/local/education/a-landmark-moment-burley-alumni-celebrate-schools-legacy-with-new-plaque/article_67a567f0-bdc6-11ec-b421-b7c72a1d79b1.html; and "Jackson P. Burley High School Monument Wall," The Historical Marker Database, https://www.hmdb.org/m.asp?m=246956.

4. Zyahna Bryant, "Change the Name of Lee Park and Remove the Statue," Change.Org Petition, 2016, accessed August 18, 2024, https://www.change.org/p/charlottesville-city-council-change-the-name-of-lee-park-and-remove-the-statue-in-charlottesville-va.

5. In Charlottesville, the City Council and related committees studied the physical landscape. These efforts led to the removal of the Lee statue as well as the

Stonewall Jackson statue also located in the downtown area. In 2020, at the University of Virginia, the School of Education removed the name of J. L. M. Curry—an avowed racist without any previous connection to the university. On the name change of the School of Education, see "Board of Visitors Votes to Drop 'Curry' from School Name," https://education.virginia.edu/news-stories/board-visitors-votes-drop-curry-school-name. In 2024, UVA renamed the undergraduate library from Edwin Alderman, the first UVA president who supported eugenics and spoke at the dedication of the Lee statue, to Edgar Shannon, the university's fourth president. On the library's name change, see Cecilia Mould, "Community Members React to the Renaming of Alderman Library to Shannon Library," *Cavalier Daily*, March 19, 2024, accessed August 18, 2024, https://www.cavalierdaily.com/article/2024/03/community-members-react-to-renaming-of-alderman-library-to-shannon-library#google_vignette.

6. Zyahna Bryant, "Change the Name of Lee Park and Remove the Statue," Change.Org Petition, 2016, accessed August 18, 2024, https://www.change.org/p/charlottesville-city-council-change-the-name-of-lee-park-and-remove-the-statue-in-charlottesville-va. On the experience and perspective of Wes Bellamy on the statue and politics in Charlottesville, see Bellamy, *Monumental*.

7. "Charlottesville High School," *Segregation Explorer*, accessed May 17, 2024, https://edopportunity.org/segregation/explorer/.

8. Debbie Truong, "An Online Threat of Violence Shuts Down All Charlottesville Schools," *Washington Post*, March 21, 2019, https://www.washingtonpost.com/local/education/an-online-threat-of-violence-shuts-down-all-charlottesville-schools/2019/03/21/9a94e124-4c02-11e9-9663-00ac73f49662_story.html; "BSU Walkout," YouTube, March 14, 2019, accessed September 2, 2022, https://www.youtube.com/watch?v=zW7QzNAh15k; and Alexander Hyres, "Why Charlottesville Students Walked Out—And What It Will Take To Keep Them From Doing It Again," *Washington Post, Made by History*, April 2, 2019, https://www.washingtonpost.com/outlook/2019/04/02/why-charlottesville-students-walked-out-what-it-will-take-keep-them-doing-it-again/.

9. "BSU Walkout," YouTube, March 14, 2019, accessed September 2, 2022, https://www.youtube.com/watch?v=zW7QzNAh15k.

10. "BSU Walkout," YouTube, March 14, 2019, accessed September 2, 2022, https://www.youtube.com/watch?v=zW7QzNAh15k.

11. "BSU Walkout" YouTube, March 14, 2019, accessed September 2, 2022, https://www.youtube.com/watch?v=zW7QzNAh15k.

12. "BSU Walkout," YouTube, March 14, 2019, accessed September 2, 2022, https://www.youtube.com/watch?v=zW7QzNAh15k.

13. Holden, *The Bus Stops Here*, 87–89.

14. Ginny Bixby, "Charlottesville High School Students Walk Out, Demand Action Following Texas School Shooting," *Daily Progress*, May 26, 2022, accessed January 4, 2023, https://dailyprogress.com/news/local/education/charlottesville-high-school-students-walk-out-demand-action-following-texas-school-shooting/article_ef59d656-dd45-11ec-bd5a-2f7e690c0b54.html; and Alexia Williams, "CHS Students Walk Out to Protest Against Youngkin's Transgender Policy," *CBS 19 News*, September 29, 2022, accessed January 4, 2023, https://www.cbs19news.com/story/47390107/charlottesville-high-school-walkout.

15. Hawes Spencer and Michael Levenson, "Charlottesville Removes Robert E. Lee Statue at Center of White Nationalist Rally," *New York Times*, July 9, 2021, https://www.nytimes.com/2021/07/09/us/charlottesville-confederate-monuments-lee.html; and Ben Paviour, "Charlottesville Removes Robert E. Lee Statue That Sparked A Deadly Rally," National Public Radio, July 10, 2021, https://www.npr.org/2021/07/10/1014926659/charlottesville-removes-robert-e-lee-statue-that-sparked-a-deadly-rally.

BIBLIOGRAPHY

Archival and Manuscript Collections

Charlottesville, Virginia

Albert and Shirley Small Special Collections Library at the University of Virginia
Charlottesville City Schools Division Archive and Board Papers
Charlottesville High School Library and Media Center
The Edgar Shannon Library at the University of Virginia
The Jefferson School African American Heritage Center

Films and Videos

Dickerson, Lorenzo. "Color Line of Scrimmage: Recounting the Champion 1956 Burley Bears." DVD.
Dickerson, Lorenzo, and Jordy Yaeger. "Raised/Razed." PBS, Virginia.
Hampton, Harry. "Eyes on the Prize: America's Civil Rights Movement." PBS, United States.
Toppin, Edgar Allan. "Americans from Africa: A History—Teacher's Manual, TV Lesson Guides." Richmond, Virginia, 1968.

Oral History Interviews by Teachers in the Movement

Anderson, Corlis, interview with Chenyu Wang, February 1, 2018.
Boyd, Lynn, interview with Danielle Wingfield, January 31, 2018.
Bryant, Florence Coleman, interview with Lindsey Jones, Derrick Alridge, and Alexander Hyres, December 19, 2014.
Bryant, James, interview with Danielle Wingfield, January 30, 2018.
Carter, Ann Wicks, interview with James Bryant, January 26, 2023.
Edwards, Patricia, interview with Kelly Martin and Alexander Hyres, September 19, 2017.
Fleming, Berdell, interview by Chenyu Wang and Derrick Alridge, January 29, 2018.

Gaines, John, interview with Nora Ferguson and Danielle Wingfield, September 19, 2017.
Lee, Druscilla, interview with Alexander Hyres, September 19, 2017.
Lewis, Wilbert T., interview with Derrick Alridge and Alexander Hyres, April 22, 2015.
Logan, Clevester, interview with Derrick Alridge and Nora Ferguson, September 19, 2017.
Price, Diane, interview with Danielle Wingfield and Gabriel Benn, September 19, 2017.
Price, Teresa, interview with Derrick Alridge and Chenyu Wang, September 20, 2017.
Vasser, Esther, interview with James Bryant and Derrick Alridge, September 10, 2022.

Oral History Interview Collections by Others

"From Porch Swings to Patios," Department of Community Planning, Charlottesville, Va.
"Jefferson School Interviews, Volume 1 and 2," The Jefferson School African American Heritage Center, Charlottesville, Va.
"No Playbook: School Integration During Massive Resistance," Albemarle Historical Society.
Planning Advisory Board and Students of the University of Virginia, Charlottesville, Va., 1982–1984.
"Ridge Street Oral History Project," Preservation Piedmont for the Department of Community Planning, Charlottesville, Va., December 1995.

Newspapers and Media

Blast
CBS 19 News
Charlottesville Observer
Daily Progress
Free Lance Star
The Hook
Jeffersonian
Knight Time Review
Lanetime

National Public Radio
Negro History Bulletin
New York Times
Reflector
Richmond Times-Dispatch
Segregation Explorer
Southern Workman
Washington Post
United Press International

Unpublished Manuscripts, Dissertations, Theses, and Government Documents

Alridge, Derrick, Alexander Hyres, Danielle Wingfield, and Chenyu Wang. "Black Teachers in the Long Civil Rights Movement: A Historiography" (under review).

Barksdale, James Worsham. "A Comparative Study of Contemporary White and Negro Standards in Health, Education, and Welfare, Charlottesville, Virginia." MA thesis, University of Virginia, 1949.

Bryant, Florence Coleman. "One Story about School Desegregation." Charlottesville, Va., 2004.

Buck, J. L. Blair. "The Development of Public Schools in Virginia, 1607–1952." Richmond: Commonwealth of Virginia State Board of Education, 1952.

Burks, Benjamin D. "What Was Normal about Virginia's Normal Schools: A History of Virginia's State Normal Schools, 1882–1930." PhD diss., University of Virginia, 2002.

Carkin, Philena. *The Reminiscences of Philena Carkin, 1866–1875*, Accession #11123, Albert and Shirley Small Special Collections, University of Virginia Library, Charlottesville, Va.

Conway, Ismail A. "Central Virginia Dreamkeepers: Narratives of African-American Teachers That Taught Before, During and After the *Brown v. Topeka, Kansas Board of Education* Decision." PhD diss., University of Virginia, 2000.

Crowe, Dallas R. "Desegregation of Charlottesville, Virginia Public Schools, 1954–1969: A Case Study." PhD diss., University of Virginia, 1971.

Cunningham, Candace. "'I Hope They Fire Me': Black Teachers in the Fight for Equal Education, 1910–1970." PhD diss., University of South Carolina, 2018.

De Corse, Helen Camp. "Charlottesville—a Study of Negro Life and Personality." MA thesis, University of Virginia, 1933.

Foster, Carmen. "Tension, Resistance, and Transition: School Desegregation in Richmond's North Side, 1960–63." EdD diss., University of Virginia, 2014.

Gaston, Paul, and Thomas T. Hammond. "Public School Desegregation: Charlottesville, Virginia, 1955–62." Conference on "The South: The Ethical Demands of Integration," Nashville, Tennessee, 1962.

Hadden, Jeffrey K., and Edwin E. Erickson. "Charlottesville: What We Say, What We Do, What We Hope For." Final Report of the Charlottesville Goals Study Central Piedmont Urban Observatory, 1975.

Harland Bartholomew & Associates. *Master Plan, Charlottesville, Virginia*. Atlanta, 1959.

Holt, Hunter. "Runaway Growth: A History of Development, Schools, and Wealth in Williamson County, Tennessee." PhD diss., University of Virginia, 2023.

Irwin, Marjorie Felice. "The Negro in Charlottesville and Albemarle County, an Explanatory Study." MA thesis, University of Virginia, 1929.

Johnson, Alexis. "'It Was a Time When Real Change Was Envisioned as Possible': Black Students and the San Francisco Bay Area Black Education Movement, 1961–1969." PhD diss., University of Virginia, 2023.

Jones, Thomas Jesse. *Negro Education: A Study of the Private and Higher Schools for Colored People in the United States*. Washington, D.C.: Department of the Interior, U.S. Bureau of Education, 1916.

Kirshstein, Rita J., and Paul H. Wilken. *High School Education in Charlottesville: A Survey of Values and Goals*. Charlottesville, Va., 1978.

Lee, Lauranett Lorraine. "Crucible in the Classroom: The Freedpeople and Their Teachers Charlottesville, Virginia, 1861–1876." PhD diss., University of Virginia, 2002.

May, Eleanor G., and Margo E. Hauck. "Impact of the University of Virginia on Charlottesville and Albemarle County," May 1981.

McCullum, Kristan. "Blue Hollers: A Pedagogy of Space and the Scale of Black Freedom in Kentucky Appalachia." PhD diss., University of Virginia, 2023.

Mearns, Edward A. *Civil Rights U.S.A.: Public Schools, Southern States: Virginia*. Washington, D.C.: U.S. Government Printing Office, 1962.

Nocera, Amato, and Alexander Hyres. "'A Rebel with a Cause': Ruby Gainer, Black Educators, and the Long-*Brown* Era."

Porter, Lucille Lorett. "Curriculum Transitions at Hampton Normal and Agricultural Institute, 1868–1927." PhD diss., University of Wisconsin—Madison, 2010.

Rabin, Yale. "West Main Street Charlottesville, Virginia: Present Conditions and Future Prospects." Central Piedmont Urban Observatory, July 1977.

Reese, Mary. "Race Relations and Employment in Charlottesville." Report of the Social Development Commission and Subcommittee on Race Relations and Employment, October 1985.

Salmonowicz, Michael J. "Race and Education in a Southern School System: An Organizational History of Charlottesville City Schools, 1985–2011." PhD diss., University of Virginia, 2013.

Templin, Robert. "Race Relations and Education in Charlottesville." Report of the Social Development Commission/School Board and Task Force on Race Relations and Education, October 1985.

Whitlock, James W., et al. *Charlottesville Pattern for School Improvement: A Survey Report*. Nashville: Division of Surveys and Field Services, George Peabody College for Teachers, 1973.

Wingfield-Smith, Danielle. "Navigating the 'Virginia Way': Henry L. Marsh, III, Civil Rights, and Movement Leadership." PhD diss., University of Virginia, 2018.

Yancy, R. A., et al. "Proposed Merger of Charlottesville and Albemarle County," 1969.

Yearbooks

The Chain, Charlottesville High School, 1974–1990, Charlottesville, Va.
The Chain, Lane High School, 1959–1974, Charlottesville, Va.
The Crimson, Jefferson High School, 1926–1951, Charlottesville, Va.
Jay Pee Bee, Jackson P. Burley High School, 1951–1967, Charlottesville, Va.

Articles and Books

Alkalimat, Abdul. *The History of Black Studies*. London: Pluto Press, 2021.

Alridge, Derrick P. *The Educational Thought of W. E. B. Du Bois: An Intellectual History*. New York: Teachers College Press, 2009.

———. "On the Education of Black Folk: W. E. B. Du Bois and the Paradox of Segregation." *The Journal of African American History* 100, no. 3 (2015): 473–93.

———. "Teachers in the Movement: Pedagogy, Activism, and Freedom." *History of Education Quarterly* 60, no. 1 (2020): 1–23.

Alridge, Derrick P., Jon N. Hale, Tondra Loder-Jackson, eds. *Schooling the Movement: The Activism of Southern Black Educators from Reconstruction through the Civil Rights Era*. Columbia: The University of South Carolina Press, 2023.

Alridge, Derrick P., Adah Ward Randolph, and Alexis M. Johnson. "African American Historians of Education and the Griot's Craft: A Historiography." *History of Education Quarterly* 63, no. 1 (2023): 3–31.

Anderson, James D. *The Education of Blacks in the South, 1860–1935*. Chapel Hill: The University of North Carolina Press, 1988.

Angus, David L., and Jeffrey Mirel. *The Failed Promise of the American High School, 1890–1995*. New York: Teachers College Press, 1999.

Baker, R. Scott. *Paradoxes of Desegregation: African American Struggles for Educational Equity in Charleston, South Carolina, 1926–1972*. Columbia: The University of South Carolina Press, 2006.

———. "Pedagogies of Protest: African American Teachers and the History of the Civil Rights Movement, 1940–1963." *Teachers College Record* 113, no. 12 (2011): 2777–803.

———. "Testing Equality: The National Teacher Examination and the NAACP's Legal Campaign to Equalize Teachers' Salaries in the South, 1936–63." *History of Education Quarterly* 35, no. 1 (Spring 1995): 49–64.

Baumgartner, Kabria. "'Be Your Own Man': Student Activism and the Birth of Black Studies at Amherst College, 1965–1972." *The New England Quarterly* 89, no. 2 (2016): 286–322.

———. *In Pursuit of Knowledge: Black Women and Educational Activism in Antebellum America*. New York: NYU Press, 2022.

———. "Love and Justice: African American Women, Education, and Protest in Antebellum New England." *Journal of Social History* 52, no. 3 (2019): 652–76.

———. "Searching for Sarah: Black Girlhood, Education, and the Archive." *History of Education Quarterly* 60, no. 1 (2020): 73–85.

Beauboeuf-Lafontant, Tamara. "A Movement Against and Beyond Boundaries: Politically Relevant Teaching among African American Teachers." *Teachers College Record* 100, no. 4 (1999): 702–23.

———. "A Womanist Experience of Caring: Understanding the Pedagogy of Exemplary Black Women Teachers." *The Urban Review* 34, no. 1 (2002): 71–86.

Bellamy, Wes. *Monumental: It Was Never About a Statue*. San Bernardino: BlackGold Publishing, 2019.

Berghel, Susan Eckelmann, Sara Fieldston, and Paul M. Renfro, eds. *Growing Up America: Youth and Politics Since 1945*. Athens: University of Georgia Press, 2019.

Biondi, Martha. *The Black Revolution on Campus*. Berkeley: University of California Press, 2012.

Bonastia, Christopher. "Black Leadership and Outside Allies in Virginia Freedom Schools." *History of Education Quarterly* 56, no. 4 (2016): 532–59.

———. *Southern Stalemate: Five Years without Public Education in Prince Edward County, Virginia*. Chicago: University of Chicago Press, 2011.

Boyle, Sarah-Patton. *The Desegregated Heart: A Virginian's Stand in Time of Transition*. Charlottesville: University of Virginia Press, 2001.

Bradley, Stefan M. *Harlem vs. Columbia University: Black Student Power in the Late 1960s*. Urbana: University of Illinois Press, 2010.

———. *Upending the Ivory Tower: Civil Rights, Black Power, and the Ivy League*. New York: NYU Press, 2018.

Brooks, Clayton McClure. *The Uplift Generation: Cooperation Across the Color Line in Early Twentieth-Century Virginia*. Charlottesville: University of Virginia Press, 2017.

Brown-Nagin, Tomiko. *Courage to Dissent: Atlanta and the Long History of the Civil Rights Movement*. New York: Oxford University Press, 2011.

Bryant, Florence Coleman. *Memoirs of a Country Girl*. New York: Vantage Press, 1988.

———. *Rebecca Fuller McGinness: A Lifetime, 1892–2000*. Charlottesville: The Van Soren Company, 2001.

Bryant, Zyahna. *Reclaim. A Collection of Poetry and Essays*. Charlottesville: Self-Published, 2019.

Burkholder, Zoë. *An African American Dilemma: A History of School Integration and Civil Rights in the North*. New York: Oxford University Press, 2021.

———. *Color in the Classroom: How American Schools Taught Race, 1900–1954*. New York: Oxford University Press, 2011.

———. "From Forced Tolerance to Forced Busing: Wartime Intercultural Education and the Rise of Black Educational Activism in Boston." *Harvard Educational Review* 80, no. 3 (2010): 293–327.

———. "From 'Wops and Dagoes and Hunkies' to 'Caucasian': Changing Racial Discourse in American Classrooms during World War II." *History of Education Quarterly* 50, no. 3 (2010): 324–58.

———. "'Integrated Out of Existence': African American Debates Over School Integration Versus Separation at the Bordentown School in New Jersey, 1886–1955." *Journal of Social History* 51, no. 1 (2017): 47–79.

———. "The Perils of Integration: Conflicting Northern Black Responses to the Coleman Report in the Black Power Era, 1966–1974." *History of Education Quarterly* 57, no. 4 (2017): 579–90.

Butchart, Ronald E. "'Outthinking and Outflanking the Owners of the World': A Historiography of the African American Struggle for Education." *History of Education Quarterly* 28, no. 3 (1988): 333–66.

———. *Schooling the Freed People: Teaching, Learning, and the Struggle for Black Freedom, 1861–1876*. Chapel Hill: The University of North Carolina Press, 2010.

Butchart, Ronald E., and Amy F. Rolleri. "Secondary Education and Emancipation: Secondary Schools for Freed Slaves in the American South, 1862–1875." *Paedagogica Historica* 40, nos. 1–2 (2004): 157–81.

Bynum, Thomas L. *NAACP Youth and the Fight for Black Freedom, 1936–1965*. Knoxville: The University of Tennessee Press, 2013.

Carson, Clayborne. *In Struggle: SNCC and the Black Awakening of the 1960s*. Cambridge: Harvard University Press, 1981.

Caruthers, Loyce, and Bradley Poos. "Narratives of Lincoln High School African American Graduates in Kansas City, Missouri." *Journal of Black Studies* 46, no. 6 (2015): 626–49.

Cecelski, David S. *Along Freedom Road: Hyde County, North Carolina and the Fate of Black Schools in the South*. Chapel Hill: The University of North Carolina Press, 1994.

Cha-Jua, Sundiata Keita, and Clarence Lang. "The 'Long Movement' as Vampire: Temporal and Spatial Fallacies in Recent Black Freedom Studies." *The Journal of African American History* 92, no. 2 (2007): 265–88.

Chilcoat, George W., and Jerry A. Ligon. "Discussion as a Means for Transformative Change: Social Studies Lessons from the Mississippi Freedom Schools." *Social Studies* 92, no. 5 (October 9, 2001): 213–19.

———. "'Helping to Make Democracy a Living Reality': The Curriculum Conference of the Mississippi Freedom." *Journal of Curriculum & Supervision* 15, no. 1 (1999): 43–68.

———. "Theatre as an Emancipatory Tool: Classroom Drama in the Mississippi Freedom Schools." *Journal of Curriculum Studies* 30, no. 5 (September 1998): 515–43.

———. "'We Talk Here. This Is a School for Talking.' Participatory Democracy from the Classroom out into the Community: How Discussion Was Used in the Mississippi Freedom Schools." *Curriculum Inquiry* 28, no. 2 (1998): 165–93.

Clemons, Kristal Moore. "I've Got to Do Something for My People: Black Women Teachers of the 1964 Mississippi Freedom Schools." *The Western Journal of Black Studies* 38, no. 3 (2014): 141–54.

Cole, Eddie R. *The Campus Color Line: College Presidents and the Struggle for Black Freedom*. Princeton: Princeton University Press, 2020.

Cole, Eddie R., and Cameron L. Burris-Greene. "Black Higher Education: A Historiography of Perseverance and Triumph." In *Higher Education: Handbook of Theory and Research: Volume 39*, edited by L. W. Perna, 1–53. Cham: Springer Nature Switzerland, 2023.

Coleman, Arica, L. *That the Blood Stay Pure: African Americans, Native Americans, and the Predicament of Race and Identity in Virginia*. Bloomington: Indiana University Press, 2013.

Cuban, Larry. *How Teachers Taught: Constancy and Change in American Classrooms, 1890–1980*. New York: Longman, 1993.

———. "Persistent Instruction: The High School Classroom, 1900–1980." *The Phi Delta Kappan* 64, no. 2 (1982): 113–18.

Cunningham, Candace. "'Hell Is Popping Here in South Carolina': Orangeburg County Black Teachers and Their Community in the Immediate Post-Brown Era." *History of Education Quarterly* 61, no. 1 (2021): 35–62.

Cyna, Esther. "Equalizing Resources vs. Retaining Black Political Power: Paradoxes of an Urban-Suburban School District Merger in Durham, North Carolina, 1958–1996." *History of Education Quarterly* 59, no. 1 (2019): 35–64.

———. "Schooling the Kleptocracy: Racism and School Finance in Rural North Carolina, 1900–2018." *Journal of American History* 108, no. 4 (2022): 745–66.

Danns, Dionne. "Black Student Empowerment and Chicago: School Reform Efforts in 1968." *Urban Education* 37, no. 5 (2002): 631–55.

———. "Chicago High School Students' Movement for Quality Public Education, 1966–1971." *The Journal of African American History* 88, no. 2 (2003): 138–50.

———. *Crossing Segregated Boundaries: Remembering Chicago School Desegregation*. New Brunswick: Rutgers University Press, 2020.

———. *Desegregating Chicago's Public Schools: Policy Implementation, Politics, and Protest, 1965–1985*. New York: Springer, 2014.

———. *Something Better for Our Children: Black Organizing in Chicago Public Schools, 1963–1971*. New York: Psychology Press, 2003.

———. "Thriving in the Midst of Adversity: Educator Maudelle Brown Bousfield's Struggles in Chicago, 1920–1950." *Journal of Negro Education* 78, no. 1 (2009): 3–16.

Danns, Dionne, Michelle A. Purdy, and Christopher M. Span, eds. *Using Past as Prologue: Contemporary Perspectives on African American Educational History*. Charlotte: Information Age Publishing, Inc., 2015.

Daugherity, Brian J. *Keep On Keeping On: The NAACP and the Implementation of Brown v. Board of Education in Virginia*. Charlottesville: University of Virginia Press, 2016.

Daugherity, Brian J., and Charles C. Bolton, eds. *With All Deliberate Speed: Implementing Brown v. Board of Education*. Fayetteville: University of Arkansas Press, 2008.

Daugherity, Brian J., and Brian Grogan, eds. *A Little Child Shall Lead Them: A Documentary Account of the Struggle for School Desegregation in Prince Edward County, Virginia*—Charlottesville: University of Virginia Press, 2019.

Davison, Douglas M. *Reading, Writing, and Race: The Desegregation of the Charlotte Schools*. Chapel Hill: The University of North Carolina Press, 1995.

Delmont, Matthew F. "The Plight of the 'Able Student': Ruth Wright Hayre and the Struggle for Equality in Philadelphia's Black High Schools, 1955–1965." *History of Education Quarterly* 50, no. 2 (May 2010): 204–30.

———. *Why Busing Failed: Race, Media, and the National Resistance to School Desegregation*. Oakland: University of California Press, 2016.

Dennis, Ashley D. "'The Intellectual Emancipation of the Negro': Madeline Morgan and the Mandatory Black History Curriculum in Chicago during World War II." *History of Education Quarterly* 62, no. 2 (2022): 136–60.

Devlin, Rachel. *A Girl Stands at the Door: The Generation of Young Women Who Desegregated America's Schools*. New York: Basic Books, 2018.

Dewing, Rolland. "Teacher Organizations and Desegregation." *The Phi Delta Kappan* 49, no. 5 (1968): 257–60.

Dingus, Jeannine. "'Doing the Best We Could': African American Teachers' Counterstory on School Desegregation." *Urban Review* 38, no. 3 (September 2006): 211–33.

Dougherty, Jack. "From Anecdote to Analysis: Oral Interviews and New Scholarship in Educational History." *The Journal of American History* 86, no. 2 (1999): 712–23.

———. *More Than One Struggle: The Evolution of Black School Reform in Milwaukee*. Chapel Hill: The University of North Carolina Press, 2004.

———. "'That's When We Were Marching for Jobs': Black Teachers and the Early Civil Rights Movement in Milwaukee." *History of Education Quarterly* 38, no. 2 (1998): 121–41.

Douglas, Andrea, Scot French, Paul M. Gaston, Patrice Preston-Grimes, and Lauranett L. Lee, eds., *Pride Overcomes Prejudice: A History of Charlottesville's African American School*. Charlottesville: The Jefferson School African American Heritage Center, 2013.

Driskell, Jay Winston. *Schooling Jim Crow: The Fight for Atlanta's Booker T. Washington High School and the Roots of Black Protest Politics*. Charlottesville: University of Virginia Press, 2014.

Du Bois, W. E. B. *Black Reconstruction in America*. New York: Free Press, 1998.

———. "Does the Negro Need Separate Schools?" *The Journal of Negro Education* 4, no. 3 (1935): 328–35.

Ellison, Ralph. *Invisible Man*. New York: Random House, 1952.

Erickson, Ansley T. "Building Inequality: The Spatial Organization of Schooling in Nashville, Tennessee, after Brown." *Journal of Urban History* 38, no. 2 (2012): 247–70.
———. "Case Study as Common Text: Collaborating In and Broadening the Reach of History of Education." *History of Education Quarterly* 56, no. 1 (2016): 125–33.
———. "Desegregation's Architects: Education Parks and the Spatial Ideology of Schooling." *History of Education Quarterly* 56, no. 4 (2016): 560–89.
———. "How/Should We Generalize?" *History of Education Quarterly* 60, no. 1 (2020): 86–97.
———. *Making the Unequal Metropolis: School Desegregation and Its Limits*. University of Chicago Press, 2016.
Erickson, Ansley T., and Ernest Morrell, eds. *Educating Harlem: A Century of Schooling and Resistance in a Black Community*. New York: Columbia University Press, 2019.
Ewing, Eve L. *Ghosts in the Schoolyard: Racism and School Closings on Chicago's South Side*. Chicago: The University of Chicago Press: 2018.
Fader, Daniel N., and Elton B. McNeil, *Hooked On Books: Program and Proof*. New York: Berkeley Medallion Books, 1967.
Fairclough, Adam. "'Beine in the Field of Education and Also Being a Negro ... Seems ... Tragic': Black Teachers in the Jim Crow South." *The Journal of American History* 87, no. 1 (2000): 65–91.
———. *A Class of Their Own: Black Teachers in the Segregated South*. Cambridge: Belknap Press of Harvard University Press, 2007.
———. "The Costs of Brown: Black Teachers and School Integration." *The Journal of American History* 91, no. 1 (2004): 43–55.
———. *Race & Democracy: The Civil Rights Struggle in Louisiana, 1915–1972*. Athens: University of Georgia Press, 2008.
———. *Teaching Equality: Black Schools in the Age of Jim Crow*. Athens: University of Georgia Press, 2001.
Fenderson, Jonathan, James Stewart, and Kabria Baumgartner. "Expanding the History of the Black Studies Movement: Some Prefatory Notes." *Journal of African American Studies* 16 (2012): 1–20.
Fenwick, Leslie T. *Jim Crow's Pink Slip: The Untold Story of Black Principal and Teacher Leadership*. Cambridge: Harvard Education Press, 2022.
Foster, Michèle. *Black Teachers on Teaching*. New York: New Press, 1997.
Fountain, Aaron. "Building a Student Movement in Naptown: The Corn Cob Curtain Controversy, Free Speech, and the 1960s and 1970s High School Student Activism in Indianapolis." *Indiana Magazine of History* 114, no. 3 (2018): 202–37.

Franklin, John H. *From Slavery to Freedom: A History of Negro Americans.* 3rd ed. New York: Alfred A. Knopf, 1967.

Franklin, Vincent P. "In Memoriam, Edgar Allan Toppin, Ph.D." *The Journal of African American History* (2004): 187.

———. "Patterns of Student Activism at Historically Black Universities in the United States and South Africa, 1960–1977." *The Journal of African American History* 88, no. 2 (April 2003): 204–17.

———. "'They Rose and Fell Together': African American Educators and Community Leadership, 1795–1954." *Journal of Education* 172, no. 3 (1990): 39–64.

———. *The Young Crusaders: The Untold Story of the Children and Teenagers Who Galvanized the Civil Rights Movement.* Boston: Beacon Press, 2021.

Franklin, Vincent P., and James D. Anderson. *New Perspectives on Black Educational History.* New York: G. K. Hall and Co., 1978.

Freeman, R. B. "Political Power, Desegregation, and Employment of Black Schoolteachers." *Journal of Political Economy* 85, no. 2 (1977): 299–322.

French, Scot A. "African American Civic Activism and the Making of Jefferson High School, 1865–1922." In *Pride Overcomes Prejudice: A History of Charlottesville's African American School*, edited by Andrea Douglas, Scot French, Paul M. Gaston, Patrice Preston-Grimes, and Lauranett L. Lee, 31–63. Charlottesville: The Jefferson School African American Heritage Center, 2013.

Fultz, Michael. "African-American Teachers in the South, 1890–1940: Growth, Feminization, and Salary Discrimination." *Teachers College Record* 96, no. 3 (1995): 1–25.

———. "African American Teachers in the South, 1890–1940: Powerlessness and the Ironies of Expectations and Protest." *History of Education Quarterly* 35, no. 4 (1995): 401–22.

———. "'As Is the Teacher, So Is the School': Future Directions in the Historiography of African American Teachers." *Rethinking the History of American Education* (2008): 73–102.

———. "The Displacement of Black Educators Post-Brown: An Overview and Analysis." *History of Education Quarterly* 44, no. 1 (2004): 11–45.

———. "'The Morning Cometh': African-American Periodicals, Education, and the Black Middle Class, 1900–1930." *The Journal of Negro History* 80, no. 3 (1995): 97–112.

———. "Teacher Training and African American Education in the South, 1900–1940." *The Journal of Negro Education* 64, no. 2 (1995): 196–210.

Gaston, Paul. *"Sitting In" in the 'Sixties: An Historian's Memoir.* Charlottesville: Self-published, 1999.

Givens, Jarvis R. *Fugitive Pedagogy: Carter G. Woodson and the Art of Black Teaching.* Cambridge: Harvard University Press, 2021.

———. "'He Was, Undoubtedly, a Wonderful Character': Black Teachers' Representations of Nat Turner during Jim Crow." *Souls* 18, nos. 2–4 (2016): 215–34.

———. *School Clothes: A Collective Memoir of Black Student Witness.* Boston: Beacon Press, 2023.

———. "'There Would Be No Lynching If It Did Not Start in the Schoolroom': Carter G. Woodson and the Occasion of Negro History Week, 1926–1950." *American Educational Research Journal* 56, no. 4 (2019): 1457–94.

Givens, Jarvis R., and Ashley Ison. "Toward New Beginnings: A Review of Native, White, and Black American Education through the 19th Century." *Review of Educational Research* 93, no. 3 (2023): 319–52.

Goldstein, Dana. *The Teacher Wars: A History of America's Most Embattled Profession.* New York: Doubleday, 2014.

Gordon-Reed, Annette. *The Hemingses of Monticello: An American Family.* New York: W. W. Norton & Company, 2008.

Graham, Gael. *Young Activists: American High School Students in the Age of Protest.* DeKalb: Northern Illinois University Press, 2006.

Green, Hilary. *Educational Reconstruction: African American Schools in the Urban South, 1865–1890.* New York: Fordham University Press, 2016.

Grundy, Pamela. *Color and Character: West Charlotte High and the American Struggle Over Educational Equality.* Chapel Hill: The University of North Carolina Press, 2017.

Haines, Michael R. *Historical, Demographic, Economic, and Social Data: The United States, 1790–2000.* Ithaca: Cornell University Center for Social Sciences.

Hale, Jon N. "'The Fight Was Instilled in Us': High School Student Activism and the Civil Rights Movement in Charleston." *The South Carolina Historical Magazine* 114, no. 1 (2013): 4–28.

———. *The Freedom Schools: Student Activists in the Mississippi Civil Rights Movement.* New York: Columbia University Press, 2016.

———. "The Freedom Schools, the Civil Rights Movement, and Refocusing the Goals of American Education." *Journal of Social Studies Research* 35, no. 2 (2011): 259–76.

———. "Future Foot Soldiers or Budding Criminals? The Dynamics of High School Student Activism in the Southern Black Freedom Struggle." *Journal of Southern History* 84, no. 3 (2018): 615–52.

———. *A New Kind of Youth: Historically Black High Schools and Southern Student Activism, 1920–1975.* Chapel Hill: The University of North Carolina Press, 2022.

———. "'We Are Not Merging on an Equal Basis': The Desegregation of Southern Teacher Associations and the Right to Work, 1945–1977." *Labor History* 50, no. 5 (2019): 463–81.

Hale, Jon N., and Candace Livingston. "'If You Want Police, We Will Have Them': Anti-Black Student Discipline in Southern Schools and the Rise of a New Carceral Logic, 1961–1975." *Journal of Urban History* 49, no. 5 (2022): 1035–48.

Hall, Jacquelyn Dowd. "The Long Civil Rights Movement and the Political Uses of the Past." *The Journal of American History* 91, no. 4 (2005): 1233–63.

Harley, Sharon. "Beyond the Classroom: The Organizational Lives of Black Female Educators in the District of Columbia, 1890–1930." *The Journal of Negro Education* 51, no. 3 (1982): 254–65.

Harold, Claudrena N. *New Negro Politics in the Jim Crow South*. Athens: University of Georgia Press, 2016.

———. "'Of the Wings of Atalanta': The Struggle for African American Studies at the University of Virginia, 1969–1995." *Journal of African American Studies* 16 (2012): 41–69.

Harold, Claudrena N., and Louis P. Nelson, eds. *Charlottesville 2017: The Legacy of Race and Inequity*. Charlottesville: University of Virginia Press, 2018.

Hayes, Worth Kamili. *Schools of Our Own: Chicago's Golden Age of Black Private Education*. Chicago: Northwestern University Press, 2019.

Hayter, Julian Maxwell. *The Dream Is Lost: Voting Rights and the Politics of Race in Richmond, Virginia*. Lexington: University Press of Kentucky, 2017.

Heinemann, Ronald L. *Depression and New Deal in Virginia: The Enduring Dominion*. Charlottesville: University Press of Virginia, 1983.

Highsmith, Andrew R. *Demolition Means Progress: Flint, Michigan, and the Fate of the American Metropolis*. Chicago: University of Chicago Press, 2015.

Highsmith, Andrew R., and Ansley T. Erickson. "Segregation as Splitting, Segregation as Joining: Schools, Housing, and the Many Modes of Jim Crow." *American Journal of Education* 121, no. 4 (2015): 563–95.

Hines, Michael. *A Worthy Piece of Work: The Untold Story of Madeline Morgan and the Fight for Black History in Schools*. Boston: Beacon Books, 2022.

Hines, Michael, and Thomas Fallace. "Pedagogical Progressivism and Black Progressivism: A Historiographical Review." *Review of Educational Research* 93, no. 3 (2023):1–33.

Hogan, Wesley C. *On the Freedom Side: How Five Decades of Youth Activists Have Remixed American History*. Chapel Hill: The University of North Carolina Press, 2019.

Holden, Anna. *The Bus Stops Here: A Study of School Desegregation in Three Cities*. New York: Agathon Press, 1974.

Houchen, Diedre Faith. "An 'Organized Body of Intelligent Agents': Black Teacher Activism During De Jure Segregation: A Historical Case Study of the Florida State Teachers Association." *Journal of Negro Education* 89, no. 3 (2020): 267–81.

Hume, Richard L. "The Membership of the Virginia Constitutional Convention of 1867–1868: A Study of the Beginnings of Congressional Reconstruction in the Upper South." *The Virginia Magazine of History and Biography* 86, no. 4 (1978): 461–84.

Hyres, Alexander. "Barbara Johns and Beyond: Black Male Youth Activists, School Desegregation, and the Black Freedom Struggle in Virginia, 1951–1970." *The Journal of the History of Childhood and Youth* 17, no. 3 (2024): 449–66.

———. "'Dedication to the Highest of Callings': Florence Coleman Bryant and the Contours of Black Teachers' Activism in Virginia." In *Schooling the Movement: The Activism of Southern Black Educators from Reconstruction through the Civil Rights Era*, edited by Derrick P. Alridge, Jon N. Hale, and Tondra Loder-Jackson, 148–165. Columbia: The University of South Carolina Press, 2023.

———. "The Whole Mess is *American* History: Protest, Pedagogy, and Black Studies at a Desegregated High School in the South, 1967–1974." *Journal of African American History* 107, no. 1 (2022): 55–78.

Hyres, Alexander, and Kyle Steele. "Reimagining the High School Experience: The Uses and Limitations of Student-Generated Documents for Understanding the Past and Present." *Teachers College Record*, Research Note (2022): https://journals.sagepub.com/pb-assets/cmscontent/TCZ/Research%20Notes%20Collection/2022%20Research%20Notes/Reimagining%20the%20High%20School%20Experience-1656007396.pdf.

Irvine, J. J., and R. W. Irvine. "The Impact of the Desegregation Process on the Education of Black Students: A Retrospective Analysis." *The Journal of Negro Education* 76, no. 3 (2007): 297–305.

Irvine, R. W., and J. J. Irvine. "The Impact of the Desegregation Process on the Education of Black Students: Key Variables." *The Journal of Negro Education* 52, no. 4 (1983): 410–22.

Jacobs, Gregory S. *Getting Around* Brown: *Desegregation, Development, and the Columbus Public Schools*. Columbus: Ohio State University Press, 1998.

James, Michael E. *The Conspiracy of the Good: Civil Rights and the Struggle for Community in Two American Cities, 1875–2000*. New York: Peter Lang, 2005.

Johnson, Karen A. *Uplifting the Women and the Race: The Educational Philosophies, and Social Activism of Anna Julia Cooper and Nannie Helen Burroughs*. New York: Garland Pub., 2000.

Johnson, Karen A., Abul Pitre, and Kenneth L. Johnson, eds. *African American Women Educators: A Critical Examination of Their Pedagogies, Educational Ideas, and Activism from the Nineteenth to the mid-Twentieth Century.* New York: R&L Education, 2014.

Johnson, Kimberley S. *Reforming Jim Crow: Southern Politics and State in the Age Before Brown.* Oxford: Oxford University Press, 2010.

Jones, Brian. *The Tuskegee Student Uprising: A History.* New York: NYU Press, 2024.

Jones-Wilson, Faustine C. *A Traditional Model of Educational Excellence: Dunbar High School of Little Rock, Arkansas.* Washington, D.C.: Howard University Press, 1981.

Kaestle, Carl F. *Pillars of the Republic: Common Schools and American Society, 1780–1860.* New York: Farrar, Straus and Giroux, 2011.

Karpinski, Carol F. *A Visible Company of Professionals: African Americans and the National Education Association during the Civil Rights Movement.* New York: Peter Lang, 2008.

Katz, William Loren. *Eyewitness: The Negro in American History—A Living Documentary of the Afro-American Contribution to U.S. History.* New York: Pittman Publishing Corporation, 1967.

———. *Teacher's Guide to American Negro History.* Chicago: Quadrangle Books, 1968.

Kelly, Hilton. "'Just Something Gone, but Nothing Missing': Booker T. Washington, Nannie Helen Burroughs, and the Social Significance of Black Teachers Theorizing Across Two Centuries." *Educational Studies* 48, no. 3 (2012): 215–19.

———. *Race, Remembering, and Jim Crow's Teachers.* New York: Routledge, 2010.

———. "'The Way We Found Them to Be': Remembering E. Franklin Frazier and the Politics of Respectable Black Teachers." *Urban Education* 45, no. 2 (2010): 142–65.

———. "What Jim Crow's Teachers Could Do: Educational Capital and Teachers' Work in Under-Resourced Schools." *The Urban Review* 42, no. 4 (2010): 329–50.

Kinchen, Shirletta J. *Black Power in the Bluff City: African American Youth and Student Activism in Memphis, 1965–1975.* Knoxville: University of Tennessee Press, 2016.

King, Shannon. "The Limited Presence of African-American Teachers." *Review of Educational Research* 63, no. 2 (1993): 115–49.

Kitzmiller, Erika M. *The Roots of Educational Inequality: Philadelphia's Germantown High School, 1907–2014.* Philadelphia: University of Pennsylvania Press, 2021.

Kluger, Richard. *Simple Justice: The History of* Brown v. Board of Education *and Black America's Struggle for Equality*. New York: Vintage Books, 1977.

Kridel, Craig. *Progressive Education in Black High Schools: The Secondary School Study, 1940–1946*. Columbia: The Museum of Education, University of South Carolina, 2015.

Krug, Edward A. *The Shaping of the American High School, 1920–1941*. Madison: University of Wisconsin Press, 1972.

Labaree, David F. *The Making of an American High School: The Credentials Market and the Central High School of Philadelphia, 1838–1939*. New Haven: Yale University Press, 1988.

Ladson-Billings, Gloria. *The Dreamkeepers: Successful Teachers of African American Children*. Hoboken: John Wiley & Sons, Inc., 1994.

Lassiter, Michael D., and Andrew B Lewis. *The Moderates' Dilemma: Massive Resistance to School Desegregation in Virginia*. Charlottesville: University Press of Virginia, 1998.

Link, William A. *A Hard Country and a Lonely Place: Schooling, Society, and Reform in Rural Virginia, 1870–1920*. Chapel Hill: The University of North Carolina Press, 1986.

Littlejohn, Jeffrey L., and Charles Howard Ford. *Elusive Equality: Desegregation and Resegregation in Norfolk's Public Schools*. Charlottesville: University of Virginia Press, 2012.

Litwack, Leon F. *Been in the Storm So Long: The Aftermath of Slavery*. New York: Vintage, 1980.

———. *Trouble in Mind: Black Southerners in the Age of Jim Crow*. New York: New Vintage, 1999.

Loder-Jackson, Tondra. "Bridging the Legacy of Activism across Generations: Life Stories of African American Educators in Post–Civil Rights Birmingham." *Urban Review* 43, no. 2 (2011): 151–74.

———. "Hope and Despair: Southern Black Women Educators Across Pre- and Post–Civil Rights Cohorts Theorize About Their Activism." *Educational Studies* 48, no. 3 (2012): 266–95.

———. *Schoolhouse Activists: African American Educators and the Long Birmingham Civil Rights Movement*. Albany: State University of New York Press, 2015.

Malone, Carry F. "Before *Brown*: Cultural and Social Capital in a Rural Black School Community, W. E. B. Du Bois High School, Wake Forest, North Carolina." *North Carolina Historical Review* 85, no. 4 (October 2008): 416–47.

Manheim, Frank T., and Shayla C. Nunnally. "Black High Schools of High Quality Prior to Desegregation." *The Journal of Negro Education* 92, no. 1 (2023): 3–15.

Martin, Rachel Louise. *A Most Tolerant Little Town: The Explosive Beginning of School Desegregation*. New York: Simon & Schuster, 2023.

Mayo, Jr., J. B. "Quiet Warriors: Black Teachers' Memories of Integration in Two Virginia Localities." *Multicultural Perspectives* 9, no. 2 (2007): 17–25.

McCluskey, Audrey Thomas. *A Forgotten Sisterhood: Pioneering Black Women Educators and Activists in the Jim Crow South*. Lanham: Rowman & Littlefield, 2014.

McCrae, Elizabeth Gillespie. *Mothers of Massive Resistance: White Women and the Politics of White Supremacy*. New York: Oxford University Press, 2018.

McCullum, Kristan L., and Derrick P. Alridge. "Toward a Critical History of Education: The Uses of the Past and Its Possibilities for the Present." In *Handbook of Critical Education Research*, edited by Michelle D. Young and Sarah Diem, 377–94. New York: Routledge, 2023.

McGuire, Danielle L. *At the Dark End of the Street: Black Women, Rape, and Resistance—A New History of the Civil Rights Movement From Rosa Parks to the Rise of Black Power*. New York: Alfred A. Knopf, 2010.

Milner, H. Richard, and Tyrone C. Howard. "Black Teachers, Black Students, Black Communities, and *Brown*: Perspectives and Insights from Experts." *Journal of Negro Education* 73, no. 3 (2004): 285–97.

Miraya Ross, K., and Jarvis R. Givens. "The Clearing: On Black Education Studies and the Problem of 'Antiblackness.'" *Harvard Educational Review* 93, no. 2 (2023): 149–72.

Moore, John H. *Ablemarle, Jefferson's County, 1727–1976*. Charlottesville: University of Virginia Press, 1976.

Morgan, Iwan, and Philip Davies, eds. *From Sit-Ins to SNCC: The Student Civil Rights Movement in the 1960s*. Gainesville: University Press of Florida, 2012.

Morris, Jerome E. "Forgotten Voices of Black Educators: Critical Race Perspectives on the Implementation of a Desegregation Plan." *Educational Policy* 15, no. 4 (2001): 575–600.

Morris, Jerome E., and Carla R. Monroe. "Why Study the US South? The Nexus of Race and Place in Investigating Black Student Achievement." *Educational Researcher* 38, no. 1 (2009): 21–36.

Morris, Jerome E., Benjamin D. Parker, and Luimil M. Negrón. "Black School Closings Aren't New: Historically Contextualizing Contemporary School Closings and Black Community Resistance." *Educational Researcher* 51, no. 9 (2022): 575–83.

Morris, Vivian Gunn, and Curtis L. Morris. *The Price They Paid: Desegregation in an African American Community*. New York: Teachers College Press, 2002.

Moses, Robert, Mieko Kamii, Susan McAllister Swap, and Jeffrey Howard. "The Algebra Project: Organizing in the Spirit of Ella." *Harvard Educational Review* 59, no. 4 (1989): 423–44.
Moss, Hilary J. *Schooling Citizens: The Struggle for African American Education in Antebellum America*. Chicago: University of Chicago Press, 2009.
Murray, Alana D. *The Development of the Alternative Black Curriculum, 1890–1940: Countering the Master Narrative*. New York: Springer, 2018.
Nocera, Amato. "'May We Not Write Our Own Fairy Tales and Make Black Beautiful?': African American Teachers, Children's Literature, and the Construction of Race in the Curriculum, 1920–1945." *History of Education Quarterly* 63, no. 1 (2023): 32–58.
———. "'More than Equivalent to a Year of College': Hubert Harrison and Informal Education in Harlem's New Negro Movement." *Teachers College Record* 122, no. 3 (2020): 1–32.
———. "Negotiating the Aims of African American Adult Education: Race and Liberalism in the Harlem Experiment, 1931–1935." *History of Education Quarterly* 58, no. 1 (2018): 1–32.
Nocera, Amato, Kyle P. Steele, and John Hensley. "Standardization, White Supremacy, and Racial Self-Definition: African American Secondary Schools in Rural North Carolina, 1920–1954." *Harvard Educational Review* 94, no. 2 (2024): 259–85.
Patterson, James T. Brown v. Board of Education: *A Civil Rights Milestone and Its Troubled Legacy*. Oxford: Oxford University Press.
Pawlewicz, Diana D'Amico. *Blaming Teachers: Professionalization Policies and the Failure of Reform in American History*. New Brunswick: Rutgers University Press, 2020.
Payne, Charles M. *I've Got the Light of Freedom: The Organizing Tradition and the Mississippi Freedom Struggle*. Oakland: University of California Press, 2007.
———. "'The Whole United States Is Southern!': *Brown v. Board* and the Mystification of Race." *The Journal of American History* 91, no. 1 (2004): 83–91.
Peeples, Edward H. *Scalawag: A White Southerner's Journey Through Segregation to Human Rights Activism*. Charlottesville: University of Virginia Press, 2014.
Perlstein, Daniel H. *Justice, Justice: School Politics and the Eclipse of Liberalism*. New York: Peter Lang, 2004.
———. "Minds Stayed on Freedom: Politics and Pedagogy in the African-American Freedom Struggle." *American Educational Research Journal* 39, no. 2 (2002): 249–77.
———. "Teaching Freedom: SNCC and the Creation of the Mississippi Freedom Schools." *History of Education Quarterly* 30, no. 3 (1990): 297–324.

Perrillo, Jonna. *Uncivil Rights: Teachers, Unions, and Race in the Battle for School Equity*. Chicago: University of Chicago Press, 2012.

Pierson, Sharon Gay. *Laboratory of Learning: HBCU Laboratory Schools and Alabama State College Lab High in the Era of Jim Crow*. New York: Peter Lang, 2014.

Pratt, Robert R. *The Color of Their Skin: Education and Race in Richmond, Virginia, 1954–89*. Charlottesville: University Press of Virginia, 1993.

———. "New Directions in Virginia's Civil Rights History." *The Virginia Magazine of History and Biography* 104, no. 1 (Winter 1996): 149–56.

Preston-Grimes, Patrice. "Fulfilling the Promise: African American Educators Teach for Democracy in Jim Crow's South." *Teacher Education Quarterly* 37, no. 1 (2010): 35–52.

———. "Teaching Democracy Before *Brown*: Civic Education in Georgia's African American Schools, 1930–1954." *Theory & Research in Social Education* 35, no. 1 (2007): 9–31.

Purdy, Michelle A. "Blurring Public and Private: The Pragmatic Desegregation Politics of an Elite Private School in Atlanta." *History of Education Quarterly* 56, no. 1 (2016): 61–89.

———. "Courageous Navigation: African American Students at an Elite Private School in the South, 1967–1972." *The Journal of African American History* 100, no. 4 (2015): 610–35.

———. *Transforming the Elite: Black Students and the Desegregation of Private Schools*. Chapel Hill: The University of North Carolina Press, 2018.

Ramsey, Sonya Y. *Bertha Maxwell-Roddey: A Modern-Day Race Woman and the Power of Black Leadership*. Gainesville: University Press of Florida, 2022.

———. "Caring Is Activism: Black Southern Womanist Teachers Theorizing and the Careers of Kathleen Crosby and Bertha Maxwell-Roddey, 1946–1986." *Educational Studies* 48, no. 3 (2012): 244–65.

———. *Reading, Writing, and Segregation: A Century of Black Women Teachers in Nashville*. Urbana: University of Illinois Press, 2008.

———. "'We Will Be Ready Whenever They Are': African American Teachers' Responses to the *Brown* Decision and Public School Integration in Nashville, Tennessee, 1954–1966." *The Journal of African American History* 90, no. 1–2 (2005): 29–51.

Randolph, Adah Ward. "'It Is Better To Light A Candle Than To Curse The Darkness': Ethel Thompson Overby and Democratic Schooling in Richmond, Virginia, 1910–1958." *Educational Studies* 48, no. 3 (2012): 220–43.

———. "The Memories of an All-Black Northern Urban School: Good Memories of Leadership, Teachers, and the Curriculum." *Urban Education* 39, no. 6 (2004): 596–620.

———. "Presidential Address: African-American Education History—A Manifestation of Faith." *History of Education Quarterly* 54, no. 1 (2014): 1–18.

Randolph, Adah Ward, and Dwan V. Robinson. "De Facto Desegregation in the Urban North: Voices of African American Teachers and Principals on Employment, Students, and Community in Columbus, Ohio, 1940–1980." *Urban Education* 54, no. 10 (2019): 1403–30.

Rasmussen, Chris. "Creating Segregation in the Era of Integration: School Consolidation and Local Control in New Brunswick, New Jersey, 1965–1976." *History of Education Quarterly* 57, no. 4 (2017): 480–514.

Reese, William J. *The Origins of the American High School*. New Haven: Yale University Press, 1999.

Rickford, Russell John. *We Are an African People: Independent Education, Black Power, and the Radical Imagination*. New York: Oxford University Press, 2016.

Rodgers, Frederick A. *The Black High School and Its Community*. Lexington: Lexington Books, 1975.

Rojas, Fabio. *From Black Power to Black Studies: How a Radical Social Movement Became an Academic Discipline*. Baltimore: Johns Hopkins University Press, 2007.

Rury, John L., and Shirley A Hill. *The African American Struggle for Secondary Schooling, 1940–1980: Closing the Graduation Gap*. New York: Teachers College Press, 2012.

———. "An End of Innocence: African-American High School Protest in the 1960s and 1970s." *History of Education* 42, no. 4 (2013): 486–508.

Ryan, James E. *Five Miles Away, A World Apart: One City, Two Schools, and the Story of Educational Opportunity in Modern America*. New York: Oxford University Press, 2010.

Sanders, Crystal. *A Chance for Change: Head Start and Mississippi's Black Freedom Struggle*. Chapel Hill: The University of North Carolina Press, 2016.

———. *A Forgotten Migration: Black Southerners, Segregation Scholarships, and the Debt Owed to Public HBCUs*. Chapel Hill: The University of North Carolina Press, 2024.

———. "'Money Talks': The Elementary and Secondary Education Act of 1965 and the African-American Freedom Struggle in Mississippi." *History of Education Quarterly* 56, no. 2 (2016): 361–67.

———. "More Than Cookies and Crayons: Head Start and African American Empowerment in Mississippi, 1965–1968." *The Journal of African American History* 100, no. 4 (2015): 586–609.

Saunders, James Robert, and Renae Nadine Shackelford. *Urban Renewal and the End of Black Culture in Charlottesville, Virginia: An Oral History of Vinegar Hill*. New York: McFarland, 2005.

Schneider, Jack. *Excellence for All: How a New Breed of Reformers Is Transforming America's Public Schools*. Nashville: Vanderbilt University Press, 2011.

Schumaker, Kathryn. *Troublemakers: Students' Rights and Racial Justice in the Long 1960s*. New York: NYU Press, 2023.

Sellers, T. J. "New $1,400,000 High School Dedicated" *New Journal and Guide*, March 29, 1952, A5.

Shelton, Jon. *Teacher Strike! Public Education and the Making of a New American Political Order*. Champaign: University of Illinois Press, 2017.

Shircliffe, Barbara J. *The Best of That World: Historically Black High Schools and the Crisis of Desegregation in a Southern Metropolis*. Cresskill: Hampton Press, 2006.

———. *Desegregating Teachers: Contesting the Meaning of Equality of Educational Opportunity in the South Post-Brown*. New York: Peter Lang, 2012.

———. "Desegregation and the Historically Black High School: The Establishment of Howard W. Blake in Tampa, Florida." *Urban Review* 34, no. 2 (2002): 135–58.

———. "Lines Were Drawn: Remembering Court-Ordered Integration at a Mississippi High School." *Journal of American History* 104, no. 2 (2017): 545–47.

———. "Rethinking Turner v. Keefe: The Parallel Mobilization of African-American and White Teachers in Tampa, Florida, 1936–1946." *History of Education Quarterly* 52, no. 1 (2012): 99–136.

———. "'We Got the Best of That World': A Case for the Study of Nostalgia in the Oral History of School Segregation." *The Oral History Review* 28, no. 2 (2001): 59–84.

Simmons, Marion Woodfork. *An Oasis in Caroline County, Virginia, 1903–1969*. Woodfork Genealogy LLC, 2011.

Simpkins, Francis Butler, Spotswood Hunnicut, and Sidman P. Poole. *Virginia: History, Government, and Geography*. New York: Charles Scribner's Sons, 1957.

Smith, J. Douglas. *Managing White Supremacy: Race, Politics, and Citizenship in Jim Crow Virginia*. Chapel Hill: The University of North Carolina Press, 2002.

Smith, Lucille Stout. *Unforgettable: Jackson P. Burley High School, 1951–1967*. Richmond: Self-published, 2021.

Span, Christopher M. *From the Cottonfield to the Schoolhouse: African American Education in Mississippi, 1862–1875*. Chapel Hill: The University of North Carolina Press, 2012.

Spruill, A. W. "The Negro Teacher in the Process of Desegregation of Schools." *The Journal of Negro Education* 29, no. 1 (1960): 80–84.

Steele, Kyle P. *Making a Mass Institution: Indianapolis and the American High School*. New Brunswick: Rutgers University Press, 2020.

Steele, Kyle P., ed. *New Perspectives on the History of the Twentieth-Century American High School*. New York: Springer Nature, 2021.

Stern, Walter C. *Race and Education in New Orleans: Creating the Segregated City, 1764–1960*. Baton Rouge: LSU Press, 2018.

———. "School Violence and the Carceral State in the 1970s: Desegregation and the New Educational Inequality in Louisiana." *Journal of Southern History* 89, no. 3 (2023): 483–534.

———. "'We Got to Fight for What We Want': Black School Rebellions in Louisiana, 1965–1974." *Teachers College Record* 125, no. 3 (2023): 319–49.

Stewart, Alison. *First Class: The Legacy of Dunbar, America's First Black Public High School*. Chicago: Chicago Review Press, 2013.

Tarter, Brent. *The Grandees of Government: The Origins and Persistence of Undemocratic Politics in Virginia*. Charlottesville: University of Virginia Press, 2013.

Taylor, Alan. *Thomas Jefferson's Education*. New York: W. W. Norton & Company, 2019.

Theoharis, Jeanne. *A More Beautiful and Terrible History: The Uses and Misuses of Civil Rights History*. Boston: Beacon Press, 2018.

Thuesen, Sarah Caroline. *Greater Than Equal: African American Struggles for Schools and Citizenship in North Carolina, 1919–1965*. Chapel Hill: The University of North Carolina Press, 2013.

Tillman, Linda C. *The Sage Handbook of African American Education*. Thousand Oaks: Sage Publications, 2008.

———. "(Un)Intended Consequences? The Impact of *Brown v. Board of Education* Decision on the Employment Status of Black Educators." *Education and Urban Society* 36, no. 3 (2004): 280–303.

Titus, Jill Ogline. *Brown's Battleground: Students, Segregationists, and the Struggle for Justice in Prince Edward County, Virginia*. Chapel Hill: The University of North Carolina Press, 2011.

Todd-Breland, Elizabeth. "Barbara Sizemore and the Politics of Black Educational Achievement and Community Control, 1963–1975." *The Journal of African American History* 100, no. 4 (2015): 636–62.

———. *A Political Education: Black Politics and Education Reform in Chicago Since the 1960s*. Chapel Hill: The University of North Carolina Press, 2018.

Vance, Joseph C. "Freedmen's Schools in Albemarle County During Reconstruction." *Virginia Magazine of History and Biography* 61 (October 1953): 430–38.

Vinovskis, M. *From A Nation at Risk to No Child Left Behind: National Education Goals and the Creation of Federal Education Policy*. New York: Teachers College Press, 2009.

Walker, Dara. "Learning to Struggle, Learning to Govern: How Black Youth Marshaled Education to Navigate Urban Transformations in the Motor City, 1967–1972." *Journal of Urban History* 51, no. 2 (2025): 431–448.

Walker, Dara, Alexander Hyres, and Jon Hale, eds. *Youth in the Movement: High School Student Activism in Twentieth Century America*. New Brunswick: Rutgers University Press, forthcoming.

Walker, Vanessa Siddle. "African American Teaching in the South: 1940–1960." *American Educational Research Journal* 38, no. 4 (2001): 751–79.

———. "Black Educators as Educational Advocates in the Decades Before *Brown v. Board of Education*" *Educational Research* 42, no. 4 (2013): 207–22.

———. *Hello Professor: A Black Principal and Professional Leadership in the Segregated South*. Chapel Hill: The University of North Carolina Press, 2009.

———. *The Lost Education of Horace Tate: Uncovering the Hidden Heroes Who Fought for Justice in Schools*. New York: The New Press, 2018.

———. "Organized Resistance and Black Educators' Quest for School Equality, 1878–1938." *Teachers College Record* 107, no. 3 (2005): 355–88.

———. "School 'Outer-Gration' and 'Tokenism': Segregated Black Educators Critique the Promise of Education Reform in the Civil Rights Act of 1964." *Journal of Negro Education* 84, no. 2 (2015): 111–24.

———. *Their Highest Potential: An African American School Community in the Segregated South*. Chapel Hill: The University of North Carolina Press, 1996.

———. "Valued Segregated Schools for African American Children in the South, 1935–1969: A Review of Common Themes and Characteristics." *Review of Educational Research* 70, no. 3 (2000): 253–85.

Walker, Vanessa Siddle, and Ulysses Byas. "The Architects of Black Schooling in the Segregated South: The Case of One Principal Leader." *Journal of Curriculum and Supervision* 19, no. 1 (2003): 54–72.

Wallenstein, Peter. *Cradle of America: A History of Virginia*. 2nd ed. Lawrence: University Press of Kansas, 2014.

Watkins, William. *The White Architects of Black Education: Ideology and Power in America, 1865–1954*. New York: Teachers College Press, 2001.

Webber, Thomas L. *Deep Like the Rivers: Education in the Slave Quarter Community, 1831–1865*. New York: W. W. Norton & Company, 1978.

Wells, Amy Stuart. *Both Sides Now: The Story of School Desegregation's Graduates*. Berkeley: University of California Press, 2009.

Wilkerson, Doxey A. "The Negro School Movement in Virginia: From 'Equalization' to 'Integration.'" *The Journal of Negro Education* 29, no. 1 (1960): 17–29.

Williams, Heather Andrea. *Self-Taught: African American Education in Slavery and Freedom*. Chapel Hill: The University of North Carolina Press, 2005.

Williamson-Lott, Joy Ann. "The Battle over Power, Control, and Academic Freedom at Southern Institutions of Higher Education, 1955–1965." *The Journal of Southern History* 79, no. 4 (2013): 879–920.

———. *Black Power on Campus: The University of Illinois, 1965–75*. Urbana: University of Illinois Press, 2003.

———. *Jim Crow Campus: Higher Education and the Struggle for a New Southern Social Order*. New York: Teachers College Press, 2018.

———. *Radicalizing the Ebony Tower: Black Colleges and the Black Freedom Struggle in Mississippi*. New York: Teachers College Press, 2008.

Willis, Vincent D. *Audacious Agitation: The Uncompromising Commitment of Black Youth to Equal Education After* Brown. Athens: University of Georgia Press, 2021.

———. "'Let Me In, I Have the Right to be Here': Black Youth Struggle for Equal Education and Full Citizenship After the *Brown* Decision, 1954–1969." *Citizenship Teaching & Learning* 9, no. 1 (2013): 53–70.

Wingfield, Danielle. "Movement Lawyers: Henry L. Marsh's Long Struggle for Educational Justice." *University of Richmond Law Review* 56 (Spring 2022): 1339–410.

Wingfield, Marshall. *A History of Caroline County: From Its Formation in 1727 to 1924*. Trevvet Christian, 1924.

Woyshner, Christine. "Black Civic Organizations and the Quest for Education: The Improved Benevolent and Protective Order of Elks of the World, 1898–1954." *The Journal of African American History* 108, no. 4 (2023): 576–99.

———. "Civic Education in Informal Settings: Black Voluntary Associations as Schools for Democracy, 1898–1959." *Theory & Research in Social Education* 52, no. 3 (2024): 458–79.

———. "'No Unfavorable Comments from Any Quarter': Teaching Black History to White Students in the American South, 1928–1943." *Teachers College Record* 114, no. 10 (2012): 1–23.

Wraga, W. G. "Clinical Technique, Tacit Resistance: Progressive Education Experimentation in the Jim Crow South." *History of Education Quarterly* 59, no. 2 (2019): 227–56.

Wright, Dwayne C. "Black Pride Day, 1968: High School Student Activism in York, Pennsylvania." *Journal of African American History* 88, no. 2 (2003): 151–62.

Von Daacke, Kirt. *Freedom Has a Face: Race, Identity, and Community in Jefferson's Virginia*. Charlottesville: University of Virginia Press, 2012.

Yacovone, Donald. *Teaching White Supremacy: America's Democratic Ordeal and the Forging of Our National Identity*. New York: Pantheon Books, 2022.

Zehmer, James, Jessica E. Sewell, and Andrew Johnston. *Educated in Tyranny: Slavery at Thomas Jefferson's University*. Charlottesville: University of Virginia Press, 2019.

Zimmerman, Jonathan. "Storm over the Schoolhouse: Exploring Popular Influences upon the American Curriculum, 1890–1941." *Teachers College Record* 100, no. 3 (1999): 602–26.

——. *Whose America? Culture Wars in the Public Schools*, 2nd. ed. Chicago: University of Chicago Press, 2022.

Zinn, Howard. *SNCC: The New Abolitionists*. Chicago: Haymarket Books, 2013.

INDEX

Locators in italics indicate a figure. Locators in bold indicate a table.

ability tracking, 101, 124
"abroad mentorship," 52
activism: *Blast* and, 91; curriculum reform and, 94–95; educational opportunities and, 4–5; educators and, 85, 88–89, 95; equalization movement and, 10, 52–53, 55; *Knight Time Review* incident and, 114–17; LHS and, 88–92, 94; Little Rock Nine and, 98–99; Massive Resistance campaign and, 60, 82, 86; Moton High School and, 59; "movement centers" and, 10; "Safeway Riots" and, 114–15; sit-in protests and, 70–74; statue removal and, 129, 133, 153–54n5; "The Wrecking Crew" and, 89–90; voting and, 69. *See also* Black freedom struggle; protest
"African American" (terminology), 135n1
African American history course (CHS), 132
Afro-American Club (LHS), 87–88
Albemarle County Schools Division, 21, 53, 76
Albemarle Training School, 43
Alexander, Charles, 2–3, 10, 13, 85, 89, 126–27
Allen, Frankie, 66
Almond, J. Lindsey, 60
American high school, 5–6, 8–9, 29–31

"Americans from Africa" (course), 93–94
Association for the Study of Negro Life and History, 51–52
athletics/sports, 48–49, 66–67, 114. *See also* extracurricular activities

Barringer, Paul, 23
basement schools, 79–80, 86
Battle, John S., 58
"Black" (terminology), 135n1
Black Culture Week (LHS), 106–7
Black education (general): access to advanced curriculum and, 27–31; Black inferiority myth and, 23; Caroline County and, 45–47; Civil War expansion of, 18–19; desire for higher education and, 28; "Hampton-Tuskegee idea" and, 20; knowledge of civil rights and, 41; literacy rates and, 40; out-of-town schools and, 31–32; prohibition of, 17–18; Virginia legislature and, 22–23
Black education (high school): access in South to, 29–31; BHS and, 6, 53; Black Studies elective course and, 95–100; books and, 27–28, 50; community advocacy for, 32–34; fight for, 9; Great Depression and, 44; JHS curriculum and, 50–52; Johnson advocacy for, 35–36;

184 | Index

Black education (high school) (cont.)
meetings about establishing, 31;
memorialization and, 128; petition
for, 34–35; travel for, 31–32; Union
High School and, 46–47. *See also
individual schools*

Black educators: BHS and, 64–65,
74–75; Black freedom struggle and,
2–5, 10, 13, 127; Black Studies and,
92, 101–2, 120; CHS and, 120–23;
covert curriculum and, 27–28;
desegregation and, 61, 63, 84, 125;
economic security and, 21; equalization movement and, 52–53;
Jefferson Elementary and, 21, 27;
lack of support for, 108; LHS and,
84, 105, 108; memory of Black high
schools and, 128; opening/closing of
schools and, 6; racism and, 122–23;
terminology, 135n5; TIM Project
and, 9; training of, 28; white educator alliances with, 85. *See also
individual educators*

Black freedom struggle: churches and,
8; contexts of, 68; desegregation in
Charlottesville and, 68–70; high
schools and, 8, 30–31; Little Rock
Nine and, 97–99; movement centers
and, 5, 10, 53; protest and pedagogy
in, 17, 19; role of Black educators/
students in, 3–5; terminology and,
135–36n6; "The Charlottesville
Twelve" and, 2, *11*, 12–13, 89.
See also activism; protest

Black History Pathway, 128

Black History Week, 51–52

Black History Week programs,
100–101, 105, 120–21

Black History Week protests (LHS),
102–4

Black literature at LHS, 102

Black National Anthem, 102, 106

Black students: ability tracking and,
101–2, 115; access to education
and, 29–32, 40, 43, 53; access to
materials and, 27–28, 50, 92;
Afro-American Club and, 87–88;
Black History Week and, 102–3;
Black Studies courses and, 94,
99–100, 106–7; carnival incident
and, 92; curriculum reform and,
94–95; Depression era and jobs of,
48; desegregation and, 60, 82, 84;
desegregation burdens and, 74,
79–80, 82; discrimination and,
114–15; equalization movement
and, 61; "Freedom of Choice"
program and, 82–83; Hampton
Institute and, 20; impact of reform
and, 107–8; *Knight Time Review*
incident and, 116–19; legacy of,
88–90; LHS enrollments and, **80**,
83–84, 109; NAACP tutoring and,
69–70; The Raiders Club and,
90–91; sit-ins and, 73; statue
removal and, 129, 133, 153–54n5;
"The Charlottesville Twelve" and, 2,
11, 12–13, 89; Virginia and success
of, 46. *See also* activism; Black
education; *individual students*

Black Student Union (CHS), 131, 133

Black Studies elective course (LHS),
95–100

Blast (newspaper), 91

Booker T. Washington Park Recreational Center, 41

Brown v. Board of Education, 10, 59

Bryant, Florence C., 1–3, 10, 45–47,
51, 112, 118–19, 125–27

Bryant, James, 90–91

Bryant, Zyahna, 7, 12, 127–30, *131*, 133
Buddy's Restaurant, 70–73
Bunn, Benjamin F., 8, 70
Burley, Jackson Price, 33–34, 56
Burley Bulletin (student newspaper), 74–75
Burley High School (BHS). *See* Jackson P. Burley High School (BHS)

Carkin, Philena, 20
carnival incident (LHS), 92
Caroline County, Virginia, 45
Central High School (Little Rock Nine), 98–99
Charlottesville, Virginia: background of, 6–8; employment opportunities/practice and, 24–26, 70; equalization movement and, 52; historical markers and, 12–13; housing segregation and, 42–43; Jim Crow and, 22–24, 68; legacy of Black high schools in, 132–33; Massive Resistance and, 60; population (1890–1920), **24**; population (1930–1950), **39**; population (2020), **7**; "Race Relations" report and, 119–20; "Safeway Riots" and, 114–15; sit-ins and, 70–74; statue removal and, 129, 133, 153–54n5; urban renewal and, 61–63
Charlottesville City Schools Division: advanced curriculum for African Americans and, 27–28; equalization movement and, 52–53, 55–56; formation of, 21; high schools and, 29–30; LHS closure and, 6; overcrowding and, 109–11; sale of BHS and, 76; segregation and, 34–35; system of, 7; teacher assignments and, 75–76; UVA reports and, 115
Charlottesville High School (CHS): Black educators and, 120–24; Black History program and, 120–21; Black student protests and, 114–15; contemporary protest at, 12; DeBerry and, 122; demographics of, 130; desegregation and, 10, 12; extracurricular activities and, 114; innovative high school model and, 112–13; issues with location and name of, 111–12; *Knight Time Review* incident and, 115–18; legacy of, 125–26; legacy of student protest and, 132–33; online petition video and, 130–32; opening of, 6; pedagogy and protest at, 125; prejudicial treatment and, 114; UVA reports and, 115
"Charlottesville Twelve, The," 2, *11*, 12–13, 89
Civil Rights Movement. *See* Black freedom struggle
Coles, Braxton, 43–44
Coles, Ruth, 32, 43
constitutional conventions and Black education (Virginia), 21–23
Consultative Center for School Desegregation (UVA), 123
Cumming v. Richmond County Board of Education, 30
curriculum: "Americans from Africa" and, 92–95; BHS and, 64, 68; Black freedom struggle and, 84; Black Studies elective course and, 95–100; CCS development of high school, 29–30, 34; challenging status quo through, 4–5; CHS and, 112–13, 115, 120–21, 131–32; covert efforts

curriculum (cont.)
to expand, 9, 27; Hampton Institute and, 20; innovative high school model and, 112–13, 115; JHS and, 39, 50–52, 68; LHS and, 85–86, 92–95, 101–3; online petition video demands and, 131–32; Scott and, 85–86; Union High School and, 46–47; UVA and, 92; Vasser and, 102–3. *See also* pedagogy
Curry, Jabez Lamar Monroe, 23, 153–54n5

Daily Progress, The (newspaper), 41
DeBerry, Garwin, 60, 122
De Corse, Helen Camp, 42
Deluxe Glee Club, 49
desegregation: BHS and, 74–75; Black student school choices and, 60–61; Black Studies elective and, 98–99; Charlottesville and, 68; CHS and, 10; "Freedom of Choice" program and, 82–83; increase of opportunities and, 6; LHS and, 10, 79–81; Massive Resistance and, 60; NAACP and, 69–71; "Race Relations" report and, 119; school overcrowding and, 109–11; urban renewal and, 61–63

"educators" (terminology), 135n5. *See also* Black educators
Edwards, Patricia, 61, 74, 124
employment opportunities in Charlottesville during Jim Crow, 24–26
equalization movement, 10, 52–53, 55
extracurricular activities: access to, 43, 47, 60, 81–82, 114; BHS and, 64–65; class photos and, 142n28; community building and, 48–49; space for, 41, 56, 110. *See also* athletics/sports

"Eyes on the Prize" (documentary), 121
Eyewitness (Katz), 95–98

Faulkner, Alberta Hall, 63–64
Ferguson, George, 31, 61–62, 117
First Baptist Church, 8, 31–33, 70
Fleming, Berdell McCoy, 10, 66, 73–74
Franklin, John Hope, 95–98
Franklin, Laura, 32
"Freedom of Choice" program, 82–83
From Slavery to Freedom (Franklin), 95–98
Fuller, Rebecca. *See* McGinness, Rebecca Fuller

Gardner, Anne, 19
Garrett, David H., 116–17
Gaston, Paul, 70–73
General Education Board, 29
Gibbons, Isabella, 19, 22
Gilmore, William, 48, 54
Goffney, Rudolph, 47–49, 51
"Great Society" speech, 68

Hampton Institute, 20, 28
"Hampton-Tuskegee idea," 20
historical markers (Charlottesville), 12–13. *See also* statue removal
Hooked on Books (Fader and McNeil), 87
Huegal, John E., 103, 112, 116

industrial training protests (Jefferson Colored Graded/Elementary School), 33
Inge, Thomas J., 31, 33–34
innovative high school model (CHS), 112–13

Jackson, French, 79–80
Jackson P. Burley High School (BHS): athletics at, 66–67; community involvement and, 66; curriculum and, 64–65; desegregation and, 60–61, 74–75; design and construction of, 56–58; educational staff at, 63–64; establishment of, 53, 55–56; extracurricular activities and, 64–65; Fleming on, 73; JHS and, 68; memorialization and, 128; as "movement center," 10; NAACP and, 69–70; national events and, 68; opening and closing of, 6, 58; sale of, 76; urban renewal and, 62–63; UVA and, 67; vocational education and, 65, 67; yearbook and, 67–68
James, John Henry, 22
Jay Pee Bee (yearbook), 64, 67–68
Jefferson, Thomas, 7–8, 19
Jefferson Colored Graded/Elementary School: advanced curriculum and, 27–28; approach of, 26–27; Black teachers and, 21; bond for expansion of, 35–37; building replacement for, 30; Civil War and, 18; employment opportunities and, 25–26; industrial training and, 33; LHS overcrowding and, 110; opening of, 19–20; student preparation and, 80–81; terminology and, 135n1
Jefferson High School (JHS): access to, 40, 43; BHS and, 68; books and, 50; Bryant and, 47; curriculum and, 39, 50–52; enrollments at, 44; equalization movement and, 10; extracurricular activities and, 48–49; impact of, 48, 54; Negro History Week and, 52; opening and closing of, 6, 37, 52; Patron's Day Exhibit and, 50; proximity to gas plant, 44; Vinegar Hill and, 24
Jim Crow, 22–26 *passim*, 30, 42, 68. *See also* segregation
Johns, Barbara, 59
Johnson, Floyd, 71–72
Johnson, James G., 33–37
Johnson, Van, 90
Johnson, William, 72
Jones, Clarice, 99–100

Katz, William Loren, 95–98
King, Martin Luther, Jr., 71
Knight Time Review (student newspaper), 112, 115–18

Lane High School (LHS): ability tracking and, 101; Afro-American Club and, 87–88; Alexander and, 2; "Americans from Africa" and, 93–94; Black Culture Week and, 106–7; Black educators and, 84–85; Black History Week and, 100–104, 105; Black student activism and, 88–92, 94, 102–4; Black student enrollments at, **80**; Black student experiences at, 79–82; Black Studies elective course and, 95–100; closure of, 6; curriculum reform and, 92–95; desegregation and, 4–5, 10, 60–61, 74–75, 82, 107–8; equalization movement and, 53; historical markers and, 12; image of, 83; Lewis and, 107; as "movement center," 10; overcrowding and, 109–11; Scott courses and, 86–87; Vasser courses and, 101–2; white educator allies and, 85–86
Lanetime (student newspaper), 91, 115

Lewis, Michael, 107
Lewis, Wilbert T., 123–24, 125–26
literacy rates, 40, 86–87
Little Rock Nine, 98–99
Long, Clarence M., 32–33
lynching, 22

Martin, Donald, 73, 79–82
Martin, John, 79–80
Massive Resistance campaign, 60, 82, 86
McCoy, Gladys, 75–76
McGinness, Rebecca Fuller, 9, 26–28, 52
memorialization of Black high schools, 128
methodology, 8–9
Midway School, 29–30, 34–35
Mitchell, Henry B., 104
Monacan Indians, 7
Monticello, 8
Moton High School, 59
Mount Zion African Methodist Episcopal (AME), 8
movement centers, 5, 10, 53

NAACP (Charlottesville chapter), 8, 69–71, 89
newspapers, 41, 49; *Blast*, 91; *Burley Bulletin*, 74–75; *The Daily Progress*, 41; *Knight Time Review*, 112, 115–18; *Lanetime*, 91, 115; *The Reflector*, 41
"Notehand" (course), 84–85

online petition video (CHS), 130–32
overcrowding of schools, 109–11

Parent Teacher Association (PTA), 33–34
Patron's Day Exhibit (JHS), 50

pedagogy: Black Studies and, 94–96, 99; civic education and, 68; covert, 27–28, 32; Diane Price and, 121, 125; Hampton Institute and, 20; historical memory and, 127–28; *Hooked on Books* and, 87; as protest, 4–5, 9–10, 28, 40, 50, 52, 64, 102, 125; *for* protest, 4–5, 10, 125; protest *as*, 4–5, 59, 129; protest *for*, 4, 33, 41, 53, 59, 94, 107, 129; rote learning and, 27, 51; use of term, 4. *See also* curriculum
petition for high school education, 34–35
Price, Diane, 10, 105–6, 120–22, 125
Price, Teresa, 10, 48, 49, 67, 70, 84–86
protest: as pedagogy, 4–5, 59, 129; *for* pedagogy, 4, 33, 41, 53, 59, 94, 129; pedagogy *as*, 4–5, 9–10, 28, 40, 50, 52, 64, 102, 125; pedagogy *for*, 4–5, 10, 107, 125. *See also* activism

"Race Relations and Education in Charlottesville" (Templin), 119–20
Racial Integrity Act, 23
Raiders Club, The, 90–91
Rap Sessions (LHS), 106
Reaves, Booker, 10, 38–40, 44–45, 52, 62
Reflector, The (newspaper), 41
reports on Charlottesville (UVA), 115
Robert E. Lee statue removal, 129, 133
Rock Hill Academy, 83–84, 109
Rodgers, Frederick, 115
Rodgers report, 115
Ryan, Stanley, 99

"Safeway Riots," 114–15
school divisions (Virginia), 21. *See also* Albemarle County Schools Division; Charlottesville City Schools Division

Scott, Susan Cone, 85–88
segregation, 21–23, 34–35, 40–43, 55, 68–71. *See also* desegregation; Jim Crow
Shelton, John, 28
Sherman, Anthony, 95–97, 99
sit-in protests, 70–74
Social Development Commission and Task Force, 119–20
South (region), 5, 9, 17–19, 29–30, 46. *See also* equalization movement; Jim Crow; Massive Resistance campaign; sit-in protests
sports. *See* athletics/sports
statue removal, 129, 133, 153–54n5
St. John Elementary School, 45–46
Stratton, Cindy, 117–18

"teachers" (terminology), 135n5. *See also* Black educators
Teachers in the Movement (TIM), xiv, 9
Tonsler, Benjamin, 9, 17–22, 27–28
Toppin, Edgar A., 92–94, 120
Turner, Corlis, 89

Union High School, 46–47
Unite the Right rally, 129–30
University of Virginia (UVA): BHS and, 67; Charlottesville reports and, 115; curriculum reform and, 92; Curry and, 23; establishment of, 7–8; inequality and, 35; student demographics and, 101
U.S. Constitution, 68

Vasser, Esther, 10, 101–2, 104–5, 108
Venable Elementary School, 12, 37
Vinegar Hill (Charlottesville neighborhood), 24, 61–63
Virginia Council on Human Relations (VCHR), 70–71
Virginia legislature, 17–18, 21–23
voting, 65, 68–69

Walsh, Human W., 59
"warm demander" archetype, 121
Washington, Booker T., 20
Washington, D.C., 31
Williams, Eugene, 69, 88
Williams, Lorraine, 84, 86
Woodson, Carter G., 51–52
"Wrecking Crew, The," 89–90
Wright, James, 95

yearbooks, 9, 49, 63, 65, 67–68, 96

Politics and Culture in the Twentieth-Century South

A Common Thread: Labor, Politics, and Capital Mobility in the Textile Industry
by Beth English

"Everybody Was Black Down There": Race and Industrial Change in the Alabama Coalfields
by Robert H. Woodrum

Race, Reason, and Massive Resistance: The Diary of David J. Mays, 1954–1959
edited by James R. Sweeney

The Unemployed People's Movement: Leftists, Liberals, and Labor in Georgia, 1929–1941
by James J. Lorence

Liberalism, Black Power, and the Making of American Politics, 1965–1980
by Devin Fergus

Guten Tag, Y'all: Globalization and the South Carolina Piedmont, 1950–2000
by Marko Maunula

The Culture of Property: Race, Class, and Housing Landscapes in Atlanta, 1880–1950
by LeeAnn Lands

Marching in Step: Masculinity, Citizenship, and The Citadel in Post–World War II America
by Alexander Macaulay

Rabble Rousers: The American Far Right in the Civil Rights Era
by Clive Webb

Who Gets a Childhood? Race and Juvenile Justice in Twentieth-Century Texas
by William S. Bush

Alabama Getaway: The Political Imaginary and the Heart of Dixie
by Allen Tullos

The Problem South: Region, Empire, and the New Liberal State, 1880–1930
by Natalie J. Ring

The Nashville Way: Racial Etiquette and the Struggle for Social Justice in a Southern City
by Benjamin Houston

Cold War Dixie: Militarization and Modernization in the American South
by Kari Frederickson

Faith in Bikinis: Politics and Leisure in the Coastal South since the Civil War
by Anthony J. Stanonis

Womanpower Unlimited and the Black Freedom Struggle in Mississippi
by Tiyi M. Morris

New Negro Politics in the Jim Crow South
by Claudrena N. Harold

Jim Crow Terminals: The Desegregation of American Airports
by Anke Ortlepp

Remaking the Rural South: Interracialism, Christian Socialism, and Cooperative Farming in Jim Crow Mississippi
by Robert Hunt Ferguson

The South of the Mind: American Imaginings of White Southernness, 1960–1980
by Zachary J. Lechner

The Politics of White Rights: Race, Justice, and Integrating Alabama's Schools
by Joseph Bagley

The Struggle and the Urban South: Confronting Jim Crow in Baltimore before the Movement
by David Taft Terry

Massive Resistance and Southern Womanhood: White Women, Class, and Segregationist Resistance
by Rebecca Bruckmann

I Lay This Body Down: The Transatlantic Life of Rosey E. Pool
by Lonneke Geerlings

Partners in Gatekeeping: How Italy Shaped U.S. Immigration Policy Over Ten Pivotal Years, 1891–1901
by Lauren Braun-Strumfels

Radical Volunteers: Dissent, Desegregation, and Student Power in Tennessee
by Katherine J. Ballantyne

Nuggets of Gold: Further Processed Chicken and the Making of the American Diet
by Patrick Dixon

Southern by the Grace of God: Religion, Race, and Civil Rights in Hollywood's American South
by Megan Hunt

Great Times Down South: Deep South Tourism Promotion in the Carter Era
by Guiliano Santangeli Valenzani

Protest and Pedagogy: Charlottesville's Black Freedom Struggle and the Making of the American High School
by Alexander D. Hyres

www.ingramcontent.com/pod-product-compliance
Lightning Source LLC
Chambersburg PA
CBHW020828230426
43666CB00007B/1151